Felony Arrests

Their Prosecution and Disposition in New York City's Courts

Felony Arrests

Their Prosecution and Disposition in New York City's Courts

Revised Edition with a Foreword by Malcolm Feeley

Vera Institute of Justice

Vera Institute of Justice
New York

Longman
New York and London

FELONY ARRESTS
Their Prosecution and Disposition in New York City's Courts

Longman Inc., 19 West 44th Street, New York, N.Y. 10036
Associated companies, branches, and representatives
throughout the world.

Copyright © 1977 by Vera Institute of Justice.

Copyright © 1981 by Longman Inc.

All rights reserved. No part of this publication may be
reproduced, stored in a retrieval system, or transmitted
in any form or by any means, electronic, mechanical,
photocopying, recording, or otherwise, without the prior
permission of the publisher.

Developmental Editor: Irving E. Rockwood
Editorial and Design Supervisor: Joan Matthews
Interior Design: Freeman Craw
Cover Design: Dan Serrano
Manufacturing and Production Supervisor: Robin B. Besofsky
Printing and Binding: Fairfield Graphics

Library of Congress Cataloging in Publication Data

Main entry under title:

Felony arrests, their prosecution and disposition
    in New York City's courts.

    (Professional studies)
    Includes bibliographical references.
    1. Criminal law—New York (City) 2. Criminal
justice, Administration of—New York (City)
3. Criminal courts—New York (City) I. Vera
Institute of Justice. II. Series: Professional
studies (New York)
KFX2007.F44   1981   345.747'102   80-26233
ISBN 0-582-28195-4
ISBN 0-582-28187-3 (pbk.)

Manufactured in the United States of America

9   8   7   6   5   4   3   2   1

Contents

Acknowledgments	ix
Foreword	xi
Introduction	xxi
1. The Deterioration of Felony Arrests	1
Dispositions	6
The Process of Reaching Dispositions	14
Factors Explaining Dispositions of Felony Arrests	19
Summary	21
2. Assault, Rape, Murder and Attempted Murder	23
Assaults	23
Fact Patterns in Assaults	23
Deterioration of Assault Arrests	24
Factors Explaining Dispositions of Assault Arrests	27
Prior Relationship Assaults	31
Stranger Assaults	36
Rape	42
Murder and Attempted Murder	52
Murder and Manslaughter	53
Attempted Murder	57
Summary	61
3. Robbery	63
Fact Patterns in Robberies	63
Deterioration of Robbery Arrests	64
Factors Explaining Dispositions of Robbery Arrests	65
Prior Relationship Robberies	65
Stranger Robberies	73
Evidentiary Problems	75
Archetypal Robberies	76
Summary	77
4. Burglary	81
Fact Patterns in Burglaries	82
Deterioration of Burglary Arrests	83
Factors Explaining Dispositions of Burglary Arrests	84
Prior Relationship Burglaries	86
Stranger Burglaries of Commercial Premises	89
Stranger Burglaries of Residential Premises	92
Summary	95

5. Grand Larceny 96
    Fact Patterns in Grand Larcenies 97
    Deterioration of Grand Larceny Arrests 97
    Factors Explaining Dispositions of Grand Larceny Arrests 100
        Auto Theft 100
        Other Larcenies 105
Summary 112

6. Criminal Possession of Dangerous Weapons: Guns 115
    Fact Patterns in Gun Possession Cases 116
    Deterioration of Gun Possession Arrests 117
    Factors Explaining Dispositions of Gun Possession Arrests 120
Summary 130

7. Reflections on the Study 133

Epilogue: 1980 141

Appendix: Note on Methodology 147

Figures and Tables

Figure 1. Disposition of 1971 Felony Arrests in the Criminal Process . . 1
Figure 2. Felonies Reported to the Police and Persons Arrested for Felonies, by Type of Felony 5
Figure 3. The Course to Disposition of Felony Arrests 7
Figure 4. Proportion of Convictions in Cases Reaching Disposition, by Charge at Arrest 8
Figure 5. Type of Plea of Those Convicted by Plea, for Each Type of Felony Charge 10
Table A. Crime Class and Maximum Sentence for Each Major Charge in Its Various Degrees 11
Table B. Crime Class of Guilty Pleas, by Crime Class of Felony Charged at Arrest 13
Figure 6. Sentence Following Conviction, by Type of Felony Charged at Arrest: Percent Given Each Sentence 14
Figure 7. Dispositions, by Stage of the Process Where Disposition is Reached 16
Table C. Types of Sentence Promise and Participation of the Bench in Negotiated Pleas 18
Table D. Relationship Between Victim and Defendant, by Felony Charged 19
Table E. Proportion of Dismissals Due to Complainant Non-Cooperation, by Crime 20
Table F. Disposition of Current Felony Charge, by Defendant's Prior Record 21
Figure 8. Dispositional Pattern for Felony Assault Arrests Compared to All Felony Arrests 25
Figure 9. The Course to Disposition for Felony Assault Arrests . . . 26
Table G. Prior Relationships in Assault Cases and Case Outcomes . . 27
Figure 10. Deterioration of Prior Relationship Assault Arrests and Stranger Assault Arrests 28
Table H. Sentences in Assault Cases, by Relationship of Victim to Defendant 29
Table I. Injuries in Assault Cases, by Relationship of Victim to Defendant 29
Table J. Use of Weapons in Assault Cases, by Relationship of Victim to Defendant 31
Figure 11. Dispositional Pattern for Robbery Arrests Compared to All Felony Arrests 64
Figure 12. The Course to Disposition for Robbery Arrests 66

Table K. Prior Relationships in Robbery Cases 67
Figure 13. Deterioration of Prior Relationship Robbery Arrests and Stranger Robbery Arrests 68
Table L. Sentences Following Arrests for Stranger Robberies, by Defendants' Arrest Records 74
Figure 14. Dispositional Pattern for Burglary Arrests Compared to All Felony Arrests 83
Figure 15. The Course to Disposition for Burglary Arrests 85
Figure 16. Deterioration of Prior Relationship Burglary Arrests and Stranger Burglary Arrests 86
Table M. Prior Relationships in Burglary Cases 87
Figure 17. Dispositional Pattern for Grand Larceny Arrests Compared to All Felony Arrests 98
Figure 18. The Course to Disposition for Grand Larceny Arrests . . . 99
Table N. Dispositions in Grand Larceny Cases, by Nature of Property Taken 106
Table O. Nature of Prior Relationships in Non-Car Grand Larceny Cases 106
Figure 19. Dispositional Pattern for Handgun Possession Arrests Compared to All Felony Arrests 118
Figure 20. The Course to Disposition for Felony Gun Possession Arrests 119
Table P. Sentences in Gun Possession Cases, by Prior Criminal Record 131
Figure 21. The Course to Disposition for 1977 Felony Arrests, Compared with the Course to Disposition for 1971 Wide Sample Arrests 143

Acknowledgments

This monograph concerns the process by which felony arrests are handled in the New York City criminal courts. It describes the deterioration of cases that takes place as they make their way toward final disposition. More importantly, it explores some underlying patterns which tend to explain how and why that deterioration takes place. It is not an effort to assess blame for a situation which, by agreement of all concerned, has become a critical issue of public policy. Rather, it is an effort to identify and understand the complex factors that have prevented the criminal justice system from having the effect that society desires.

The monograph is based on research conducted by the Vera Institute of Justice that was presented in a 1975 report to the New York State Division of Criminal Justice Services entitled, *A Criminal Justice System Under Stress*. Hans Zeisel conceived and designed the research and supervised the data collection which resulted in that report.

Lucy N. Friedman participated in that work with Dr. Zeisel and oversaw the initial presentation of that report. Her patience and hard work also helped to resolve a number of conceptual and practical problems, conflicts in the data, and difficult choices of interpretation which played an important role in shaping the original research into this present monograph.

The task of building upon the rich, sometimes vexing results of the earlier research to construct this monograph fell heavily on the capable shoulders of Michael Smith. Tension between the need for professional thoroughness and the need for clarity was exceptionally great in this task, but Mr. Smith's perceptiveness, experienced pen—and stamina—were invaluable in bringing together the present work.

We are deeply indebted to Patricia M. Wald for her guidance and labor throughout the entire effort. Ms. Wald was generous beyond measure with her wisdom and with her time, working long, late hours on drafts of the monograph. The study bears the mark of her incisiveness and good sense.

Jessica de Grazia supervised the interviewing and the field research. Nan C. Bases and Steven Brill helped in organizing and presenting the data. Thanks are also due to members of the Vera staff, in particular John MacWillie and Susan Singleton for their skilled analysis of the data and Paul Strasburg for final editing of the manuscript. We are grateful to Judith Douw, Rosemary Johnston and Sandra Walker for typing the manuscript and the drafts that preceded it.

Special recognition must be given to the contribution of the late Paul Lazarsfeld. He was the mentor of us all, a friend, and a constructive critic of this work.

In addition, we want to thank the New York State Division of Criminal Justice Services of the Law Enforcement Assistance Administration for underwriting the original research, and the Ford Foundation for its general support to Vera over the years and for its special assistance in making possible the publication of this monograph.

But above all, our debt is to the police officers, defense attorneys, prosecutors and judges who offered their time and opinions and searched their memories and records for our interviewers; and to the interviewers themselves who harvested so much data so well.

It is our hope that the publication of this monograph, which raises more questions than it attempts to answer, will stimulate others to explore this dimension of the criminal justice process and carry the work further.

December 1976 *Herbert Sturz*

Foreword

Studies of criminal courts almost always include a discussion of the high drop-off rate between arrest and final disposition. Only a handful of cases eventually lead to conviction on the original charges, and of those only a minute fraction are resolved through trial—a pattern that has come to be known as the "funnel of justice." To this extent, the findings in *Felony Arrests* are no different than those in dozens of other studies. However, what is distinctive about this book is its careful examination of how and why this attrition occurs. Typically it is attributed to one of two factors: Either the police were guilty of mistakes at arrest or the court has been forced to make shortcuts owing to congestion, incompetence, or carelessness. The truth of the matter, as this study of New York City's criminal courts makes abundantly clear, is that neither of these popular explanations is correct. Although containing more than a grain of truth, they overstate and oversimplify, and in so doing they perpetuate half-truths, myths about the functioning of the criminal justice system. Such errors are common and have a powerful effect. They lead to incorrect diagnoses of problems and questionable proposals for reform. They miss the obvious even as they search for the elusive. And as will be seen, these errors are fostered even by those closest to the criminal process.

It is for these reasons that *Felony Arrests* is so important and deserving of the attention of the larger audience which, one hopes, will be reached by this new Longman edition. This is a careful study, detailing *what* actually occurs as felony cases wend their ways through the criminal process, and *why* they are handled as they are. As such, it is an important corrective to the common misunderstandings and conventional views of the criminal process.

Felony Arrests is a study of a single city, New York City, and one can legitimately ask, how much can we generalize from it? We might be tempted to answer "not much," since the portrait presented here is now several years old and examines a city whose size and complexity make it distinctive if not unique. However, it would be a shame to dismiss these findings as being out of date, or as revealing no general insights into the criminal process. As shown in the *Epilogue,* which reports on more recent data, the dispositional pattern of felony arrest cases in New York has remained remarkably stable in the period since completion of the original Vera study, this despite the several and often dramatic changes in the way these cases are processed.

The more problematic question is, to what extent do these findings from such a distinctive city yield insight into the nature of the criminal justice system in general? Obviously at one important level, every city is unique, but the question is, how *distinctive*? The ways prosecutors are appointed, judges selected, police assigned, and the ways each works with the others vary significantly from city to city, and clearly affect the ways courts operate. Yet if researchers ask the right questions and concern themselves with the generic, *underlying* factors and processes, a study of a single setting can yield great insights of a general nature. While particular details vary from place to place, there are contours, tensions, and processes that are common to all. This study focuses on these basic and generic concerns, and as such yields important generalizable insights.

On the other hand, I do not mean to suggest that this portrait of New York City's courts describes in detail the criminal process throughout America. As James Q. Wilson, Martin Levin, and others have so convincingly demonstrated, the criminal justice system reflects to a considerable extent the values and expectations of the local political culture.[1] What it does is to identify those types of factors that go into decision making in the courts.

The most obvious finding in this study is the high attrition rate in criminal cases. Roughly 44 percent of all felony arrests are dropped outright, either by the prosecutors or judges. Of those remaining, only one-quarter lead to convictions on felony charges, and of those convicted, fewer than 10 percent are sentenced to prison for felony terms. Furthermore, only a handful of all cases (less than 3 percent) are adjudicated by trial, the vast majority being resolved through guilty pleas. In this sense, New York City's "funnel of justice" is similar to that of most other cities, and incidentally not markedly different from the pattern for many small towns. This similarity to other courts reinforces the position that despite New York's distinctiveness, the findings reported here shed insight into the operations of the courts in other settings as well.

The most intriguing findings in this study were the high number of felony arrests which involved people with prior relationships and how this fact affected the court's decision making. The study's concluding reflections summarize this issue in succinct fashion:

The study found an obvious but often overlooked reality: criminal conduct is often the explosive spillover from ruptured personal relations among neighbors, friends and former spouses. . . . [T]he reluctance of the complainants in these cases to pursue prosecution . . . accounted for a larger proportion of the high rate of dismissal than any other factor. . . . It also has an effect on the sentences ultimately imposed in those cases that survive the adjudicating process. Judges and prosecutors, and in some instances police officers, were outspoken in their reluctance to prosecute as full-scale felonies some cases that erupted from quarrels between friends or lovers. . . . Thus, where prior relationship cases survived dismissal, they generally received lighter dispositions than stranger cases.[2]

When these factors are taken into account, the study concludes, one can detect a rough sense of proportionate justice that pervades the system. Serious stranger-to-stranger felonies—"real felonies" in the language of the study—are treated seriously and conviction results in stiff sentences; in contrast, "technical felonies" among family, friends, and lovers are usually downgraded, at times leading to dismissals and often resulting in reduced charges and light sentences.

While one might dispute the wisdom and at times the accuracy of this classification the Vera researchers imposed on the cases, what this study makes abundantly clear is that the nature of relationships between accused and victim is a salient factor in the minds of criminal justice officials. They look beyond the formal charges and strength of evidence to assess the *incident* itself, making complex judgments about "contributing" factors and circumstances. Despite the formalities and procedure of the criminal process, they are concerned, as well, with *substantive* justice. It is this concern, the study reports, that leads to much of the drop-off and differential treatment of felony cases.

When first reported, these findings were discounted by many scholars whose own research suggested other explanations for the high drop-off and differential treatment of criminal cases. Standard explanations focus on the self-interest of officials, the organizational imperative to cope with congestion and heavy caseloads and the need for a smooth functioning routine. Thus it was not surprising that a study which emphasized considerations of *justice* was greeted with skepticism.

While it may be that these different explanations are a result of which jurisdictions were examined, it is more likely that they reflect the different methods and concerns of various researchers. A good deal of research on criminal courts is motivated by a zeal for due process, and focuses upon the lack of trials, the infrequency of formal motions, charge reductions, and the like as a means of exploring the *gap* between theory and practice. Finding few formal motions, fewer trials, frequent charge reductions, and a rapid pace in the courtroom, it is easy for researchers to conclude that concern for due process has all but been abandoned in favor of self-serving interests. This view is reinforced by sociological theory which holds that there is a tendency for large-scale organizations to abandon formal goals in the interest of maintaining group cohesion and individual self-interest.

Studies of criminal courts emphasizing such concerns employ a variety of different methods and techniques, but they share one important feature in common: They have rarely asked officials why they handle individual cases as they do. These researchers *infer* motive rather than *ascertain* it, and it is for this reason, I believe, that they tend to discount or overlook considerations of "justice." In contrast, this study follows the sage advice of the late Paul Lazarsfeld: If you want to know why people do something, "ask them!" This research has done just that. It painstakingly drew two samples of cases, systematically interviewed officials who played a role in handling these cases, and carefully reconstructed *reasons* for decisions in each case at each stage of the criminal process. The authors of this study are well aware of the dangers that such an approach could lead to self-serving rather than truthful responses, but the consistent pattern and "logic" they find suggests otherwise. The results can be taken as an accurate description of factors shaping disposition.

What one sees depends upon what one is looking for, where one looks, and how one listens, and it may be this that accounts for differences between the findings in this study and those in so many other studies. Still such variances are not so much in opposition as they are complementary to each other. *Felony Arrests* suggests the importance of still another, often overlooked set of factors; it does *not* refute the findings of others who emphasize case pressures, political culture, social background factors, or organizational self-interest as partial explanations for courtroom behavior. As such, it reinforces the obvious need for researchers to use a multiplicity of techniques and methods.

One might argue that prior relationship should *not* be a significant factor in determining case outcomes, that a truly even-handed system of law should proceed without regard to such particularistic factors. But whether we like it or not, those who invoke and administer the law do in fact take such relationships into consideration. Why? Most obviously because they often have an eye to *future* relationships between legal antagonists, and see that strict and continued invocation of the law can be an impediment in those relations.

While students of criminal courts have rarely focused on such considerations, researchers of other legal institutions have. Studies of police practices consistently reveal the importance of these considerations. In fact, one of the primary functions of the police is to try to cool down disputants who know each other without having to make an arrest. All studies systematically investigating police encounters with suspects report that the police are much less likely to arrest when the parties to a dispute are related to or know each other.[3] Indeed, "good" police work often consists of resolving such disputes through negotiation, compromise, or temporary separation even though there may be probable cause for arrest. Such practices are so widespread that they have led one researcher to give his book on police the subtitle *Streetcorner Politicians*.[4] *Felony Arrests* shows that even when arrests have been made, these same considerations continue to be applied by the prosecutor and the court.

This reluctance to invoke the full force of the law in disputes among acquaintances is not limited to police, prosecutors, and the criminal law. Research on civil law reveals a similar reluctance to employ the law in disputes among acquaintances. Stewart Macaulay has found that the full force of the law is rarely used in business, either to define relationships or resolve disputes.[5] Even though businesses relied on their attorneys to draft contracts and monitor their performance, he found, many such contracts contain boiler plate language that is probably unenforceable in court. Furthermore, in the event of disputes arising under these contracts few businesses went to court or even threatened to do so. Most businesspeople, he found, prefer the handshake to the contract, and informal discussion and compromise to litigation in the event of dispute. Two overriding factors account for this: the desire for future relationships and considerations of reputation, both of which are jeopardized by *formal* insistence on *rights*. Even to draw up a careful contract, he found, generates a considerable amount of ill will. Among other things, a "good" contract is likely to anticipate all the ways one's business partner could cause problems, and as such it fosters suspicion and distrust. More general is the desire to limit disputes and maintain harmonious relations, thereby creating a strong incentive to keep the dispute "within the community," as it were.

We see, then, a general pattern. While the law plays a significant role in defining expectations and shaping boundaries, and stands as the "ultimate weapon," it is but one of several forms of social control.

Like the studies of police practices and Macaulay's work on contractual relations in business, the central findings in the Vera study all fit this pattern. Each of them suggests that when there is another basis for social control, there is a reluctance to invoke the full force of the law even when there is a clear basis for doing so. Donald Black has found that this is a general tendency across *all* cultures and has phrased it in general propositional form. He asserts that "relational distance predicts and explains the quantity of law. . . . Law is inactive among intimates, increasing [in use] as the [social] distance between people increases. . . ."[6]

We are accustomed to think of the criminal justice sanction as an awesome power, and indeed it is. But it is also something of a clumsy giant. While it wields enormous powers—the possibility of death, lengthy prison terms, the stigma of conviction—these are nevertheless a limited range of responses which are further constrained by the ambiguity of language itself. Applicable for some offenders, sanctions may not be appropriate for others, and no matter how carefully drawn, a statute inevitably fails to fully capture precisely what its authors intend. Aiming to proscribe one type of conduct, the law inadvertently draws other conduct within its definition.

This study nicely depicts what officials do when confronted with these problems. They use their discretion; they distinguish between "technical" and "real" felonies (i.e., those incidents which have all the elements of a felony but nevertheless are regarded by all concerned not as "crimes" but "social problems" which are best coped with elsewhere, and those "serious" incidents which are properly handled by the courts), and develop alternative plans accordingly. No doubt readers will disagree, perhaps vigorously, with how this particular distinction is drawn, but no one can disagree with the fundamental finding of this study: that a broad spectrum of behavior, involving incidents of widely varying seriousness, stemming from quite different causes, and invested with a wide range of social significance, can be and often is given the same label when formally defined as a crime; and that what the law simplifies, public officials complicate. It is this, the study finds, which leads to so much of the differential handling of seemingly similar cases.

Traditionally, prosecutors and judges have accommodated these concerns through the exercise of their charging and sentencing discretion, but within recent years this discretion has come under increased attack. Plea bargaining has been challenged as a self-serving device employed by prosecutors and defense attorneys who are more interested in their own concerns than those of the accused or the victim. But increasingly, scholars are coming to realize that the same discretion that permits such abuses also facilitates other objectives as well. Much of what is "negotiated" deals with the meaning of the facts, and takes into consideration the nature of

Foreword xvii

the incident as well.[7] *Felony Arrests* makes a major contribution to this growing literature.

Similarly, judicial sentencing discretion has also come under fire recently as a source of problems for the courts and prisons, and the response has been a growing tendency to "rationalize" and restrict judicial decision making at this stage through legislation mandating minimum, determinate, or presumptive sentences.[8] Although each of these schemes is quite different, they share one element in common: increased restrictions on judicial discretion at sentencing.

The rich details in this study suggest why such reforms in plea bargaining and sentencing are likely to create some problems even as they seek to solve them. While this study does not and cannot lead to the conclusion that prosecutorial or judicial sentencing discretion should not be curtailed, it does point out the great variety of conduct and situations which can be characterized by the same formal offense, and in so doing reveals an important truth about the limits of the language of law and the functions of discretion. It reveals a considerably more complicated process than so many advocates of reform, particularly of sentence reform, seem to realize.

But to acknowledge, as this study does, that once the nature of prior relationships is taken into consideration, one can detect a pattern of rough justice in the courts, is not to conclude that there are no problems. The study also reveals a careless and haphazard process. The courts in New York City are complex, busy, and confusing institutions; decisions are made split-second; information is often incomplete; inferences are drawn from negatives. For instance, this study reports that when complainants do not appear at scheduled court appearances, prosecutors are inclined to drop charges on the belief that the complainant-victim does not want to press the case because differences have been patched up or restitution has been made. But such an inference can be and often is wrong; nonappearance can also mean that the complainant has been intimidated by the accused, has misunderstood directions from the prosecution, or has been waiting patiently in the wrong courtroom.

If we accept for the moment that prior relationship and the wishes of the complainant *should be* taken into consideration in establishing charges and sentencing, then we must also ask how this information can be obtained in a systematic manner. Clearly the haphazard process described in this study is inadequate. Similarly, to say that a rough sense of proportionate justice prevails in New York's courts says nothing about the appropriateness of the proportions or how they are timed. It may be that overall the courts are too slow, or too harsh, or too lenient—taking too long to come to decision, discounting across the board certain serious offenses, and treating others too harshly. Or perhaps it fails to appreciate the intimidation that husbands or former husbands exert over women who are complainants. Here too, the study makes no judgments, but does raise important questions for further consideration.

Even though *Felony Arrests* seeks to understand the criminal process from the perspective of official participants, it would be a mistake to read this book as a justification of the status quo, a defense of current practices. While the study does show that a consideration of justice plays a larger role than is generally thought, it also reveals a system with a great many serious problems. If it fails to conclude with an appeal for "comprehensive reform" or a list of major changes, this is because the study recognizes just how complex and deep-seated the problems confronting the criminal courts are. It depicts a system struggling along more effectively than many imagine, but one with an immensely complicated set of nagging problems, ones which are not likely to be effectively tackled by "more resources," "better personnel," "stricter sentencing standards," or the "abolition of plea bargaining," solutions with great popular appeal but likely to miss their mark in this little-understood and immensely complex process. While the study does not offer any solutions to the problems it depicts, it does provide a more accurate portrait of that process than has hitherto been available. And to the extent that solutions cannot be found until problems are first diagnosed, this study makes a major contribution to the improvement of the criminal justice system. It also suggests that improvement is likely to be achieved piece-meal through incremental adjustments; in the aggregate such efforts are likely to be much more effective than many more celebrated "comprehensive" reforms, which while glamorous are likely to be premised on false assumptions.

Finally, as good as it is, *Felony Arrests* is not the definitive study of criminal courts. Indeed it is not likely that a definitive study can ever be written; the criminal process is too varied, too complicated for any single work to capture its essence. However, this study is important, and is one of the truly outstanding books on the criminal courts that have been published in the past decade. Its most distinctive features are that it successfully challenges a number of myths about the operations of the criminal process, and that it returns our attention to the fact that the law is a normative ordering, an enterprise designed to apply the values of the community. As flawed as this institution is in pursuing the latter function, *Felony*

Arrests shows that this goal has not been altogether forgotten, even if it must make itself felt in a variety of not-so-obvious ways.

It is also an important study of discretion; it reminds us that however much we try, the law must remain an imprecise instrument for expressing our aims and defining our behavior. As such it is an important reminder of the limits of order.

But it is an incomplete study, one which raises questions even as it answers them. The researchers impose their classifications—"real" and "technical" felonies—upon the cases rather than letting them emerge from the views of official decision makers. Even as it yields an important insight, such an a priori classification obscures the *process* by which these crucial distinctions are made. Thus the study raises important questions for further research: How do officials understand and distinguish serious from not-so-serious cases? How do they *learn* this? To what extent is there actually a *consensus* among all participants that "prior relationship" cases are less serious than "stranger" cases? What *constitutes* "relationships"? What other factors aside from prior relationships are included in "technical" not-so-serious cases? How do officials draw inferences from limited and incomplete information?

Like many good books, *Felony Arrests* raises as many questions as it answers, and as such should be an invaluable stimulus for fruitful future research.

Madison, Wisconsin *Malcolm Feeley*
May 1980

1. James Q. Wilson, *Varieties of Police Behavior* (Cambridge: Harvard University Press, 1968); Martin Levin, *Urban Politics and the Criminal Courts* (Chicago: University of Chicago Press, 1977).
2. Pp. 141–142, *Felony Arrests*.
3. See, e.g., Albert Reiss, *The Police and the Public* (New Haven: Yale University Press, 1971); Donald Black, "The Social Organization of Arrest," *Stanford Law Review*, 23 (June 1971): 1087–1111; and Herman Goldstein, *Policing in a Free Society* (Cambridge, Mass.: Ballinger Books, 1978).
4. William K. Muir, *Police: Streetcorner Politicians* (Chicago: University of Chicago Press, 1977).
5. Stewart Macaulay, "Noncontractural Relations in Business: A Preliminary Study," *American Sociological Review*, 28 (February 1963): 55–67.

6. Donald Black, *The Behavior of Law* (New York: Academic Press, 1976), p. 41. Black goes on to note that this effect is "curvilinear," in that law decreases as relations begin to reach "the point at which people live in entirely separate worlds" (p. 41).

7. See, e.g., Malcolm M. Feeley, *The Process Is the Punishment: Handling Cases in a Lower Criminal Court* (New York: Russell Sage Foundation, 1979); Lief Carter, *The Limits of Order* (Lexington: Lexington Books, 1974); Pamela Utz, *Settling the Facts* (Lexington: Lexington Books, 1978); Arthur Rosett and Donald Cressey, *Justice by Consent* (Philadelphia: Lippincott, 1976); and Jerome Skolnick, *Justice without Trial* (New York: John Wiley & Sons, 1966).

8. See, e.g., Andrew von Hirsch, *Doing Justice: The Choice of Punishments* (New York: Hill and Wang, 1976).

Introduction

Former New York City Police Commissioner Patrick V. Murphy, in a 1972 address to the Association of the Bar of the City of New York, assigned to the courts "the giant share of the blame" for what he said was a disturbing rise in crime in the city. To support his charge, the Commissioner recounted the final dispositions in 136 recent arrests for felonious possession of handguns: not one retained its felony status through to conviction, only 53 of the defendants received jail or prison sentences, and the average sentence was one month. "No wonder," the Commissioner concluded, "so many people of criminal intent carry handguns in New York City."*

Although Commissioner Murphy's figures provided striking evidence of the deterioration of felony arrests in court, they did not address the more fundamental issue of why this deterioration takes place. Actually, the outcome of felony arrests depends on many factors, including the "quality" of the arrest and the legal accuracy of the original charge; the sufficiency of evidence to support the original charge (at a later time when it must be presented to court); the willingness of complainants, victims and witnesses to pursue the case; the relative burdens on the prosecutor, the defense counsel and the defendant himself in holding out for trial; the acumen of the prosecutor and the defense counsel in negotiating a disposition when neither side is willing to wait for or risk losing at trial; the judge's feelings about how much punishment or rehabilitation the particular defendant deserves or needs for the crime he has committed; and the legal limits of the penal law on what punishment can be imposed and on the discretion within those limits invested in the judge.

The importance of such factors as these in the final disposition of cases is illustrated by two felony arrests dismissed in New York City in 1973. In the first, a gun possession charge of the kind Commissioner Murphy referred to, the arresting officers themselves explained the dismissal in the following way:

"We got a radio call that there had been a fight on the street and that there was a man with a gun. We had a description of the man and his car and we found someone who fitted. He said, yes, he had been in a fight with some drunk over a parking place. We placed him under arrest and searched the car. But there wasn't any gun. And the complaining witness never showed or made contact with us again. We check out every gun call, but this will happen nine times out of ten on a radio call—and it's we, the police, who

---
* *Record of the Association of the Bar of the City of New York,* Vol. 27, no. 1, January 1972, p. 26.

turn out to be the bad guys. This complainant probably just wanted the defendant locked up for his own satisfaction."

The second case involved an alleged first degree robbery.

An auxiliary police officer watched a woman approach a man as he emerged from a liquor store. It was dark. The officer thought he saw a knife flash in her hand, and the man seemed to hand her some money. She fled, and the officer went to the aid of the victim, taking him to the hospital for treatment.

The officer saw the woman on the street a few days later and arrested her for first degree robbery on the victim's sworn complaint. It was presumably a "high quality" arrest—identification of the perpetrator by an eye-witness, not from mugshots or a line-up, but in a crowd. Yet, shortly thereafter, this apparently airtight case was dismissed on the prosecutor's motion.

What the victim had not explained to the police was that this defendant, an alcoholic, had been his girlfriend for the past five years; that they had been drinking together the night of the incident; that she had taken some money from him and got angry when he took it back; that she had flown into a fury when he then gave her only a dollar outside the liquor store; and that she had slashed at him with a pen knife in anger and run off. He had been sufficiently annoyed to have her charged with robbery, but, as the judge who dismissed the case said, "He wasn't really injured. Before it got into court they had kissed and made up." In fact, the victim actually approached the defense attorney before the hearing and asked him to prevail upon the judge and the Assistant District Attorney (ADA) to dismiss the charges against his girlfriend.

No one wanted conviction and punishment in this case except the ADA, who acknowledged that prosecution on the robbery complaint was impossible but added: "I wish they would do something about people using the courts to settle their personal quarrels. . . . It's too bad there isn't a way to penalize these people."

Are these cases typical of felonies that come to court? Do they contain the seeds of an explanation for the perceived ineffectiveness of the criminal process? Or do "real" felons—predatory, hardened criminals—make up a large share of the courts' caseload, and do they also pass through the system relatively unscathed?

If accused felons go unpunished too often, is it because most cases are weak to begin with, like the two cited? Is it because complainants refuse to press charges, using the criminal justice system for its police (arrest) ca-

Introduction xxiii

pacity, not its court (adjudicating) capacity? Or does the problem lie in laxness on the part of prosecutors and judges?

What role is played by another commonly cited factor, court congestion? Extensive delays between arrest and disposition require many defendants who wish to go to trial to spend lengthy periods in pretrial detention, and tempt prosecutors to rely on delay and pretrial detention, rather than on the merits of the case, in striking a plea bargain. Delay in the congested system can also benefit a defendant at liberty who can wait for the prosecutor's case to develop weaknesses as memories and witnesses fade away. Prosecutors, defense counsel and judges have little time to devote to individual cases; each is burdened by inadequate resources, a factor likely to affect judgment. Clearly, these are not the conditions under which we want felony charges to be disposed. They undermine our confidence in the ability of the criminal process to produce just outcomes. But a basic question remains: Are the *results*—the bulk of the dispositions—in rough accord with our notions of justice for the individual and of safety for the public, or are they not?

Analysis of all these questions is needed not only to clarify our understanding but to lay the groundwork for changes, if needed, in policy and resource allocation. If high rates of dismissal or plea bargaining to lesser offenses are attributable primarily to court congestion, the remedy would seem to be an influx of funds for the creation of new court, prosecutorial, and defense resources. But if, in fact, most cases brought into the system are not of a serious nature, and if most cases are disposed of in a satisfactory way despite the congestion, it would be unwise to concentrate resources on enlarging the system's capacity or on restructuring it *as if* the system were dealing primarily with "real," predatory felonies. It would be better to introduce administrative controls, diversion efforts and a conflict resolution capacity to deal quickly and constructively with the cases that will not, and should not, result in prison terms; and to concentrate on policing and preventive measures aimed at bringing more of the dangerous criminals before the courts and making commission of serious crime more difficult.

This monograph reports on the results of two studies undertaken by the Vera Institute of Justice in 1973–74 in an attempt to dig below the surface generality of crude statistics in order to understand what actually happens to felony arrests in the criminal process and why. First, Vera researchers gathered and analyzed court records—from arrest through disposition—for a probability sample of 1,888 cases out of approximately 100,000 that were commenced by arrests on felony charges, covering every major crime category in the four major boroughs of New York City in 1971. (This sample is referred to as the "wide" sample.) Second, Vera researchers conducted interviews with the principal officials—police officers, prosecutors, defense attorneys and judges—involved in an additional probability sample of 369 felony arrests* reaching dispositions in 1973, in order to determine the reasons for dispositions. (This sample is referred to as the "deep" sample.) The majority of arrests for cases in the deep sample were made in 1972 and 1973, not long before our interviews.† Although these cases were brought to court three or more years ago, recent court data indicate that, in general, the mix of cases and the way in which they are handled remain much the same today.

The wide sample was used to identify the layers in the process at which deterioration of charges occurs and to quantify it; the deep sample provided a close look at the material in those layers. The deep sample is not a true subsample of the wide sample, however. Consequently, we cannot be certain that every pattern revealed in the deep sample explains deterioration of felony cases generally. But the two samples are sufficiently well matched for us to place some confidence in the general applicability of deep sample findings that emerged with particular clarity. (A note on the research methodology used in drawing the two samples, and on methodological difficulties, is provided in the Appendix.)

The general findings from the wide sample are presented first, in the following chapter, so that the reader can gain an overall impression of how the system operates. The five chapters after that describe in some detail what happened to felony arrests, crime by crime. In these chapters, statistical results are interwoven with excerpts and summaries from the deep sample interviews. That collection of candid views from decision-makers across a sample of felony prosecutions affords an unusual opportunity to understand the workings of a much-maligned and much-misunderstood process.

Much of what we found was startling. In half of all the felony arrests for crimes against the person, the victim had a prior relationship with the defendant. Prior relationships were frequent in cases of homicide and assault, where they were expected, as well as in cases of robbery, where they were not. Even in property crimes, prior relationships figured in over a third of the cases. This unanticipated level of prior relationships proved significant to the outcome of cases.

---

* "Felonies" are crimes carrying a maximum sentence of more than a year in prison.
† There were a few exceptions. The most notable was a 1958 arrest in which the defendant was originally found unfit to stand trial. The case was returned to court in 1973. This case is described in some detail on pp. 55 and 56, *infra*.

Introduction

Another finding, also surprising, was the relative infrequency of cases involving recidivists. Forty percent of the defendants had no prior record of arrests, and another 40% had never been sentenced to prison. On the whole, cases against defendants with prior records were treated more seriously and evidenced less deterioration. The interplay of these two major factors—prior relationship and prior record—varied from crime to crime.

The net conclusion drawn from these data is that although court congestion is an important factor, particularly as it affects defendants held in pretrial detention, and although the criminal process certainly suffers weaknesses that should be corrected, a more fundamental cause of high rates of deterioration in felony arrests as they proceed through court lies in the nature of the cases themselves. Often the facts prove insufficient to sustain the original felony charges. Equally important, however, the incidents that give rise to arrest are frequently not the kind that the court system is able to deal with satisfactorily. At the root of much of the crime brought to court is anger—simple or complicated anger between two or more people who know each other. Expression of anger results in the commission of technical felonies, yet defense attorneys, judges and prosecutors recognize that in many cases conviction and prison sentences are inappropriate responses. High rates of dismissal or charge reduction appear to be a reflection of the system's effort to carry out the *intent* of the law—as judges and other participants perceive it—though not necessarily the letter of the law.

Because our society has not found adequate alternatives to arrest and adjudication for coping with inter-personal anger publicly expressed, we pay a price. The price includes large court caseloads, long delays in processing and, ultimately, high dismissal rates. These impose high financial costs on taxpayers and high personal costs on defendants and their families. The public pays in another way, too. The congestion and drain on resources caused by an excessive number of such cases in the courts weakens the ability of the criminal justice system to deal quickly and decisively with the "real" felons, who may be getting lost in the shuffle. The risk that they will be returned to the street increases, as does the danger to law-abiding citizens on whom they prey.

A prerequisite for ameliorating this situation is a better understanding of the nature of the problems the courts are asked to deal with and a more realistic assessment of the capacities and limitations they bring to the task. In the course of interviewing for the deep sample study, one of Vera's researchers was told by a judge:

"I don't see any value in another study about plea bargaining. What use is the information without input from the people being studied? In Criminal Court

there is a subculture unrelated to the rest of the world. The rest of society has no idea of what goes on in court. How can you understand what I am thinking when I see a defendant before me? You will only get the bare outlines of it, and you can't really understand it."

The judge is both right and wrong: right in implying that understanding of the realities of criminal court is essential to constructive change; wrong in doubting that understanding is possible. This monograph attempts to introduce new evidence and raise considerations that have been inadequately examined. But it provides only partial insight to some critical issues, such as the impact of bail status and court congestion on the disposition of cases, and does not deal at all with others, including the subculture of defendants and victims, the impact of race, the processing of juvenile crimes, the role of private and Legal Aid defense counsel, or the effect of differing prosecutorial practices from one borough to another. It will serve its intended purposes, however, if it stimulates further reflection and research on these issues.

Felony Arrests

Their Prosecution and Disposition in New York City's Courts

1 The Deterioration of Felony Arrests

New York City police made 100,739 felony arrests in 1971.* Extrapolating from data in Vera's wide sample, Figure 1 provides a graphic representation of the deterioration—the reduction or dismissal of charges, or the imposition of non-felony sentences on those found guilty—which occurred in the three-quarters of arrests that proceeded to disposition in the criminal process.†

Figure 1 shows that only 56% of felony cases entering the criminal justice system resulted in conviction for some offense; 44% were dismissed or acquitted. Only 15% of all cases resulted in conviction for a felony. While 27%

* The data in this monograph—whether from our samples or from New York City Police Department records—cover the four major boroughs of New York City but exclude Staten Island.

† There was no criminal process disposition for 25% of the wide sample felony arrests. (Footnote continued on page 2.)

Figure 1. Disposition of 1971 Felony Arrests in the Criminal Process

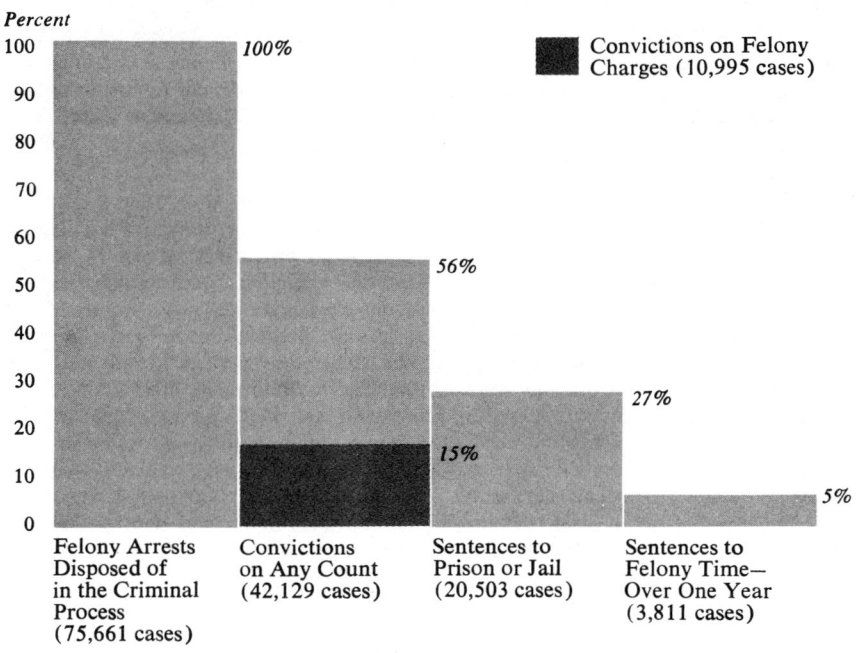

Source: Wide Sample Data (1971); Vera Institute Felony Disposition Study.

of all defendants received sentences to jail or prison, only 5% were given prison sentences (more than one year) prescribed for felonies.*

Data as striking as these give the impression that dangerous criminals are released in large numbers soon after being arrested. To gauge whether that impression is accurate, it is necessary to know whether the people being arrested are, in fact, dangerous criminals—"real" felons. The bulk of this monograph is devoted to answering that question, and the answer appears to

---

Figure 1, therefore, is extrapolated from the dispositions of 1,382 of the 1,888 felony arrests in the sample. Forty cases were eliminated from the 1,888 because the files could not be located. The remaining 466 cases are accounted for as follows:

Diverted to Family Court—260
   (juveniles under 16 or relatives of victims) 14%
Failed to Appear—106 . . . . 6%
Case Still Pending—37 . . . . 2%
Youthful Offenders—56[a] 3%
Abated before Disposition
   (death or insanity of defendant, etc.) 7 . . . . [b]

The extrapolation from which Figure 1 is derived involves "weighting" the wide sample data to account for differences between the boroughs. See Appendix.

a. Under New York Criminal Procedure Law § 720.10, a youth between 16 and 19 years old is eligible for youthful offender treatment if the charge is not an A felony and if he has not previously been convicted of a felony. Youthful offender treatment means that the case record is sealed, and thus such cases were excluded from the study.

b. Less than .5%.

---

* A jail sentence of one year or less is considered "misdemeanor time," and a sentence of more than one year is considered "felony time" although most prisoners are eligible for release by the Parole Board before the maximum sentence is served. A "NACC" sentence (i.e., committal to custody of the Narcotics Addiction Control Commission—now known as ODAS, the Office of Drug Abuse Services) is theoretically 36 months for misdemeanors and 60 months for felonies, but because discharge from NACC is in practice nearly assured before the end of 12 months, these sentences are considered "misdemeanor time." A "walk" is any sentence that has the immediate effect of releasing the defendant: probation, conditional and unconditional discharge, or a fine. In this monograph, sentences to "time served" (i.e., time spent in custody before the imposition of sentence) are termed "misdemeanor time" or "felony time" sentences depending on the length of time already served. Thus a sentence of "time served plus three years probation" is not a "walk," and it is "felony time" if the defendant has been in custody for more than 365 days. If, on the other hand, a defendant who has spent time in jail before sentence is sentenced to probation and no mention was made at sentencing of "time served," the sentence is recorded as a "walk." Whenever our data clearly indicate that the defendant was in custody before sentence and that this fact affected disposition, mention is made of it in the text.

be that in large measure they are not. That conclusion, in turn, raises another question: Are the people arrested on felony charges and processed through the criminal justice system representative of the people who are committing felonies? Unfortunately, this is a more complicated question, and one that this study cannot answer satisfactorily.

In New York City, the odds that a felony complaint will lead to an arrest appear to be about one in 5: in 1971, New Yorkers reported 501,951 felonies to the police, but the police made only 100,739 felony arrests. Arrests do not necessarily clear complaints on a one-for-one basis, however. A single felony arrest may account for several reported felonies. For example, one of the arrested felons in the deep sample was convicted of six separate rapes and was strongly suspected of other reported sex felonies and a murder. On the other hand, several felony arrests may account for only one reported crime. In some crime categories, the tendency is for a single defendant to be charged with more than one crime, and in other categories the tendency is for co-defendants to be charged with a single crime. The net balance in 1971 was that the 100,739 felony arrests "cleared" only 111,824 of the 501,951 reported felonies.*

Surveys of crime victims in recent years have indicated that only about half of the incidents that might be recorded as felonies are actually reported to the police.† Although it is impossible to know for certain whether unreported crimes are similar to crimes that victims do report to the police, victim survey literature suggests that the less serious crime, and the crime for which the victim feels he cannot provide meaningful information that could lead to an arrest, are the ones that most often go unreported. Thus, it seems highly unlikely that "real" felons are committing only crimes that are not reported. (Felonies that do not involve victims are probably overlooked on an even

---

* Although the 1971 clearance rate for all reported felonies (22%) is close to the arrest rate (20%), the rates do not correspond well within separate felony categories. For example, the arrest rate for rape was 48% but the clearance rate was 31%; the arrest rate for burglary was 9% but the clearance rate was 16%; and the arrest rate for robbery was 19% while the clearance rate was 25%.

† See *Crime in the Nation's Five Largest Cities*, U.S. Department of Justice, Law Enforcement Assistance Administration, National Criminal Justice Information and Statistics Service; and, *Crime in Eight American Cities* and *Crimes and Victims, A Report on the Dayton-San Jose Pilot Survey of Victimization* (Government Printing Office, Washington, D.C., 1974.)

larger scale. The most obvious omissions from recorded crimes include innumerable felonious possessions of drugs, including marijuana, narcotics sales and technically felonious possessions of loaded weapons that remain unseen in dressers and closets.)

The ratio of reported felonies to arrests varies greatly by type of offense. This is illustrated graphically in Figure 2.

Not surprisingly, the arrest rate for reported victimless felonies is far greater than the arrest rate for felonies in which there is a victim-complainant; in victimless felonies the discovery, the "report" and the arrest are often made simultaneously by the police themselves.* It is also not surprising that crimes of personal violence, which entail some contact between victim and assailant, result in arrest more often than non-violent property crimes, in which the victim is less likely to see the perpetrator or be able to identify him. But even for robberies and assaults there are wide gaps between the number of offenses reported and the number of persons arrested.

In short, it is quite possible that many serious felons are never caught. It may also be that some "real" felons are arrested on relatively minor charges and dealt with as if they were not dangerous because their more serious offenses are not known to the police and courts.

Determining whether "real" felonies are disproportionately excluded from court processing would require, at a minimum, a comparative analysis of cleared and uncleared incidents of reported crime. Such a comparison is not possible here because the data on which this study is based relate only to incidents that have been cleared by arrest.† Nevertheless, some of the

---

* As seen in Figure 2, forgery has a high arrest rate (78%) when compared to the other non-violent property crimes. This is in part explained by the large number of forgery felonies that are really "victimless" in the sense used here; that is, felonies for which there is no complainant to report the crime except the investigating or arresting officer. Sixty-nine percent of the forgery arrests in our deep sample resulted from possession of altered driving licenses and similar documents. Check forging accounted for most of the rest. (It should be noted that forgery will be the most serious charge in check forgery cases only if the amount of the check is less than $250. If it is more, the top charge will be grand larceny.)

† About one-quarter of the arrests are not disposed in the criminal courts—for instance, some are transferred to Family Court and others remain pending because the defendant jumped bail—and these, too, are not discussed in this study. We can make guesses about whether such cases were more or less likely to be "real" felonies (e.g., serious charges may be overrepresented among cases pending two years after arrest, whereas minor transgressions may be overrepresented among cases in which the defendant is judged a youthful offender), but the data in this study do not allow us to know for sure.

Figure 2. Felonies Reported to the Police and Persons Arrested for Felonies, by Type of Felony

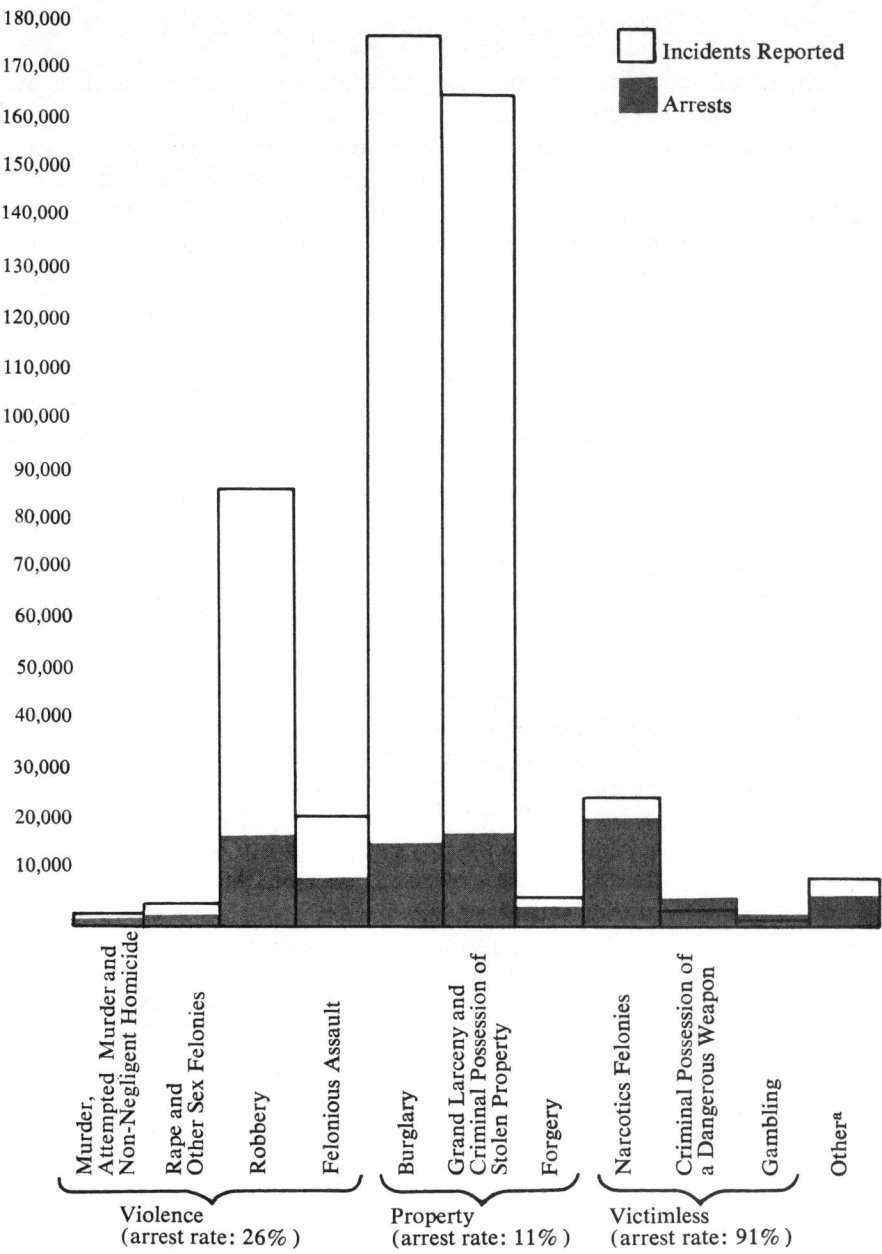

Source: New York City Police Department, "Crime Comparison Report" (for December 1971), and NYPD Crime Analysis Section, "Key Sheets" (for December 1971).

a. Included in "Other" are kidnapping, coercion, arson, perjury, bribery, bail jumping, falsifying records, etc.

results of this research do contain provocative implications regarding the proportion of court cases involving truly predatory crimes. For example, as noted in the first chapter, the analysis revealed a surprisingly high incidence of prior relationships between victims of felonies and defendants. This raises the possibility that stranger felonies, which might be regarded as more serious and more frightening, are less often cleared by an arrest and processed by the criminal justice system. Arrest is, after all, more likely to follow when the victim knows and can lead the police to the alleged felon.

In the balance of this chapter, data from the deep and wide samples will be examined more closely to gain an overall understanding of the manner in which felony arrests proceed to disposition in New York City's criminal justice system. Later chapters will focus on specific felony categories and on the characteristics of offenses and offenders in each category.

Dispositions

The wide sample data suggest, by extrapolation, that 75,661 of the 100,739 felony arrests in 1971 in the four major boroughs of New York reached disposition in the criminal process. Using the same extrapolation technique, Figure 3 maps the routes taken by those cases to disposition.

Only 15% of defendants in the wide sample were convicted of a felony and only 4% went to disposition without a reduction or dismissal of the original charge or acquittal at trial. Although few (2.3%) of the wide sample cases went to trial, more than half of those that did resulted in acquittals. Those convicted at trial stood a roughly even chance of being convicted of a felony (as contrasted with a lesser offense), but more than half of those convicted of a felony at trial walked.

Forty-three percent of the felony arrests were disposed of by dismissal.*
Fifty-five percent of the defendants pled guilty, and three-quarters of those

---

* In this monograph, a case disposed of by "Adjournment in Contemplation of Dismissal" (ACD) is considered a dismissal. Under New York Criminal Procedure Law § 170.55, a non-felony prosecution in the Criminal Court may be "adjourned in contemplation of dismissal . . . without date ordered with a view to ultimate dismissal of the accusatory instrument in furtherance of justice." After a felony charge has been reduced to a misdemeanor, a motion for an ACD may be made by the defendant, the prosecutor, or the court. Usually an ACD is conditioned on the defendant's not being rearrested within a six-month period, but theoretically the judge could impose other conditions prerequisite to ultimate dismissal. The court may not order an ACD if the defendant: "has previously been granted an ACD; has previously been convicted of any offense involving dangerous drugs; has previously been convicted of a crime and the district
(continued on page 9)

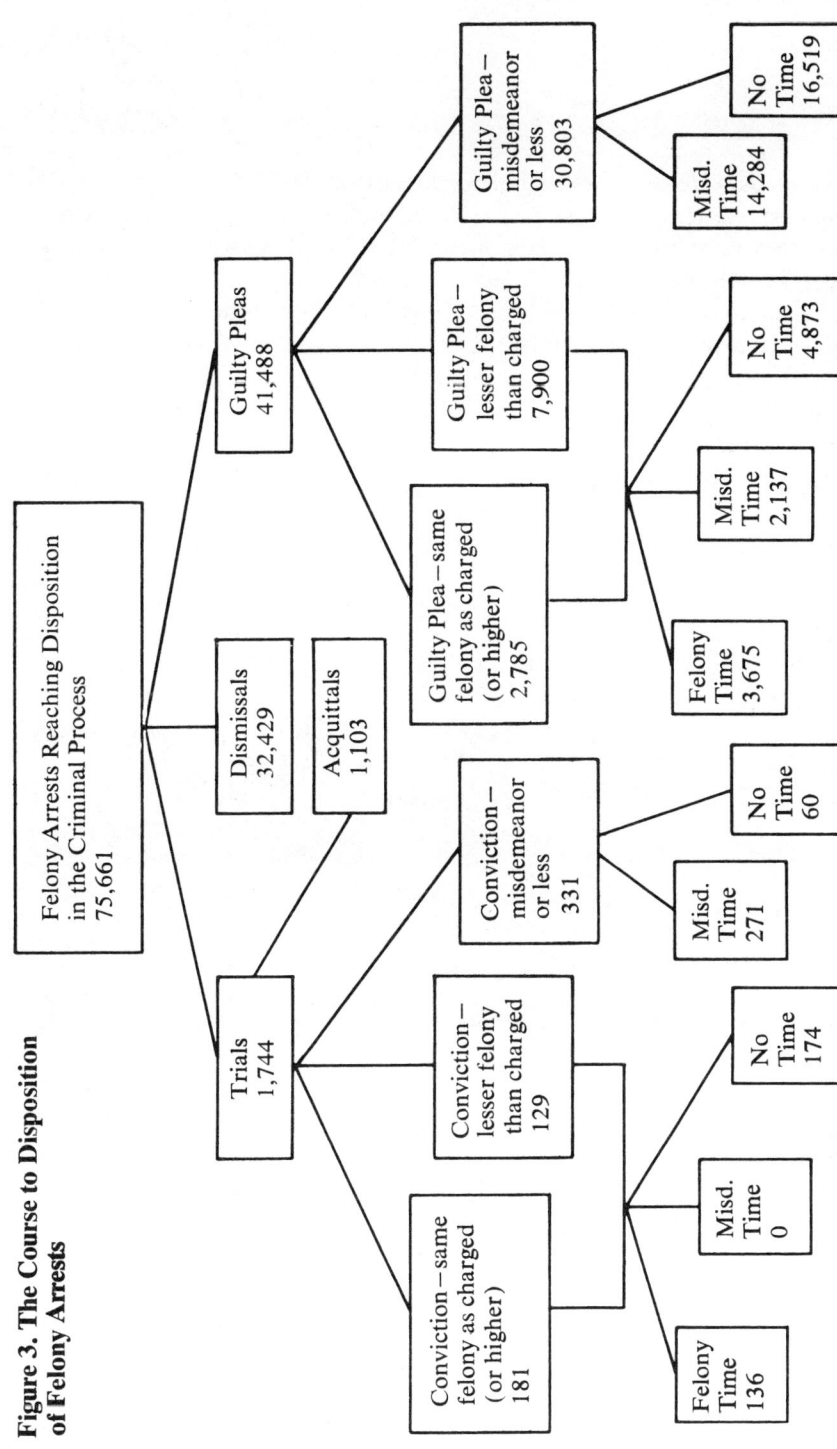

Figure 3. The Course to Disposition of Felony Arrests

Source: Wide Sample Data (1971); Vera Institute Felony Disposition Study.

guilty pleas were to misdemeanors or violations. Half of those convicted by plea, and one-third of those convicted at trial, walked out of court without being sentenced to jail or prison. Most (81%) of those who did get time got misdemeanor time (one year or less).

The pattern of disposition varied, however, among the different felonies charged at arrest. Figure 4 breaks down, by the category of arrest charge, the

Figure 4. Proportion of Convictions in Cases Reaching Disposition, by Charge at Arrest

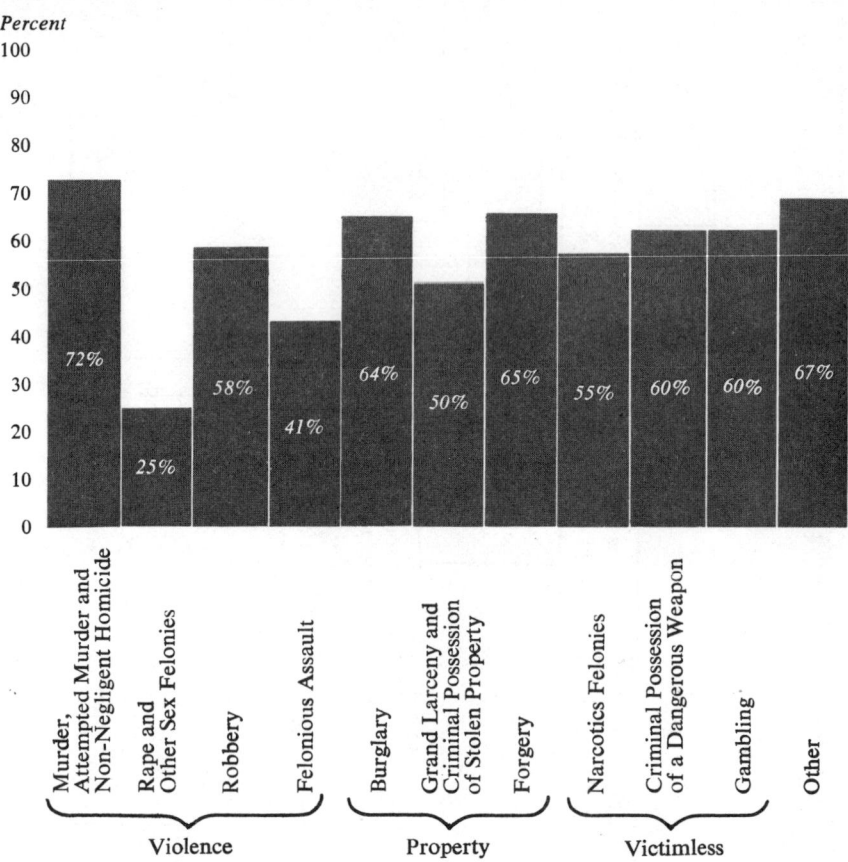

Source: Wide Sample Data (1971); Vera Institute Felony Disposition Study.

rate at which defendants were convicted of any kind of offense—felony, misdemeanor or less.

Only 25% of rape arrests resulted in any kind of conviction. Factors explaining this low conviction rate are explored in the next chapter. Otherwise, felonies of violence show conviction rates declining with the lessening seriousness of the crime, from 72% for homicide arrests to 41% for assaults. But rates of conviction for the remaining felonies show only moderate variation and no obvious pattern.

A clearer pattern does emerge, however, when one examines the incidence of various kinds of guilty pleas that were made in each crime category, as in Figure 5, page 10.

Figure 5 suggests that when a guilty plea disposes of a case commenced by felony arrest, the seriousness of the felony charged at arrest is reflected in the level (felony or misdemeanor) of the plea. Thus, roughly half the guilty pleas in cases commenced by robbery arrests are felony pleas, but only 10% of guilty pleas in gambling cases are pleas to felony charges. Generally, misdemeanor pleas are more common in property and victimless crimes than in the violent crimes. The point is not just that robbery (a violent crime) is generally considered more serious than gambling (a victimless crime). It is also that charges can be reduced in the more serious felonies without hitting the misdemeanor level.

Felony charges in Figures 4 and 5 are arrayed from left to right within each of the broad categories (violent, property, victimless), in decreasing order of maximum sentence authorized by the Penal Law for the most serious degree of the felony. These statutory gradations of seriousness, between and within each type of felony, are the currency of the plea bargaining process and figure prominently throughout the discussion in this monograph. For reference, the statutory scheme is presented in Table A, page 11. (In addition to prison sentences, judges are authorized to give non-prison sentences such as probation except on conviction of an A felony.)

---

attorney does not consent to an ACD on the current offense; or has previously been adjudicated a youthful offender on the basis of any act involving dangerous drugs and the district attorney does not consent." (New York Criminal Procedure Law (C.P.L.) § 170.56(1)).

10 Felony Arrests

Figure 5. Type of Plea of Those Convicted by Plea, for Each Type of Felony Charge

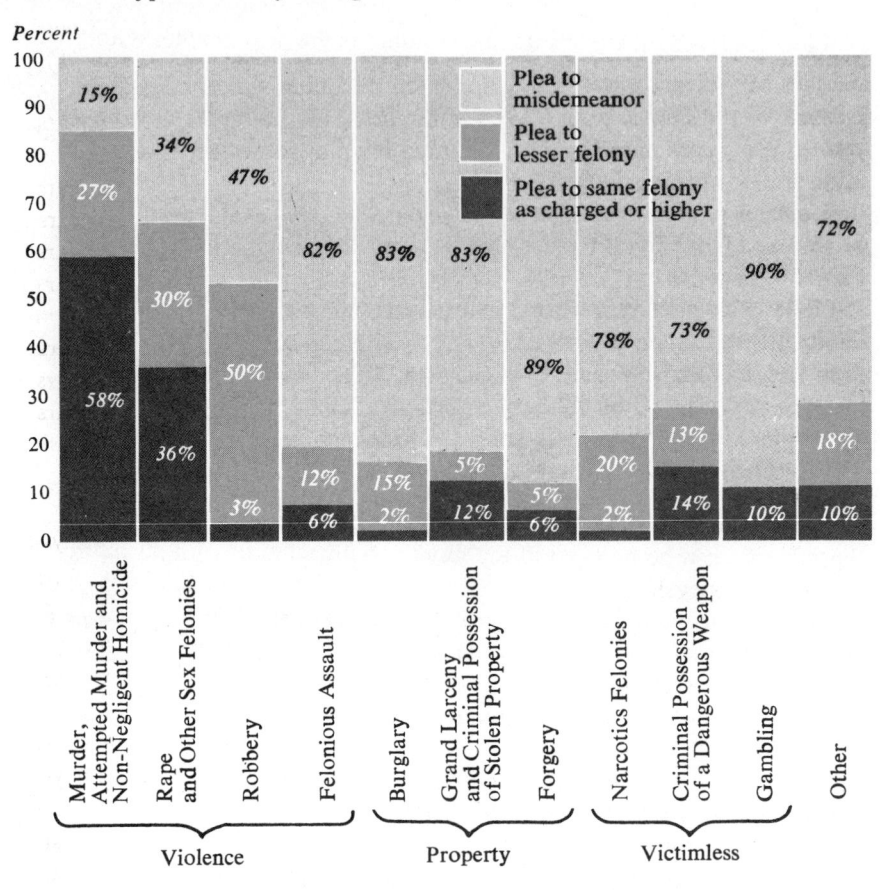

Percent

Legend:
- Plea to misdemeanor
- Plea to lesser felony
- Plea to same felony as charged or higher

Charge	Plea to same felony as charged or higher	Plea to lesser felony	Plea to misdemeanor
Murder, Attempted Murder and Non-Negligent Homicide	58%	27%	15%
Rape and Other Sex Felonies	36%	30%	34%
Robbery	3%	50%	47%
Felonious Assault	6%	12%	82%
Burglary	2%	15%	83%
Grand Larceny and Criminal Possession of Stolen Property	12%	5%	83%
Forgery	6%	5%	89%
Narcotics Felonies	2%	20%	78%
Criminal Possession of a Dangerous Weapon	14%	13%	73%
Gambling	10%	—	90%
Other	10%	18%	72%

Groupings: Violence (Murder... through Felonious Assault); Property (Burglary through Forgery); Victimless (Narcotics Felonies through Gambling).

Source: Wide Sample Data (1971); Vera Institute Felony Disposition Study.

Table A: Crime Class and Maximum Sentence for Each Major Charge in its Various Degrees[a]

	Charge	Degree	Crime Class	Maximum Sentence[b]
Violent	Murder	—	**A felony**	Life
	Manslaughter	First	B felony	25 years
		Second	C felony	15 years
	Rape	First	**B felony**	25 years
		Second	D felony	7 years
		Third	E felony	4 years
	Sexual Misconduct	—	A misdemeanor	1 year
	Robbery[c]	First	**B felony**	25 years
		Second	C felony	15 years
		Third	D felony	7 years
	Assault	First	**C felony**	15 years
		Second	D felony	7 years
		Third	A misdemeanor	1 year
	Menacing	—	B misdemeanor	90 days
	Harassment	—	Violation[d]	15 days
Property	Burglary	First	**B felony**	25 years
		Second	C felony	15 years
		Third	D felony	7 years
	Criminal Trespass	First	D felony	7 years
		Second	A misdemeanor	1 year
		Third	B misdemeanor	90 days
		Fourth	Violation[d]	15 days
	Grand Larceny	First	**C felony**	15 years
		Second	D felony	7 years
		Third	E felony	4 years
	Criminal Possession of Stolen Property	First	D felony	7 years
		Second	E felony	4 years
		Third	A misdemeanor	1 year
	Forgery	First	**C felony**	15 years
		Second	D felony	7 years
		Third	E felony	4 years

(continued on page 12)

Charge	Degree	Crime Class	Maximum Sentence[b]
Narcotics (Sale or Possession)	First	**A felony**	Life
	Second	B felony	25 years
	Third	C felony	15 years
Criminal Possession of Dangerous Weapons[e] ...	—	**D felony**	7 years
Gambling	First	**E felony**	4 years
	Second	A misdemeanor	1 year

(Victimless)

Source: Penal Law of the State of New York, 1971.

a. There were no amendments to the Penal Law between 1971 and 1973 that would change the information presented in this table, except with regard to narcotics felonies, for which the changes were substantial. The 1971 provisions are presented here.

b. The Penal Law also authorizes the court to impose minimum terms of imprisonment as well as non-prison sentences:

A felony—at least 15 years, no more than 25 years (judge must set).

B felony—at least 1 year, no more than 8⅓ years (or leave to discretion of Parole Board).

C felony—at least 1 year, no more than 5 years (or leave to discretion of Parole Board).

D felony—at least 1 year, no more than 2⅓ years (or leave to discretion of Parole Board).

E felony—not less than 1 year, set by Parole Board only (or judge may set a definite maximum term of up to one year).

c. Although the second and third degrees of robbery are higher level felonies than the second and third degrees of rape, rape is rated as a more serious felony in this monograph because the deep sample cases suggest it is more often charged in the first degree (92%) than is robbery (53%).

d. A violation is technically not a crime under the Penal Law.

e. There are a number of E felony and A misdemeanor variations, and the crime becomes a B felony if the weapon possessed is any explosive substance with intent to use the same against the person or property of another.

Table B makes use of these statutory gradations, rather than the generic names of the various felonies, to show the relationship between the level of the initial charge and the level of the ultimate plea.

Table B makes it apparent that, in general, the higher the level of felony charged at arrest, the less deterioration there was in the course to disposition. For example, when a guilty plea was obtained in cases commenced by arrest for an A felony, reduction of the charge was less likely and the extent of re-

Table B: Crime Class of Guilty Pleas, by Crime Class of Felony Charged at Arrest

Class of Felony Charged at Arrest	\.	Class of Crime to Which Guilty Plea Made							
		A fel.	B fel.	C fel.	D fel.	E fel.	A misd.	B misd.	Violation[a]	Infraction[a]
A		31%	9%	9%	22%	16%	12%	—	—	—
B		—	5	9	23	25	29	7	3	—
C		—	2	1	14	13	53	11	7	—
D		—	—	—	5	10	51	19	14	1
E		—	—	1	4	8	52	20	9	5

Source: Wide Sample Data (1971); Vera Institute Felony Disposition Study.

a. Violations and infractions are technically considered not to be crimes under the Penal Law.

duction was less than when the initial charge was for a lower crime class. B felony charges were more elastic, although 62% of the pleas in such cases were felony pleas. Cases commenced with C felony charges or below were much more likely to end in misdemeanor pleas. Seventy-one percent of pleas in the C felony arrest cases were to misdemeanors or less. The rate of pleas to misdemeanors or less was 85% in the D felony cases and 86% in the E felony cases.

Figures 4 and 5 and Table B, taken together, suggest proportionality. The chances of dismissal, of misdemeanor plea, and of charge reduction generally are related in a rough way to the seriousness of the initial charge. This suggestion of proportionality is further reinforced by evidence from the wide sample regarding sentences imposed on defendants following conviction.

As Figure 6 (page 14) shows, the more serious the offense charged at arrest in each general category, the stiffer is the sentence likely to be following conviction, whether the conviction was for the felony originally charged, a lesser felony, or a misdemeanor. For example, more than 85% of convicted defendants charged initially with homicide or rape drew felony time, whereas only 31% of convicted defendants charged initially with assault drew any time at all—and only 7% drew felony time.

As noted earlier, however, it is necessary to examine the specific crimes and actors, not just the charge labels or the sentences, to understand whether court processes are working rationally. Before turning to that examination, it may be useful to describe the process by which dispositions are reached in New York's criminal justice system.

Figure 6. Sentence Following Conviction, by Type of Felony Charged at Arrest: Percent Given Each Sentence

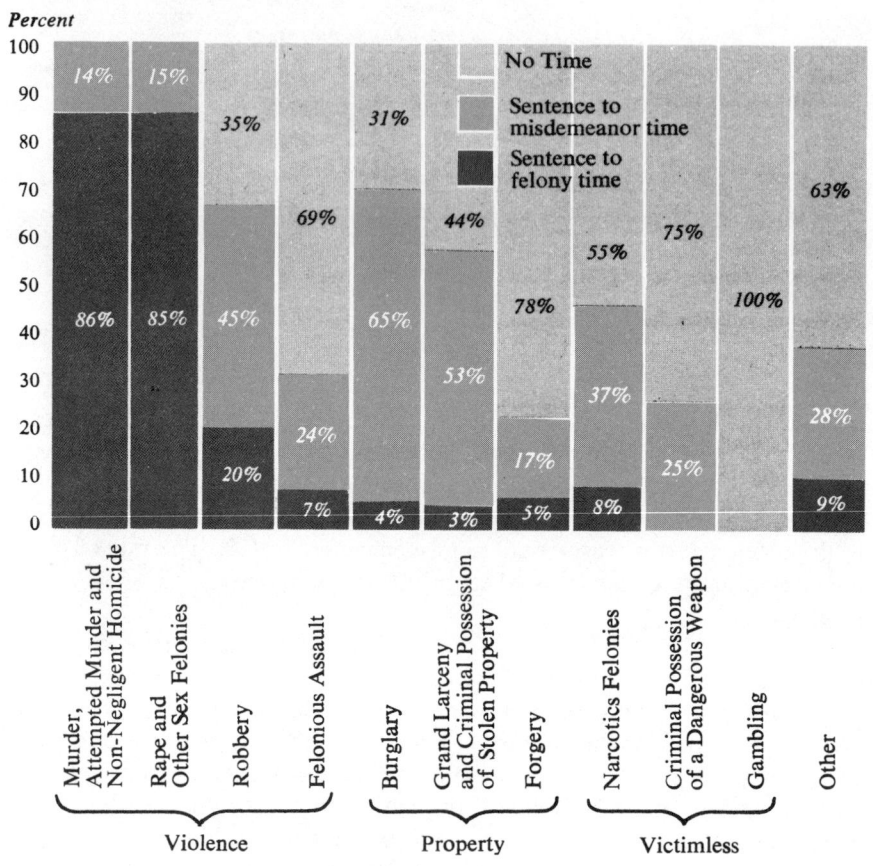

Percent

Legend:
- No Time
- Sentence to misdemeanor time
- Sentence to felony time

Category	Felony time	Misdemeanor time	No time
Murder, Attempted Murder and Non-Negligent Homicide	86%		14%
Rape and Other Sex Felonies	85%		15%
Robbery	20%	45%	35%
Felonious Assault	7%	24%	69%
Burglary	4%	65%	31%
Grand Larceny and Criminal Possession of Stolen Property	3%	53%	44%
Forgery	5%	17%	78%
Narcotics Felonies	8%	37%	55%
Criminal Possession of a Dangerous Weapon		25%	75%
Gambling			100%
Other	9%	28%	63%

Groupings: Violence (Murder, Rape, Robbery, Felonious Assault); Property (Burglary, Grand Larceny and Criminal Possession of Stolen Property, Forgery); Victimless (Narcotics Felonies, Criminal Possession of a Dangerous Weapon, Gambling)

Source: Wide Sample Data (1971); Vera Institute Felony Disposition Study.

The Process of Reaching Dispositions

New York City's Police Department makes most, but not all, felony arrests; the Transit Police, Housing Police and Port Authority Police also bring felony charges to the courts for processing. There is a city-wide Criminal Court, with separate court facilities in each borough, for processing misdemeanors. The maximum jail sentence that may be imposed in Criminal Court is one year. The Criminal Court also handles felony cases at their first arraignment and preliminary hearing. Each borough has a Supreme Court to dispose of felony cases not screened out by the Criminal Court or by the Grand Jury. There is no jurisdictional bar, however, to a misdemeanor disposition being reached once a case is in the Supreme Court.

The arresting officer first takes a felony case to the Criminal Court Complaint Room where an Assistant District Attorney (ADA) reviews the charge. The Complaint Room ADA is empowered to raise, reduce or dismiss the charge on the spot, or to have the case transferred to Family Court if the defendant is a juvenile or the crime arose from a dispute between family members. The ADA can also decide to request a dismissal at arraignment, which is invariably granted by the court.

From the Complaint Room, the case goes on to the Arraignment Part in the Criminal Court. A plea to a misdemeanor or lesser offense can be taken at the Arraignment Part, and cases can be dismissed there either at the request of the ADA or, less frequently, on the judge's own initiative.

If the felony case is not disposed of by dismissal or by guilty plea to a misdemeanor at the Arraignment Part, it goes one of two routes: to the Criminal Court Trial Part for disposition, if the charge was reduced to a misdemeanor in the Complaint Room or at arraignment; or to a preliminary hearing, if the charge remains a felony as it comes out of the Arraignment Part. The purpose of the preliminary hearing is to enable a judge to determine after hearing testimony (usually the complainant's) whether there is reasonable cause to send the case on to the Grand Jury. At the Criminal Court preliminary hearing stage, a felony case can be disposed of by dismissal or by plea to a misdemeanor or violation.

Cases in which the felony charge survives preliminary hearing are sent on to the Grand Jury where the defendant may be indicted or the charge dismissed or reduced to a misdemeanor and sent back to the Criminal Court Trial Part. If the Grand Jury indicts, the case is sent to Supreme Court Arraignment (where dispositional activity is insignificant), and then to the Pretrial Conference Part. If no plea is negotiated at the pretrial conference, the case proceeds to the Supreme Court Trial Part where it can be disposed of by a dismissal, plea or trial by judge or by jury. A plea or a conviction at trial in Supreme Court may be for a misdemeanor or a felony.

The manner in which cases commenced by felony arrest flow through the system is depicted in Figure 7, next page.

It can be seen that only 23% of the felony arrests disposed of in the criminal process reached their dispositions in the Supreme Court; conversely, the great majority were disposed of in the Criminal Court either by dismissal or

Figure 7. Dispositions, by Stage of the Process Where Disposition is Reached

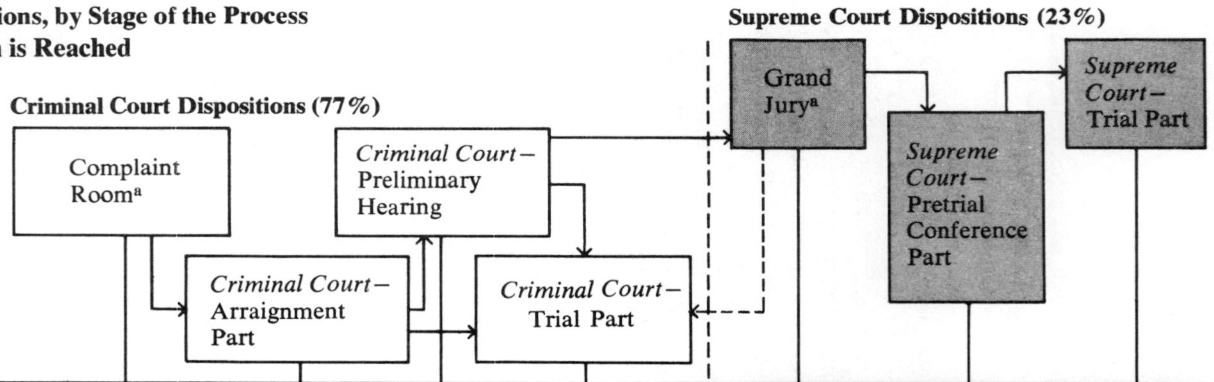

Criminal Court Dispositions (77%)

Supreme Court Dispositions (23%)

	Complaint Room[a]	Criminal Court– Arraignment Part	Criminal Court– Preliminary Hearing	Criminal Court– Trial Part	Grand Jury[a]	Supreme Court– Pretrial Conference Part	Supreme Court– Trial Part
Percent of Cases Reaching Disposition that Reach Disposition at this stage:	1%	15%	52%	9%	1%	11%	11%
Percent of Cases Reaching Disposition at this Stage that were disposed of by							
Dismissal	100%	28%	50%	17%	100%	5%	6%
Guilty Plea	0	72%	50%	70%	0	95%	63%
Trial	0	0	0	13%	0	0	31%

Sources:[a] Wide Sample Data (1971), Vera Institute Felony Disposition Study; and Deep Sample Data (1973), Vera Institute Felony Disposition Study.

a. Because the deep sample data do not include cases disposed of by dismissal in the Complaint Room or Grand Jury, the wide sample is used to show percentage that reaches disposition at those stages. The distribution of dispositions by plea, trial or dismissal within each of the other stages is found by reference to the deep sample only because the wide sample data are not sufficiently detailed. Because the two samples are combined to produce this illustration, the percentages taking certain routes to trial are different from the percentages shown in, for instance, Figure 3 above.

The Deterioration of Felony Arrests

by guilty plea (necessarily to a misdemeanor charge after the felony arrest charge was reduced). Only 4.6% of the felony arrests in the deep sample were disposed of by Criminal or Supreme Court trial.* In addition:

- The more serious the charge, the more likely the case was to be disposed of in Supreme Court rather than Criminal Court. Sixty-eight percent of homicide arrests, 34% of rape arrests and 37% of robbery arrests reached disposition in the higher court. Seventeen percent of burglaries, 14% of grand larcenies and only 9% of forgeries were disposed of there.

- If a case got to Supreme Court, it was far less likely to be dismissed than a case which reached disposition in Criminal Court. Seventy-six percent of Supreme Court dispositions† were by plea of guilty, while only 10% were dismissed there. The rest went to trial. In contrast, 56% of cases remaining in Criminal Court resulted in guilty pleas, but 43% were dismissed.‡

- The highest level of dispositional activity anywhere in the process is found at the Criminal Court "preliminary hearing" stage—the sometimes extended period after Criminal Court arraignment and before the Grand Jury either indicts on felony charges, dismisses, or sends the case back, as a misdemeanor, to a Criminal Court Trial Part. Fifty-two percent of the sample cases were disposed of at the preliminary hearing stage, and half of these dispositions were dismissals.

Data in the deep sample also reveal the distribution of prison sentences imposed at the different stages in the process. In both the Supreme Court and the Criminal Court, approximately half of those who were convicted got no jail or prison time.** Forty-eight percent of those convicted in Criminal Court were sentenced to jail (the mean time of sentences was nine months).

---

* The proportion of felony arrests going to trial was greater in the deep sample (4.6%) than in the wide sample (2.3%). The difference may be attributed to a steadily increasing trial rate in New York City as well as to methodological problems. (See Appendix.)

† Including cases disposed of by Grand Jury dismissal.

‡ Including cases disposed of by dismissal in the Complaint Room.

** Pretrial custody may, however, have served as a "time" sentence for those who waited until late in the Supreme Court stages to plead guilty, and then got walks. When the sentence was expressly to time served, it emerges in our data as "time," but only in some of the deep sample cases (where interviews reveal the bail/custody status of the defendant in the period before disposition and the effect that status had on the disposition) do we know that a defendant who walked at sentence had actually done time first. Where we know this, it is noted in the case summaries of the following chapters.

Table C: Types of Sentence Promise and Participation of the Bench in Negotiated Pleas

Explicit Sentence Promise	**72%**
(Defense counsel and prosecutor agree on sentence and judge accepts	16%)
(Judge participates in working out sentence agreement	56%)
Implicit Sentence Promise	**21%**
Made by allowing a plea to—	
(A misdemeanor (maximum one year)	17%)
(B misdemeanor or less (maximum three months)	4%)
No Sentence Promise nor Reduction of Charge to Misdemeanor	**7%**

Source: Deep Sample Data (1973); Vera Institute Felony Disposition Study.

Fifty percent of those convicted in Supreme Court were given time (the mean time was four years). Surprisingly, defendants had a greater chance of doing some time if they pled guilty at arraignment in Criminal Court than at any other stage in that court.*

Although 20% of the deep sample cases reached disposition in a Trial Part of the Criminal or Supreme Court, only 4.6% were actually tried. "Plea bargaining" took place at every stage of the process. There are, of course, instances in which the prosecution offered reduction of charges in order to clear the case from an overloaded system, and the defendant accepted and pled guilty in order to avoid further pretrial custody or the possibility of felony conviction and a prison sentence. In many cases, however, although the dispositions were reached in a congested system and were therefore often delayed or rushed, the results seem to be determined more by factors inherent in the cases themselves than by a need to clear calendars.

Before looking at those factors, it is interesting to note the incidence of various types of assurances which defendants in the deep sample received when they entered their guilty pleas. Table C, above, summarizes this information.

In 72% of cases disposed of by guilty plea, the defendant had been expressly promised a particular sentence, or an upper limit on his sentence, as

---

* Again, some of those who pled guilty at a later Criminal Court stage and were sentenced to a walk may in fact have been in pretrial custody, and thus have done some time, although they were not expressly sentenced to "time served." It is one of the faults of the data in both samples that we cannot know for certain whether the defendant was in custody or had made bail at the time of sentence.

part of the plea bargain; in three-quarters of those explicit plea agreements, the judge took an active part. In the remaining 28% of cases, the defendant had no express assurance about his sentence when he pled, but in 21% of the cases disposed of by plea he was allowed to plead guilty to a misdemeanor or a lesser offense and therefore knew the upper limit of the sentence. In only 7% of cases was there neither an explicit promise made nor a plea to a misdemeanor.

Factors Explaining Dispositions of Felony Arrests

The two factors inherent in the cases themselves which judges, prosecutors and defense attorneys cited widely as affecting case outcomes were the prior relationship of the defendant and victim and the defendant's criminal history. As Table D shows, prior relationships were found in over half of all felonies involving victims. In crimes of interpersonal violence, where one might expect to find a high incidence of personal relationships, the overall rate was 56%, ranging from a high of 83% for rape to a low of 36% for robbery. Perhaps more surprising is that 35% of burglary and larceny cases also involved prior relationships between victims and defendants.

Prior relationships included husbands and wives, lovers, prostitutes and their pimps or customers, neighbors, in-laws, junkies and dealers, even land-

Table D: Relationship between Victim and Defendant, by Felony Charged

	Prior Relationship	Stranger
Violent Crimes (N=148)	56%	44%
Attempted Homicide, Manslaughter (N=16)	50	50
Rape (N=12)	83	17
Robbery (N=53)	36	64
Assault (N=67)	69	31
Property Crimes (N=107)	35%	65%
Burglary (N=44)	39	61
Grand Larceny (N=63)	32	68
Grand Larceny-Auto (N=43)	21	79
Grand Larceny-Other (N=20)	55	45
Total Victim Felonies (N=255)	47%	53%

Source: Deep Sample Data (1973); Vera Institute Felony Disposition Study.

lords and tenants. As will be seen in the following chapters, prior relationships were often mentioned by prosecutors, in the deep sample interviews, as their reason for offering reduced charges and light sentences in return for a plea of guilty. Even more commonly, prior relationships led to dismissals.

The most frequently cited reason for dismissal in prior relationship cases was lack of cooperation by the complainant. Table E shows the proportion of dismissals in each crime category which can be traced to non-cooperation. The explanation offered most often for non-cooperation was reconciliation between the victim and defendant, although often the complainant simply never appeared and his reasons were not accurately known. As Table E shows, dismissals resulting from complainant non-cooperation were much more frequent in cases in which the defendant and victim were known to each other.

A second factor of significant influence on the disposition of felony cases was the prior record of the defendant. It was often cited in deep sample interviews as the reason for a decision to dismiss or offer a particular plea and sentence. Table F, drawn from wide sample data, confirms the impression given by the deep sample interviews.

Defendants with heavier criminal histories were more likely to be convicted and, if convicted, more likely to receive heavier sentences than those with lighter or clean records. Seventy-seven percent of convicted defendants with no prior record avoided jail or prison; only 16% of convicted defendants who had previously been sentenced to prison were as fortunate.

Table E: Proportion of Dismissals Due to Complainant Non-Cooperation, by Crime

	Prior Relationship Cases	Stranger Cases	Total Proportion of Dismissals Due to Complainant Non-Cooperation
Rape	100% (n=6)	0% (n=1)	86%
Assault	92% (n=25)	40% (n=5)	83%
Robbery	75% (n=12)	50% (n=4)	69%
Burglary	75% (n=8)	100% (n=3)	82%
Grand Larceny	73% (n=11)	0% (n=11)	36%
Total	87% (n=62)	29% (n=24)	69% (n=86)

Source: Deep Sample Data (1973); Vera Institute Felony Disposition Study.

Table F: Disposition of Current Felony Charge, by Defendant's Prior Record (N=1382)

Disposition on Current Charge	No Prior Record	Arrest (No Convictions Known)	Conviction No Prison	Conviction Prison	Incidence of This Type of Disposition in Sample
Dismissal/Acquittal	54%	45%	36%	29%	44%
Conviction	46	55	64	71	56
Sentence:					
Walk	77	61	42	16	50
Misdemeanor Time	22	37	56	56	41
Felony Time	1	2	2	28	9
Incidence of this type of record in sample	39%	27%	14%	20%	

Source: Wide Sample Data (1971); Vera Institute Felony Disposition Study.

Summary

The data summarized in this chapter shed light on court processing and the factors at work in that process, but they represent only the first step in understanding that process. It is the detail of case summaries in subsequent chapters, not the gross data reported here, that brings the process to life and permits distinctions to be drawn between its rational and irrational elements.

The research on which both the broad picture and the detail are based was exploratory. An attempt was made to find some explanations for the deterioration of felony arrests, but not to find all explanations. The methodology unfortunately prevented coherent analysis of the impact of some potentially powerful factors on which further research is needed. For example, prior research has indicated that a defendant's inability to win pretrial release—on bail or on his own recognizance—has an influence, independent of all other variables, on the likelihood of conviction and on severity of sentence. Our data were not sufficient to further validate that thesis, although the influence of extended pretrial custody on the defendant's willingness to plead guilty and on the prosecutor's willingness to agree to a "walk," and the influence of extended pretrial liberty on the defendant's ability to wait for a better offer and on the prosecutor's reasons to oblige, are noted in the summaries of individual deep sample cases in the following chapters.

Similarly, we were not able systematically to go behind the initial charging decision to explore how often intentional overcharging occurs, in what kinds of cases, and what the motives for it might be. In addition, we were unable to answer other kinds of questions because of the limited size of the data base. For example, several of the felonies analyzed in later chapters carry different maximum sentences when a gun, an injury or concerted action is involved. Generally, the deep sample was too small, when cases were subclassified for these factors, either to establish or to dispel the possibility that they play a major part in shaping dispositions.

The data are sufficient, however, to raise questions about the validity of some current thinking about crime. They should provoke others to dig further into the dispositional process in order to obtain answers, both to questions raised here and to questions not yet asked.

The next five chapters explore dispositions, patterns and explanatory factors as they emerged from deep sample data for the crime categories which most concern the public and the police. The first of them is devoted to the felonies of "pure" personal violence: felonious assault, rape, murder and attempted murder. The next chapter looks at robbery, the archetypal violent felony in which physical attack is combined with larcenous motive. The following two discuss the property felonies, burglary and grand larceny. The remaining crime-category chapter is the only one devoted to a "victimless" crime (crime without a complainant), felonious possession of a handgun. This crime was chosen rather than narcotics felonies, which are generally considered more serious, because both the Penal Law and the criminal process relating to narcotics felonies have been substantially overhauled since our sampling, rendering our findings for narcotics offenses less relevant to current policy issues.* Finally, this report concludes with some reflections on the study.

---

* The effect of New York State's new drug law, which took effect on September 1, 1973, on arrests, convictions and sentences for narcotics offenses is the subject of study by the Drug Law Evaluation Project, organized under the auspices of the Association of the Bar of the City of New York and the Drug Abuse Council Inc., with funding from the National Institute of Law Enforcement and Criminal Justice of the U.S. Justice Department's Law Enforcement Assistance Administration.

2 Assault, Rape, Murder and Attempted Murder

The felonies of "pure" violence—that is, violence against the person without an obvious larcenous motive—are discussed in this chapter. Of the 369 cases in the deep sample, 67 entered the court process charged as felony assaults. Twelve were charged as rape, 9 as attempted murder and 7 as murder.

Of the crimes of "pure" violence, assault was the only one that afforded enough cases to permit a meaningful statistical breakdown. Nevertheless, the details of rape, attempted murder and murder cases contain valuable information about the factors that produce dispositions in those felonies.

Assaults

Intentionally or recklessly inflicting injury on another is assault in the third degree, an A misdemeanor punishable by up to one year in jail.* Felony assaults arise from aggravating factors (for example, assault with a weapon or dangerous instrument, assault on a police officer or fireman in the course of his duties, or assault resulting in disabling or disfiguring injuries). The most serious of assaults—in the first degree—carries a 15-year maximum sentence as a C felony.

Fact Patterns in Assaults

Thirteen of the 67 defendants in the deep sample assault cases were arrested for attacks on their friends and acquaintances. Another 12 were accused of attacking spouses or lovers. Altogether, 46 (69%) of the assault cases involved prior relationships. In 9 cases (13%), the defendant was accused of assaulting a police officer.

The defendant had no previous record of arrest for misdemeanors or felonies in 21 (46%) of the prior relationship cases and in 10 (48%) of the stranger cases. Prior arrests for assault figured in the criminal histories of defendants in 11 (24%) of the prior relationship cases and in 4 (19%) of the stranger cases.

---

* "Reckless endangerment" is a crime closely related to assault. It may be charged as a D felony against one who, "under circumstances evincing a depraved indifference to human life, recklessly engaged in conduct which creates grave risk of death to another." If the risk is only one of "serious" (rather than "grave") injury, reckless endangerment is an A misdemeanor. If, however, serious injury results from conduct falling within the reckless endangerment definition, the crime becomes first degree assault, the C felony.

Only one defendant entered our sample for arrest on D-felony reckless endangerment; his case is treated as a felonious assault and is included in this chapter.

There were injuries in about four-fifths of the assault cases, but serious injuries in 42% and permanent or disabling injuries in only 4 cases (6%). Weapons were used in 78% of the cases, but were much more common when victim and assailant had a prior relationship (93%) than when they were strangers (43%). The most commonly used weapon was a knife; 28 (42%) of the cases involved use of knives. The variety of other weapons included a brick, a rolling pin, a hammer, "assorted household throwables," and a pencil.

Only 5 defendants—all in prior relationship cases—were accused of assault with a gun. In one of these cases the gun was apparently not discharged and in another the complaining witness recanted her testimony that the defendant had used a gun. In one case a gun was discharged but caused no injury and in two—both resulting in felony convictions—injury resulted from the gunshot. The low incidence of gun assaults is partially explained by the fact that most gun attacks are charged as attempted murder rather than assault, although with the two categories combined there were still only 12 gun attacks in the deep sample assault and attempted murder cases.

To the extent that a typical felony assault arrest can be constructed, it arose from an argument between friends that erupted into a fight and involved the infliction of minor injury with whatever object was nearest at hand. And it was dismissed because the victim refused to testify.

Deterioration of Assault Arrests

The deep sample data suggest that arrests for felony assault deteriorate more dramatically than arrests for felonies in general, as Figure 8 shows.*

In Figure 2, page 5, above, it was seen that reports to the policy of felony assault are much less frequent than reports of robbery, burglary or grand larceny, but that the arrest rate is considerably higher for assault than for the other crimes. Yet Figure 8 shows that a defendant who enters the criminal process charged with a felony assault is less likely to be convicted than defendants entering the process on other felony charges. If convicted, he is less likely to be convicted of a felony; he is also less likely to get a prison

---

* The wide sample, with its larger number of cases, would have provided a sounder statistical basis for analyzing deterioration of arrest charges here and in subsequent chapters. Unfortunately, however, the wide sample did not permit analysis of critical issues, such as prior relationships, which are discussed in detail in these chapters. Consequently, deep sample data are used. Overall, statistical differences between the wide and deep samples with regard to case outcomes were not great. For an analysis of crime-by-crime differences between the two samples, see Appendix.

Figure 8. Dispositional Pattern for Felony Assault Arrests Compared to All Felony Arrests

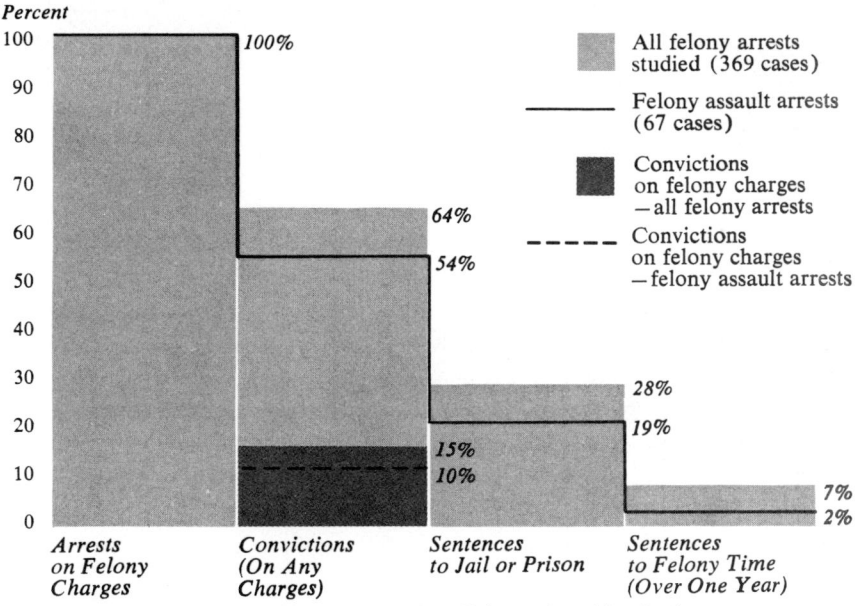

(Felony assault arrests are 18% of all felony arrests studied.)

Percent

- All felony arrests studied (369 cases)
- Felony assault arrests (67 cases)
- Convictions on felony charges — all felony arrests
- Convictions on felony charges — felony assault arrests

Arrests on Felony Charges: 100%
Convictions (On Any Charges): 64% / 54%
Sentences to Jail or Prison: 15% / 10%
Sentences to Felony Time (Over One Year): 28% / 19% / 7% / 2%

Source: Deep Sample Data (1973); Vera Institute Felony Disposition Study.

sentence and less likely to be given felony time. Thus, the criminal process does not appear to regard these cases as very serious.

The 67 deep sample cases commenced by arrest for felony assault reached their disposition by the routes shown in Figure 9 (next page). Thirty of the 67 felony assault arrests were dismissed after entering the criminal process. In only 2 of the remaining 37 was guilt resolved at trial; one ended with conviction for harassment (a violation) and a 15-day jail sentence, and the other ended in acquittal. None of the 35 who pled guilty did so to the same level of felony as had been charged. Seven pled guilty to a lesser felony charge,* but these 7 felony convictions netted only one felony time sentence—the only felony time sentence in the entire assault sample. Just over half (15) of the 28 remaining pleas were to the A misdemeanor (assault in the third degree),

---

* Two pled guilty to assault in the second degree, a D felony, and five pled guilty to attempted assault in the second degree, an E felony.

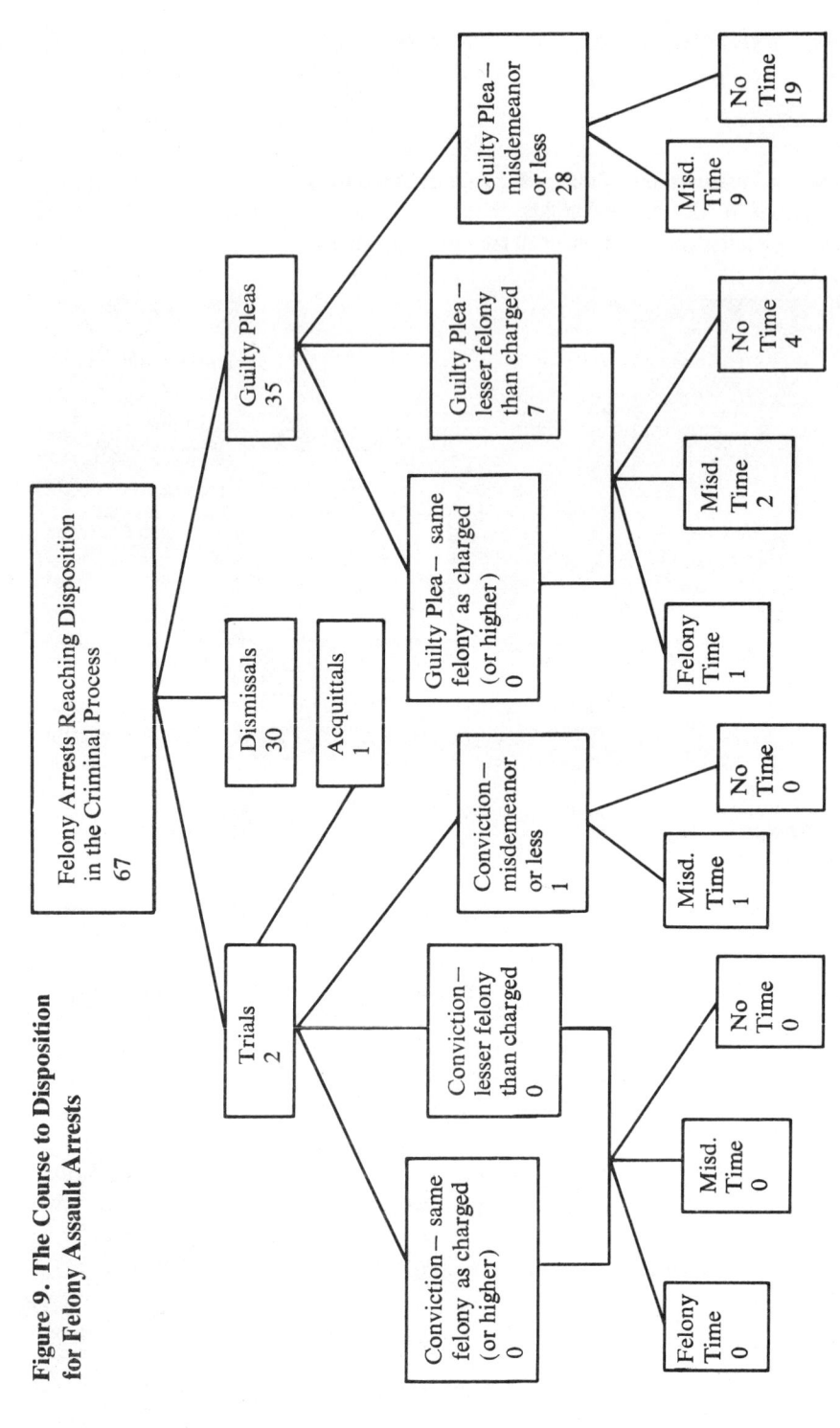

Figure 9. The Course to Disposition for Felony Assault Arrests

Felony Arrests Reaching Disposition in the Criminal Process: 67

- Dismissals: 30
- Acquittals: 1
- Guilty Pleas: 35
  - Guilty Plea—misdemeanor or less: 28
    - Misd. Time: 9
    - No Time: 19
  - Guilty Plea—lesser felony than charged: 7
    - Felony Time: 1
    - Misd. Time: 2
    - No Time: 4
  - Guilty Plea—same felony as charged (or higher): 0
- Trials: 2
  - Conviction—same felony as charged (or higher): 0
    - Felony Time: 0
    - Misd. Time: 0
    - No Time: 0
  - Conviction—lesser felony than charged: 0
  - Conviction—misdemeanor or less: 1
    - Misd. Time: 1
    - No Time: 0

Source: Deep Sample Data (1973); Vera Institute Felony Disposition Study.

while the others included 4 to B misdemeanors and 9 to mere violations. Only a third (9) of the 28 who pled to a misdemeanor or less got any time at all, and 7 of the 9 jail sentences were to 6 months or less. The 19 others who pled guilty to misdemeanors walked, as did 4 of the 7 who pled guilty to felonies.

Factors Explaining Dispositions of Assault Arrests

Assault, more than other serious felonies, is likely to be a spontaneous response to conflict arising in common life situations rather than an attack by a predatory criminal. The incidence of prior relationships between victim and assailant was therefore expected to be high among the assaults, and this was borne out by analysis of the deep sample cases. Prior relationships of some sort existed in 46 (69%) of the 67 cases. This supports the speculation in the preceding chapter that the comparatively high arrest and "clearance" rates for reported felony assaults might be explained by the relative ease of arrest in cases where the victim knows the assailant. The relationships found in the deep sample assault cases are summarized in Table G.

Deterioration of the felony arrests was substantially greater in the prior relationship cases than in the cases where victim and defendant were stran-

Table G: Prior Relationships in Assault Cases and Case Outcomes

Nature of Relationship	No. of Cases	No. Dismissed	No. Convicted
Spouses or common-law spouses	6	3	3
Lovers	6	2	4
Former spouses or lovers	2	1	1
Family and in-laws	5	4	1
Friends	8	5[a]	3
Neighbors	5	4	1
Acquaintances	5	2	3
Business[b]	7	2	5
Unspecified relationship	2	2	—
Total with Prior Relationships	46	25	21
(Total without Prior Relationships)	(21)	(6)	(15)

Source: Deep Sample Data (1973); Vera Institute Felony Disposition Study.

a. Includes one acquitted at trial.
b. These relationships were: building superintendent/tenant (two cases); car repairman/customer (two cases); cab driver/customer; store owner/customer; and prostitute/customer.

gers. Figure 10 presents a graphic comparison of the dispositional patterns.

Dismissal of assault charges in prior relationship cases was often explained, in the deep sample interviews, by the victim's refusal to press forward with the complaint. A second common explanation lay in the feeling of the judge and prosecutor that the underlying personal conflict was trivial or that an adjournment in contemplation of dismissal (ACD), with dismissal conditioned on a period of good behavior, would afford the victim sufficient protection against repetition of the attack. Conversely, the higher rate of conviction among the stranger cases can be attributed to the greater cooperation the victims offered to the prosecution. Most important in this regard is that 9 of the 21 complaining witnesses in stranger assaults were police officers. Only one of these officers failed to secure some sort of conviction

Figure 10. Deterioration of Prior Relationship Assault Arrests and Stranger Assault Arrests

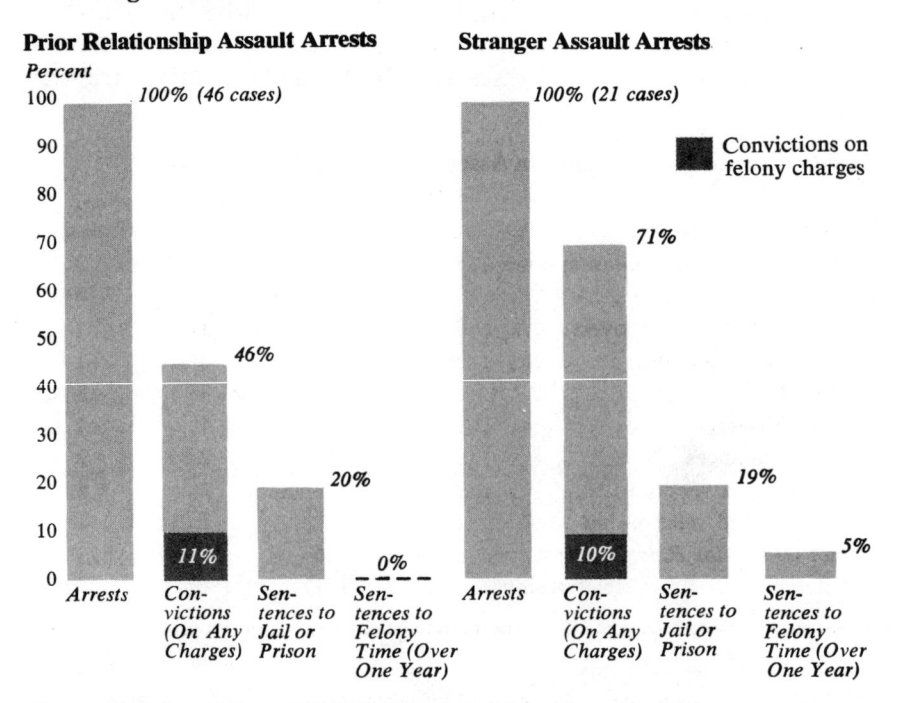

Source: Deep Sample Data (1973); Vera Institute Felony Disposition Study.

Table H: Sentences in Assault Cases, by Relationship of Victim to Defendant

	No. Convicted	Sentence Walk No.	%	Time No.	%
Prior Relationship (N=46)	21	12	57	9	43
Stranger (N=21)	15	11	73	4	27

Source: Deep Sample Data (1973); Vera Institute Felony Disposition Study.

Table I: Injuries in Assault Cases, By Relationship of Victim to Defendant

	Serious (Requiring Medical Attention) No. %	Minor (Superficial) No. %	None No. %	Unknown No. %
Prior Relationship (N=46)	21 46	18 39	5 11	2 4
Stranger (N=21)	7 33	7 33	7 33	– –

Source: Deep Sample Data (1973); Vera Institute Felony Disposition Study.

against his alleged assailant, but 5 of the 8 convictions were for violations (one for drunken driving and 4 for harassment).

Although dismissal was the most frequent disposition in prior relationship assault cases, the prior relationship cases that survived dismissal resulted in more serious dispositions than stranger cases that survived dismissal. Table H reveals that a convicted defendant in a prior relationship case was more likely to get time than a convicted defendant in a stranger case.

As Table I shows, serious injury—that is, injury requiring some medical attention, stitches or hospitalization*—was more frequent in the prior relationship cases (46%) than in stranger cases (33%). This may explain the

---

* Any injury for which the victim sought medical attention was classified as "serious" in Table I, but only four such injuries were permanent or disabling. One case (a stranger assault with a pencil that permanently damaged the victim's eye) was dismissed when the defendant was found unfit to stand trial; the other stranger defendant who inflicted permanent injury was fit to stand trial but was unbalanced and sentenced to felony time in a psychiatric hospital. Although conviction resulted in both of the prior relationship cases involving permanent injury, one defendant was allowed to plead to a violation and walked when the victim (his common-law wife) refused to appear to testify against him. The other defendant had attacked a neighbor with a bucket of lye.

more lenient sentences for stranger assaults, half of which involved police officers as victims.

The extent of injury was widely cited in the deep sample interviews by judges, prosecutors, police officers and defense attorneys as measures of the seriousness of an assault. It is not surprising, therefore, that the prior relationship cases which were more likely to involve serious injury than stranger cases were also more likely to end in a sentence to time. And this standard is, after all, embodied in the statute that raises simple assault to a felony if injury is serious or if a dangerous weapon is used.

The higher incidence of serious injuries in prior relationship cases was matched by the more frequent use of weapons, as seen in Table J.

Virtually all (93%) defendants who attacked people they knew used a weapon of some kind; over half used a knife. But less than half (43%) of those who allegedly attacked strangers used any weapon at all. There were no felony convictions and only one jail sentence among the 15 dispositions of cases in which no weapon was used.

The deep sample interviews suggest two reasons why injuries and weapons are found more frequently in the prior relationship cases and why, if convicted, a defendant has a greater chance of drawing time if the victim was someone he knew. First, the police are likely to be called to intervene in family fights or conflicts between friends and acquaintances—and are likely to arrest one of the parties—only when the conflict gets out of hand, resulting or threatening to result in injuries or involving a weapon. Thus, when a prior relationship assault case is serious enough to trigger a felony arrest and to motivate the complaining witness to cooperate with the prosecution to secure a conviction, it is also likely to be serious enough to draw time.

Second, the Penal Law makes what otherwise would be simple assault a felony if the victim is a police officer. Nine (43%) of the defendants in stranger assault cases were accused of attacking police officers. These cases were, as a group, the least serious in the assault sample. None involved the use of a weapon and there was only one serious injury to a police officer,* although a few defendants accused of assaulting officers received serious injuries themselves. The typical disposition in cases alleging assault against police officers was a plea of guilty to a violation followed by a conditional

---

* The injury in that case did not increase the sentence because the charges were dismissed. Eight people, including four police officers, were shoving each other about in a dark driveway. The prosecutor doubted he could show that the defendant was responsible for any particular assault or that the police officer's injury was a result. (See case description, page 37.)

Table J: Use of Weapons in Assault Cases, by Relationship of Victim to Defendant

	Gun	Knife	Broken Bottle or Glass	Blackjack or Club	Lye or Chemical Spray	Other
Prior Relationship (N=46)	5	24[a]	1	6	4	3[b]
Stranger (N=21)	–	4	2	1	–	2[c]

Source: Deep Sample Data (1973); Vera Institute Felony Disposition Study.

a. Two razors (used by friends who attacked each other and both of whom entered our sample) and one pair of scissors (used by a woman who attacked her cab driver) are counted as "knives."

b. One "hammer," one "sharp object" and one "assorted household throwables" are counted as "Other."

c. One pencil and one brick.

discharge. Had police officers not been involved, none of these cases would have drawn the felony label at arrest.* Thus, the pattern of deterioration of deep sample felony assault arrests seems to be a product of the high incidence of prior relationship between victim and defendant, the resulting lack of cooperation from the victims in those cases and, in the cases of assaults against strangers, the relative lack of seriousness of the attack. The detail provided by the deep sample interviews reveals more about the way these factors operate and interact.

Prior Relationship Assaults. More than half of the prior relationship cases (24 of 46) were dismissed; in 22 (92%) of these dismissals, the primary reason given in interviews was the victim's refusal to cooperate with the prosecution. An Assistant District Attorney (ADA) described one of them.

"This woman was charged on the complaint of her common-law husband. She then filed a complaint against him for assault. I don't know which of them called the police first. The charge against her was reduced in the Complaint Room to assault in the third degree [a misdemeanor]. Because they were both complainants in court, I was able to speak to them both. . . . They told me they did not wish to continue prosecution. They told me that they were both drinking and apparently they both started to insult each other. It wasn't clear who struck first, but the common-law husband struck his wife

---
* If the cases with police officer complainants are excluded, the rate of prior relationships in the remaining deep sample assaults rises to 79% and the rate of dismissal to 52%.

with a shovel, hitting her in the eye, and she struck him in the arm with an exacto knife, causing injury. Neither said they were injured seriously, though the arresting police officer had written up her assault against her husband as assault in the second degree, while his assault against her was a third degree assault. She was also charged with possession of a weapon as an A misdemeanor, which was also dropped because the husband refused to testify as to how the knife was used. The knife was not classified as a dangerous instrument per se.

"When I had satisfied myself that neither had been injured seriously, I looked at their past records. He had one previous arrest ten years ago, I don't recall for what, and she had no prior arrests. I felt that since there had not been problems with the law, and neither one had any sort of record, there was no reason to keep this case in court."

This case is typical of the prior relationship assaults in a number of ways: first, the victim was not interested in pressing for a conviction and was reconciled with the assailant after the arrest had been made; second, the victim was not entirely innocent; and third, the passion of the relationship led to infliction of injuries in the attack, but the injuries were not so obviously serious that the attack fit the definition of assault in the second degree, thus justifying a felony charge.

Dismissal because of complainant non-cooperation appears less likely to occur when the prior relationship is a business, rather than a personal, one. Only two of the seven cases involving a business relationship resulted in dismissal, and in one the dismissal followed from the filing of cross-complaints which were mutually withdrawn.

The chances of serving time were about even for the 21 defendants in prior relationship assault cases who were convicted: 9 got time and 12 walked. The 9 assailants who got time had inflicted injury *and* had used a weapon; 7 of them had prior records, and the 2 with no prior record had inflicted very serious injuries. All but one of the 9 were sentenced to less than a year.

The importance of the injury to the sentence, in cases not dismissed, is illustrated by the following case.

"At first, this case seemed very simple," according to the Legal Aid attorney. "The defendant had lived for ten years in the same building as the victim. Conflict between them had brought them to Housing Court several times before on cross-complaints. This time the assault arose when the defendant's daughter told her that the other woman had struck her. The defendant went

to the laundromat where she worked, returned with a bucket of lye used there to clean the machines, and threw it in the other woman's face. She told the police she had done it and they arrested her the next day, after the victim went to the precinct station, for first degree assault. She pled guilty to third degree assault, the misdemeanor—but that was before anyone had seen the victim in court."

The prosecutor in this case refused to be interviewed but the judge said, "The ADA wanted to know the victim's condition before reducing the charge to the misdemeanor level. But when he called the hospital they just said the victim was no longer there. So the ADA decided to accept the plea because there appeared to be nothing serious there, because the defendant had turned herself in and because of her home situation and lack of prior record."

The Legal Aid attorney continued, "There was no promise about the sentence, but I thought at the time that she would walk—probation at the worst. She was forty-three, living with her husband, and both of them were working. Six of their seven children lived with them and three of them were very sick with sickle-cell anemia. None of them had a prior record—not her, her husband or the kids. It is rare to find that in her neighborhood. The probation report recommended a conditional discharge. But at the next hearing, for sentence, the victim showed up; she is maimed for life and it is possible she'll lose sight in both eyes. The defendant might as well have shot her. No one could look at her, and she was screaming for the defendant to be sent to jail. The press had picked up on the case, and the judge indicated he would give the maximum possible on her plea—a year. She would have gotten zero to five years if she'd refused to plead and gone to trial where the jury could see those injuries. But I persuaded the judge to have a presentence conference with reports and witnesses. Her children testified about being hit by the other woman, and it was clear that the defendant had suffered years of persecution at her hands. In the end, the judge sentenced the woman to six months in jail."

The interviews reveal the shock of the judge and Legal Aid attorney at the nature and extent of the victim's injuries. But the arresting police officer was suprised that the defendant got any time at all: "This was a 'lye case.' In the South, where she comes from, this is very common. I saw her [the victim] and it's awful, but these two had been feuding for a long time, the defendant turned herself in even before we had the complaint, and she had no prior record. I didn't think they would give her jail."

When the injury is serious, the prosecutor will generally try to keep the case alive, but often his efforts cannot overcome the problems posed by a witness whose reluctance to testify is rooted in a previously amicable relationship with the defendant. Thus, in one stabbing case where the victim spent a month in the hospital with serious injuries, the ADA refused to let her withdraw the complaint for felony assault. However, the judge dismissed the case for lack of evidence at the preliminary hearing when she changed her story. There were no other witnesses.

The victim's refusal to cooperate appears to have been based in most cases on a reconciliation with the defendant, but in several cases in which the defendant filed a cross-complaint against the victim, the prosecutor's difficulties may have been caused more by the victim's fear of self-incrimination. Cross-complaints were filed in eight of the prior relationship assault cases; in seven of these, the case was dismissed becaue of victim non-cooperation. One cross-complaint case went to trial, despite the victim's reluctance to testify, because it was the District Attorney's policy in that borough not to dismiss when the assault causes serious injury. In that case, the victim refused to testify when put on the stand at trial, invoking his privilege against self-incrimination, and the defendant was acquitted.

Even if an ADA can compel a reluctant victim's presence and testimony, thereby avoiding dismissal of the case, the prior relationship may force him to settle for a lighter disposition at sentence than, in his judgment, the injuries warrant. One such case arose when a woman complained to the police that a man she used to live with had gone mad with jealousy as she was trying to break up with him, had come to her apartment, beaten her, forced her at gunpoint to return to his apartment and held her there against her will for 12 hours. The defendant was arrested on 15 charges including kidnapping, assault, burglary and illegal possession of a gun.* He had been to court before for assaulting her. When she failed to show up at court, the arresting officer went looking for her. "I couldn't find her," he said. "They had a strange relationship. I wish I'd never got involved in it."

"Both the defendant and his girlfriend were a little crazy," according to the defense attorney. *"She called this assault a 'mistake' and when the judge re-*

---

* There were too few kidnapping cases in the sample to warrant a separate treatment for them, and in this case the judge, ADA and defense attorney all agreed that, in the circumstances, the charge represented an "over-indictment." The gun possession charge was dropped when a plea was taken. The ADA wasn't interested in pressing it "because of a search problem."

fused to drop the charges she got herself a lawyer. She refused to testify at any of the hearings. I didn't think he'd be convicted by a jury, but there was certainly a risk. In spite of the relationship, the charges were very serious. Had he been convicted, he could have gotten up to 25 years in prison."

The defense attorney wanted the charges reduced to an A misdemeanor. The ADA refused. "The girl was so reluctant to testify I had to have her arrested and put in Civil Jail for five days as a material witness before I could get her to appear. She claimed she had been threatened. But I refused to go to an A misdemeanor because of the injuries. She had a fractured nose, broken teeth. He would have been convicted of assault at trial. But, given the way she had behaved, there was a chance the jury would react: 'she got what she deserved.' Without the relationship between them, the case would have been very strong. The other charges would have stuck, too, and altogether they could carry up to 25 years. But I settled for an E felony [attempted second degree assault] and a conditional discharge. Five years probation would have been better, but he was on federal probation for a credit card case and, this way, if he bothers her again within the year, he can get up to four years prison anyway."

The defense attorney found it acceptable too: "The condition was that he stay away from the girl. When he left the court the judge called for her to be brought in and explained to her to stay away from him. Still, they won't stay away from each other. It's a love-hate relationship."

The Supreme Court judge thought that "because of the relationship and all the circumstances, this case should have been taken care of downstairs [that is, a misdemeanor plea should have been offered and accepted in the lower court]. She said on the record that she was against him going to jail—that she just wanted to be left alone. In a case like this, it all depends on her testimony. In a trial, he might have been acquitted because of the relationship and she being such a reluctant witness. The conditional discharge seemed the most sensible thing to me. I've heard that he assaulted her again last week. Now it's up to her—but I doubt she'll bring him in again. These prior relationship cases should really be going to Family Court."

Most of the non-cooperating prior relationship assault victims seem simply to have changed their minds after complaining to the police in the heat of the moment. But in at least four cases, the victims refused to cooperate because they felt that the criminal process was an inappropriate response. The following are illustrative.

- A 24-year-old man with a history of mental illness went berserk and stabbed his brother with a pocket knife. An ambulance was summoned. The driver called the police, who arrested the defendant for assault and criminal possession of a dangerous weapon. The assault charge was transferred to Family Court and the weapons charge was dismissed in Criminal Court, when the brother refused to testify. Neither the brother nor the mother had wanted police involvement: they had called for the ambulance, not the police.

- A man tried to stab his former wife. The Legal Aid attorney explained the dismissal this way: "The evidence was probably excellent in this case. Most important, however, is that the guy is crazy. He's receiving counselling at Creedmore. She didn't want him to go to jail; she said he was nice so long as he didn't drink." The ADA was in agreement: "I interviewed her and she stated that he was sick, had no place to live and came back to live with her. She didn't want him to go to jail. He had been taking some pills on the night of the incident. I believe I suggested to her that the case be adjourned in contemplation of dismissal, and she was in favor of it. I felt this disposition would protect her."

It might be expected that defendants in prior relationship assault cases either would have no prior criminal record or, if they had, would have records of repeated assaults. But in fact, over half did have prior records, usually only for *non-*assaultive offenses: among the 54% with prior records, three-fifths had no previous assault arrests.* Only one defendant had a record of prior assault against the same victim. Defendants in the stranger cases were not very different in this respect: 48% had prior records, two-thirds of whom had not previously been arrested for assault.

Stranger Assaults. The 21 cases of assault against strangers were dismissed far less frequently (29%) than were the prior relationship cases (52%), and none were dismissed because of the victim's non-cooperation. One of the 6 stranger assault dismissals occurred when the defendant, who was already in prison when accused of assault on another inmate, was found to be mentally incompetent to stand trial. Another case was dismissed because the judge found the complaining witness's story incredible.

According to the ADA, *"The complainant was an off-duty corrections officer. He claimed that the defendant tried to interfere when he was arguing about his bill at a coffee shop, that he pulled his badge to identify himself and the defendant knocked it to the floor and punched him. The corrections officer's*

---

* Many of these were arrest records only; the dispositions were unknown.

gun fired twice in the ensuing struggle. When the police arrived, the corrections officer signed the affidavit as the arresting officer. The defendant said the corrections officer had been drinking in the coffee shop, had used abusive language to the waitress and had hit him over the head with the gun when he told the officer to pay and go. The defendant had two witnesses to back up his version."

The judge dismissed the charges at the preliminary hearing: "There was no case against him. I believed the defendant and his witnesses. I did not believe a word the corrections officer said."

The victim's story in the third stranger assault dismissal did not satisfy an ADA who moved to dismiss the assault charges against the co-defendants, both of whom were in our sample. He had been handed the case after a first trial ended in mistrial for reasons unconnected with the merits. The ADA who handled it initially was unavailable for an interview.

According to the ADA who moved to dismiss, "It involved a fight at Kennedy Airport. The complainant was a customs agent who drove up to a barrier erected by the defendants, who were attendants at the parking lot, in the course of their duties. The complainant wanted the barrier removed, they refused. A brawl started, and both sides say the other started it. When the customs agent got back to his car and tried to get away, the defendants thought he was trying to run them down and surrounded the car with barricades until the police came. The first ADA who handled this case was told by the police that the customs agent was afraid to press charges but did identify the defendants at the scene of the crime. I found this a little unbelievable, since the customs agent refused to sign the complaint originally—it was not signed until just before the mistrial. The whole case is strange. I don't think we had a case against them. When I talked to the complaining witness he admitted he might have thrown the first punch."

This case and the one below also illustrate the way felony charges can arise from misunderstandings that flare into fights.

Four police officers, two in plain clothes, came to the defendant's parents' home at night to arrest his brother on a complaint of sexual abuse. The defendant's family was Puerto Rican, and his mother and father did not understand English. The police gathered around the defendant's brother in the driveway. His parents emerged from the house screaming. They said later that they saw a number of strangers taking hold of their son and thought he was being attacked. The defendant came out when he heard his parents scream and jumped into what had become a yelling and shouting throng of eight people. One police officer had his jacket ripped. Another spent several weeks in the hospital.

The defendant in our sample was charged along with his parents for assault in the second degree. The Grand Jury reduced the charges to third degree assaults and the cases were then sent back to the arraignment part of Criminal Court.

The ADA said, "It must have been overcharged to begin with; more of a family scuffle than felony assault. The mother and father may have had a problem in communications with the officers, most of whom were in plain clothes, and became frustrated when they couldn't understand what was happening." The ADA acknowledged there was one problem in viewing the case this way: the police said that the son—the defendant in our sample—was the first to jump them. He was a pre-law student at Columbia and understood English perfectly well. But the ADA was certain that "it was a bullshit case. Your first thought when a Grand Jury reduces a felony charge supported by the testimony of four police officers, and sends it back down here to Criminal Court arraignment, is to dispose of it by plea. Most of the wind is blown out of your sails." The ADA was prepared to accept pleas from the three to disorderly conduct (a violation) with the promise of conditional discharges.

The defense attorney was even more surprised by the Grand Jury's action: "Since it was returned from the Grand Jury despite the cops testifying, there must have been just a load of lies in the complaint." He wanted to go for trial and was sure he could get acquittals for all three clients. He particularly did not want the son to plead to anything, as it could prevent him from practicing law. The defense attorney therefore insisted on an adjournment in contemplation of dismissal for him.

The arresting officer said he was "very angry" when the ADA, over the officer's opposition, went to his superior for permission to consent to the ACD. The officer felt it was hardly appropriate when one of the other officers had been hospitalized. But the ADA took the view that, with eight people scuffling in the dark, it would have been difficult to prove that the officer was injured intentionally or that it was the defendant who hurt him. He, too, was sure they would all have been acquitted at a trial.

The case against the son was adjourned in contemplation of dismissal. The parents pled guilty to the violation and walked.

In some stranger assault cases, such as the following, the anger that erupts into physical attack seems to have its origin in an existing conflict into which the stranger intrudes. Here, the victim finds himself on the receiving end of anger directed at another person.

A woman called the police for assistance in removing her husband from her apartment; she had obtained from the Family Court an "Order of Protection" against him and wanted it enforced. The officer who responded to the call said, "When we arrived he erupted in obvious rage; he wasn't about to cooperate. We tried to explain that we had to arrest him, by order of the Family Court, since he had violated its order. When I moved in to secure the arrest he threw a punch that sent me reeling to the floor." The defendant was charged with second degree assault. There was no injury but it was technically a felony because he hit a peace officer in the course of performing his duties. He pled guilty to harassment, a violation, and walked with a $25 fine.

It was the prosecutor who suggested the charge reduction and sentence. "This is very much the type of case we like to get rid of, because it's a family affair. There is a tendency for the police to use the felony assault charge because an officer was hit, but there wasn't any injury. I would rather have these charged as misdemeanor assault, if in fact there is any assault—otherwise harassment."

The judge thought it should have been charged as "resisting arrest," but "definitely not felony assault." He treated it as a "resisting" case at sentence and thought the fine appropriate and necessary, because this defendant's conduct showed an overall "disrespect for authority." The police officer, who appeared at first as the victim of a felonious assault, agreed: "It's a suitable plea and sentence." Those interviewed thought the disposition would have been the same if the defendant had gone to trial.

In another stranger assault case, it remains unclear whether the assault charge was a deliberate overcharge to protect the arresting officer, who had himself used more force than, according to his own account, should have been necessary, or whether the assault was in fact committed as an almost reflex response to a sudden intrusion.

Two Long Island Railroad policemen found the defendant sleeping on a park bench near, but not on, railroad property. He was drunk and disoriented when they woke him up and started firing questions at him; one of the officers was hit—not very hard—in the eye. The defendant, who appeared to have received a number of blows, said they began beating him before he was fully awake. He was charged with second degree assault, resisting arrest and loitering.

The Legal Aid attorney said, "The assault charge was added just to protect the police. Normally a policeman will charge 'resisting arrest.' I guess they wanted a felony to protect themselves after using all that force." The ADA *was more circumspect: "I don't think there was any attempt to commit an assault as the defendant had to be shaken by the police to arouse him. He hit the officer inadvertently. The officer told me he thought the defendant was dead at first—he was shaking him pretty strongly. I suppose he felt attacked. There was much police pressure in this case—they were all heated up for a felony."*

The case was disposed of by plea to harassment, a violation, and a $250 fine. The arresting officer, whose version doesn't fit well with the ADA's, *said, "I was sort of glad the charges were reduced because the defendant was out of work and really needed a job more than anything else." The* ADA *said, "I insisted on the violation to protect the officers if they did beat up the defendant—we couldn't support any other charge. And I think the defense theory [that the officers had no jurisdiction off* LIRR *property] may have had some merit. But he would have got a conviction for harassment anyway [at trial]. The fine [the maximum for harassment] will teach him to think twice about getting drunk in public. He gets nasty." The defense attorney accepted the* ADA's *offer because, "Juries don't call cops liars, and he would have been found guilty of harassment anyway, to give the cops something."*

Only 2 of the 21 stranger assaults went clearly beyond what might be counted as normal—albeit unacceptable—human reactions to moments of stress. Neither defendant walked. One had allegedly tried to cut off the victim's arm so he could no longer "use it," claiming he heard voices telling him to do so. Twice he had tried to commit suicide. He was sentenced to Greenhaven Prison for up to 6 years on its psychiatric ward. The other defendant might more accurately have been charged with robbery than with assault. The arresting officer reported that the defendant held a knife to the victim's throat while a co-defendant injured him. They were presumed to be looking for money. The defendant received a one-year sentence after pleading guilty to an A misdemeanor.* These two received the heaviest sentences handed out to defendants convicted of assault on strangers.

In addition to these two cases, only two others in the stranger assault group got any time at all. One defendant was an addict accused of a weaponless assault on a police officer that grew out of a routine traffic stop in 1968. This

---

* This sentence was to be served concurrently with another one-year sentence for conviction on an intervening burglary charge.

defendant had jumped bail, and when he was finally brought to the court in 1973 he asked his defense attorney to get him sent to NACC.

"We wanted to dispose of this case as fast as possible," said the Legal Aid lawyer, "as my client was an addict and wanted help. He had a wife and child; he was 40 years old, and his habit was beginning to rot his life." The ADA *offered a plea to an A misdemeanor assault. He had no problem with the reduction of charge: "I'm sure it was more of a harassment. Police officers always write up assaults as felonies, but this one would never have gotten by the Grand Jury."*

There is no very comfortable explanation for the last of the four stranger assault cases that drew time. This defendant went to trial, and was acquitted of the assault, but he was given a 15-day jail sentence on conviction of harassment, a violation.

The defendant went to visit a prostitute. At some point the woman called for the building's security guards to remove him from her apartment. He claimed he had already paid her and refused to leave. A struggle ensued when the two security guards removed him forcibly to hold him for the regular police, who were called to the scene. At one point he tried to flee and threw a brick in the direction of the pursuing guards. He was arrested and charged with trespass, harassment (for spitting at the guards and using abusive language) and assault in the second degree (because the brick was deemed a dangerous instrument).

The ADA *said, "This was a very weak case. There was no injury; a brick was thrown, but it landed on the ground first, and according to the guard's testimony, only touched his toe. The other guard testified he was hit on the head, but it was with his own nightstick when the defendant kicked it from his hand in the struggle. The trespass charge was dismissed when the woman failed to come to court, and the assault charge had already been reduced to [third degree] when I got the case in the jury part."*

The defendant insisted he had been struggling in self-defense and refused to plead to anything more than harassment. The ADA *said he would have liked to take the plea to harassment, but policy prevented such a reduction of charge once the case was in jury part. The judge was more explicit: "We usually avoid pleas [to reduced charges] in the jury part because then defense attorneys would go judge-shopping. If they could get [such deals] they would schedule cases for trial that they plan to dispose of by plea. The defendant in this case had a prior record of burglaries, and, although it was a weak case, there was evidence of the charge. The People were right to have brought it to trial."* In offering this assessment of the evidence, the judge conceded "*a little prejudice because the defendant was very uncooperative.*"

The jury acquitted him of the assault. According to the ADA, "*the guards told slightly conflicting stories. That, plus there were no injuries, made the jury apprehensive about a guilty verdict, which could have sent him to jail for a year.*" Why, then, the sentence for the harassment conviction? The judge said, "*Because of his prior arrests. He had a previous conviction of burglary and I thought 15 days in jail for a violation wasn't too long because he had already served 8 days before bail was lowered. I thought by placing him in jail it might tame him down.*" The defense attorney said, "*The defendant was very stubborn on trial. Apparently his conduct incensed the judge.*" The ADA agreed with the defense attorney on the reason for this sentence: "*The judge didn't like him.*"

Rape

Sexual assaults—particularly forcible rape—stir deeper fears than the altercations labeled at arrest as felony assault, and the penalty structure for sex crimes reaches higher. First degree rape, a B felony punishable by up to 25 years in prison, is defined as sexual intercourse with a female who is either taken by "forcible compulsion" or is presumed incapable of consent because she is physically helpless (for example, unconscious) or because she is less than 11 years old.*

Eleven of the twelve rape cases in the deep sample were commenced by arrest for rape in the first degree. The twelfth involved third degree rape, which is an E felony, punishable by up to four years in prison.

Prior relationships existed in 10 of the 12 rape cases and appear to have been the most important factor in the dispositions. The duration of these prior relationships ranged from a few hours to many years in a former marriage. The disposition in the latter case, a dismissal, followed upon the remarriage of defendant and complainant—perhaps the ultimate in reconciliation and victim non-cooperation with prosecution. Of the 10 prior rela-

---

* "Forcible compulsion" is either physical force that overcomes "earnest resistance" or a threat of immediate death, serious physical injury, or kidnapping. A male commits second degree rape when, being 18 years old, he engages in sexual intercourse with a female less than 14 years old. A male commits third degree rape by sexual intercourse with a female who is incapable of consent for some reason other than her youth or physical helplessness, or if he is over 21 years of age and the female is under 17.

tionship rape cases, 6 were disposed of by dismissal and 2 by guilty pleas—one resulting in a walk and the other in misdemeanor time (which was really a sentence to time served).

The other two prior relationship cases went to trial and ended with heavy felony sentences: 25 years for a man with a record of previous rapes who raped an 8-year-old neighbor, and a term of 2-to-6 years for a woman who befriended two girls whom she then lured to her boyfriend's apartment for an elaborately cruel program of sexual humiliation culminating in the rape of both girls.

The two stranger cases also went to trial. One ended in acquittal and the other, upon conviction of 12 counts of rape and other felonies, in a 30-year sentence.

The three felony time dispositions are explained by the quite horrible and unique facts of the cases, which will be described below. The remaining dispositions appear from the interviews to be explained by three factors: prior relationships, prior records of sex offenses (or lack thereof) and evidentiary problems.

Evidentiary obstacles to conviction in sex felonies need some explaining. Suspicion that vindictive or unbalanced female complainants, or children, might fabricate rape allegations against men has long been a powerful influence in this area of the law. In 1971, when the wide sample arrests were made, the New York Penal Law provided that "A person shall not be convicted of any offense defined in this article (sex offenses), or of an attempt to commit the same, solely on the uncorroborated testimony of the alleged victim" (§ 130.15). Prosecutions in 1973, the year in which deep sample cases reached disposition, were controlled by a mid-1972 amendment that spelled out what sort of corroboration would be required for conviction. The prosecution needed evidence, other than the alleged victim's testimony, "*tending to:*

(a) establish that an attempt was made to engage the alleged victim in sexual intercourse, deviate sexual intercourse, or sexual contact, as the case may be, at the time of the alleged occurrence; and

(b) establish lack of consent of the alleged victim, where such is an element of the offense" (§ 130.15(1)).

Typically, therefore, a deep sample prosecution case for rape required something such as a hospital report of bruises (indicating force) and of the presence of sperm (indicating sexual intercourse). Lack of consent might be supported by evidence of witnesses who heard screaming. When the charge was based on the victim's legal incapacity to consent because of her youth, the prosecution case had to meet the requirement of § 130.15(2), which provided: "then, in addition to the requirements of [§ 130.15(1)], the corroborative evidence shall not be sufficient to sustain a conviction unless it tends to connect the defendant with the commission of the offense or attempted offense." In other words, when medical evidence clearly establishes a six-year-old girl's claim that she has been raped, some evidence other than her own statement must be found to support her identification of the defendant as her assailant.

It has been argued that evidentiary hurdles such as these made the law virtually unenforceable against predatory rapists who take care to avoid witnesses, and that this discouraged women from taking complaints of rape to the police or pursuing them in the courts. The law in this area has recently undergone substantial revision in New York, as in other jurisdictions. Section 130.15 was repealed in 1974, leaving a requirement of corroborative evidence, for non-consensual sex crimes, only in cases where "lack of consent results solely from incapacity to consent because of the alleged victim's age, mental defect or mental incapacity" (§ 130.16).

It is not possible to project, from the deep sample data, what effect this repeal of the corroboration requirement might have on the volume and types of rape charges disposed of in the criminal process. It might be expected that a post-1974 sampling would reveal quite a different pattern of fact, processing and disposition. However, the disposition-shaping factors identified in the deep sample cases summarized below are likely to remain important to the extent that similar cases are still found in the process.

Two of the prior relationship rapes involved prostitutes as complainants. Each was disposed of by dismissal when the complaining witness failed to cooperate with the prosecution. The interviews in both cases suggest that prostitutes' claims of rape are not treated seriously. According to one police officer, there is a high volume of such complaints resulting from the lack of legality in the business of selling sex. "Often when they cry 'rape,'" he said, "they are making the police force a collection agency for contractual agreements that are unenforceable in the courts."

"Usually a prostitute cries rape when she hasn't been paid," echoed the ADA *who made the motion to dismiss in one of these cases, after the complainant failed to come to court or to respond to subpoenas for hearings. "Even if she did come to court, a jury would never believe her. This one didn't come in because she realized she would be destroyed on the stand." The arresting*

officer, a Port Authority Police Officer, was not happy about it. "This woman really had no chance once the case got to court," he said. "It was obvious the district attorney thought the case was worthless as soon as he discovered she was a prostitute."

The officer had found her cowering, naked, in a Kennedy Airport parking lot. "She was very upset, claiming she had been raped by a guy still sitting in a car nearby. She claimed he kept her in the car at gunpoint while driving to the lot—deserted at that time—and sexually assaulted her. He was groggy— practically asleep—when I went up to the car. He said she was a prostitute, they had driven there together, and he had fallen asleep after having sex— and before paying her. He figured she was angry that he refused to pay her immediately and drive her back so she could pick up another man. I couldn't tell who was telling the truth—it was a strange incident. She claimed she had been threatened with a gun, but we searched the car and didn't find it—a point against her story. But we couldn't figure out why she would be running around the parking lot with no clothes on, and why she was so very upset and nervous when we found her, if this was simply a case of a prostitute not getting payment."

The second rape charge based on a prostitute's complaint fared no better, despite the defendant in this case having a serious prior record of rapes and assaults. Again, only the arresting officer treated the matter seriously. The woman's story was that, although she had initially been approached for prostitution, the defendant forced her to accompany him to his apartment where he demanded a series of sexual services. In addition to threatening her with a knife, she said, he would command his dog to attack her whenever she refused, and she would then comply to avoid injury. The skepticism of the police officer to whom she told this story—a member of the Sex Crime Unit— was tempered by the evidence of bruises and by subsequent events. The officer went looking for the defendant when the woman reported a second incident in which the same man, encountering her in a restaurant, threatened her life because she had gone to the police about the incident in his apartment. "She was no angel," said the officer, "but he was violent and dangerous —near hysteria at times. She had a right to be protected and to see the case properly disposed of." He made the arrest for rape, although he recognized that the case was weak: there was no solid corroborating evidence, and the victim's own testimony could easily be discounted by cross-examination about her profession. He then discovered that the defendant had prior convictions for rapes and assaults. He was upset that the defendant had been released on his own recognizance at arraignment rather than held in custody where he could not threaten the woman. When she subsequently failed to appear at court, the ADA, defense lawyer and judge were untroubled by the dismissal for lack of prosecution. The police officer was angry, however.

"The guy had a 'mad rapist' psychology," he said. *"He wanted resistance, was sadistic, enjoyed using force. Sure, the case was weak—no jury would believe her rape claims because of her commercialization of sex as a product; juries sympathize with the man, especially in these circumstances. But the evidence for some form of assault, if not rape, was substantial—the bruises, etcetera. If she'd cooperated, there could have been a conviction on this. And a guy like this should be isolated, in psychiatric care. He'll probably kill a girl some day."*

At the other end of the spectrum of dismissed prior relationship cases is a woman's complaint of rape against her former husband. They had four children and, although divorced, he had visitation rights and a key to her apartment, where he slept with her from time to time.

"They must have had an argument in bed," according to the ADA, *"and she called the police to have him arrested."* After he had been indicted for rape, *"they came to the arraignment part and told the judge they were going to remarry; she wanted to drop it. This case belonged in Family Court—not Supreme Court." "I didn't believe it"* said the judge, *"and I adjourned the case, keeping it in arraignment part until I received the marriage certificate."* The document arrived, and the case was dismissed.

In four cases, the prior relationship was casual, having neither the general complexity of marriage nor the specificity of prostitution. Three were dismissed when the complaining witnesses failed to show at court. In one of these, the arrest was for third degree rape. A police officer saw some people looking up an alley and found a couple engaged in sexual intercourse when he went to investigate. The woman, in his judgment, was incompetent to consent to intercourse. She could not spell her name or remember her address and seemed wholly disoriented. There is a suggestion in the interviews that she had, in fact, escaped from a mental institution. There is also a suggestion that the police officer did not like the defendant.

"The defendant had an affirmative defense," said the Legal Aid lawyer, *"because he had met her earlier that day, she led him on, and he didn't think she was incompetent—he didn't ask her to spell her name or give him her ad-*

dress." *The defendant was unable to make bail while the woman was under observation in a mental facility. The report said she was competent and she had been released. She did not appear at court for the next hearing, and the rape charge was dismissed. The judge refused the* ADA's *motion to reduce the charge to public lewdness: "He'd already been two weeks in jail. He should have been discharged sooner."*

The second of these dismissals was caused by victim non-cooperation that was attributed in interviews to a prior relationship of an unspecified nature. In the third, the complainant had gone voluntarily to a motel with the defendant and had consensual sexual intercourse. According to the arresting officer, she claimed the defendant "went psycho" when she said she wanted to leave, slapped her around, locked her up and raped her repeatedly.

"She came to the station missing her shoes, pocketbook and sweater, and she had swollen arms and a swollen face," said the officer. "And we caught him leaving the motel with her stuff." He was arrested for rape, assault and grand larceny (the pocketbook). The ADA *later moved to dismiss at her request: "She changed her mind when the defendant convinced her he hadn't robbed her—she thought he'd taken her pocketbook when she went off to sleep. A claim of rape after consensual intercourse would not be very good anyway."*

In the fourth casual prior relationship case, the defendant, who had no record, pled guilty to an E felony. The interviews suggest that this case, like the others involving casual relationships, should have been dismissed or the defendant acquitted. Court congestion seems to have played a major part in shaping the disposition.

"This was a terribly weak case," said the ADA. *"We had a 17-year-old boy who allegedly raped two girls, 16 and 17 years old. They had gone to his apartment voluntarily and neither showed any signs of injury that would indicate force. There was no complaint until the father of one girl broke into the apartment and found them. One of the girls had already left. I believe the second girl made up the story of rape because of fear of her father, and that the first girl went along with it to cover her friend. I really don't know how this case got beyond the Grand Jury—they all knew one another and it began voluntarily."* There was no strong corroboration. The girls claimed to have been raped in different rooms.

The ADA admitted that the 20 minutes he spent on the case was a "disgracefully short period of time" and said he offered the E felony plea and a

10-month sentence "because of the suspicious nature of the charge. The defendant had been in for a while and now he would get out quickly; and we got a felony plea." The Legal Aid lawyer said, *"This is one of those cases which is not given enough attention. The defendant was in jail for 5 months. He would have had to wait 6 more months if he wanted trial."*

One other prior relationship rape was disposed of by a guilty plea to a reduced charge. The defendant, who had a prior record but not for sex offenses, was accused of rape by the 14-year-old daughter of his common-law wife. The girl's father, separated from her mother, pressed the case: "I believe my daughter's story. I know it really happened." The mother disagreed.

"This was really a Family Court squabble," according to the Supreme Court judge. *"There was a divorce action going on at the time and the girl didn't know how to react, so she made up the story about the rape."* The judge did not dismiss the case, however, and the defendant walked on a one-year conditional discharge after pleading guilty to an A misdemeanor, endangering the welfare of a child. *"There was always the possibility that he did these acts,"* said the judge, *"and the best thing to do was to condition the discharge on his keeping his hands off the girl."* The ADA was not ready to dismiss either, although he too said, *"There was nothing that pointed to rape. There was no medical corroboration. But our secret weapon was the defendant. If he went on the stand I would just cremate him. He had a history of this kind of thing."* The defense lawyer agreed: *"There was nothing to this case—it was a real stinkeroo. You need corroboration, and the medical report we received showed nothing. He had a bad record though, and I was fearful of going to trial. It was the mother telling the judge that the girl fabricated the story that knocked the charge down and got him the conditional discharge."*

Four of the twelve rape cases went to trial, including the only two that were clearly stranger rapes. In one of these stranger cases the defendant was acquitted against all odds. The disposition offers some support for fears of ADAs about taking even a strong prosecution case to trial rather than negotiating a plea to lesser charge. The first degree rape charge had been dropped at the Grand Jury stage in this case, for lack of corroboration, and the victim's testimony at trial was not that the defendant had raped her but that he had grabbed her and tried. The ADA still had a good case on first degree sexual abuse and assault, however. He offered a plea to an A misdemeanor, only because the fifteen-year-old complainant had returned home to Georgia, and he envisioned difficulties in getting her back to New York for trial. The defendant refused the bargain, and the complainant did come back to be, by all accounts, an unusually credible and cooperative witness. The defendant, insisting on his complete innocence in the face of a powerful prosecution case, defied the advice of the judge and his own lawyer, first by going to trial and then by taking the stand himself, despite a prior prison record for rape.

"I didn't know what to do," said the defense attorney. "My client had a long record, his story was unconvincing, he was crazy. He would jump up and down in the court yelling that everyone was lying [he had to be handcuffed to the rail in the courtroom]. But he was my client and insisted on his innocence, so we went to trial—handcuffs and all." The judge said, "The key to this trial was when the defendant was on the stand in his own defense. He was asked about his prior record. He stands up and says, 'I pleaded guilty in the past—five times—because I committed those crimes. This time I didn't do anything and I didn't plead because I'm not guilty.' The courtroom was stunned. The jury was impressed." The Legal Aid lawyer said, "He was just lucky. I would still argue with him to accept the A misdemeanor plea."

A second rape case that went to trial involved a prior relationship, albeit a brief one. The defendant, who got felony time, was a woman (eighteen years old) charged with two first degree rapes.

"The two girls came to New York to sightsee—not for sex and games," said the ADA. *"One was a farm girl and the other was due to marry a marine in a month's time. This defendant struck up a friendship with them by the fountain in Washington Square Park. They all spent the afternoon together and she invited them back to her apartment. She said it was because the girls asked her to get them some drugs. At her apartment, she introduced them to her boyfriend—the co-defendant in this case. He was definitely an evil man. I am amazed at the horror and humiliation of it. They gave the girls some grass, then demanded money. He broke one girl's nose when she refused. He forced them to strip. He forced them to do a series of intercourse, then he made them take* LSD. *The woman [defendant] was just standing around at this point, but she was the one who forced them to take the* LSD, *and then she played cruel jokes on them. One of the girls faked it, didn't swallow it, and when they went to sleep she got away and brought the cops. The woman had been the passive one of the co-defendants, and at first it seemed she had just gone along for the ride. She was personable, well-spoken and had no record. We didn't want to take a chance on her at trial; we wanted to make sure we got the guy. Her boyfriend had a record, engaged in*

the rape and did all the ordering around. Initially I offered her a plea as a matter of mercy and expected she'd get probation or 'time served.' She surprised me. She turned it down and at no point, even at the trial, did she try to separate from him. She decided to link herself with him and she went down with him."

The ADA said it was not until the trial that he fully realized the "woman's cruelty and her key role in provoking the whole episode." The judge said, after the trial, "At first I had no intention of putting her in jail. She was eighteen, from a southern town, and I thought she may have done it to please the co-defendant—to keep him. He was a very vicious guy and I felt she was a victim, too. But she had a central role in the crime. She was the imaginative architect. Still, it was a complete mystery why she didn't throw it all off on him."

According to the ADA, her defense attorney (who was not available for interview) seemed to think the story of the two girls was incredible and would not be believed by the jury. He was wrong. His client was convicted on both counts of first degree rape. The ADA asked for a fifteen-year sentence with a five-year minimum. "I thought that was ridiculous," said the judge. The ADA explained: "I felt she deserved time, and for practical matters I had an idea that the judge would set the maximum somewhere between five and nine years, and I knew he would set a bottom. But I felt they were going to appeal and I know it works better if the ADA recommends time. So I went high in my recommendation." She got a sentence to prison time with a two-year minimum and a six-year maximum. "I felt she ought to do two years," said the judge, "but the sentencing structure is so stupidly inflexible that I had to give the six-year maximum as well. She should now be eligible for parole after two."*

The third case to go to trial involved a defendant with a prior conviction for a sex felony and a complainant who was his 8-year-old neighbor. Neither the victim's mother nor the ADA were inclined to treat it lightly, and the defendant received the full 25-year sentence.

According to the ADA, the case was aided by the fact that the little girl was "extremely capable on the stand." Initially worried about her testimony and unaware of the defendant's 1944 prison sentence for a sex felony, the ADA

---

* The male co-defendant was also convicted on both counts and, although we do not know from our data what sentence he received, the judge did say he wished he could have imposed a ten-year minimum. (The Penal Law puts a limit of eight-and-a-half years on B felony minimums.)

had offered a plea to an E felony with a 4-year sentence. The defendant refused the offer, against his lawyer's advice. "When he was finally ready to plead," said the ADA, "I had already prepared the case. I knew he had the record, I had the medical corroboration, and it wasn't worth my while. He said he'd take 15 years, but it was just too late in my book. So he got the conviction and 25 years." The defense attorney said, "There was no defense. The evidence was strong, the complaining witness was cooperative and the defendant was a liability on the stand. It was a heinous crime."

Finally, the fourth jury trial (and second stranger case) ended in a conviction on 12 counts of rape, sodomy and burglary for four separate incidents in 1971. The defendant was a rapist for whom the law was clearly written. His conviction and 30-year prison sentence offer some indication of how the system can respond to a solid arrest of an unambiguously predatory felon of this type. Most of the story belongs to the police officer.

"We had a homicide in the Bronx. A nude young woman with semen stains on her body was strangled in her apartment. Two days earlier a woman down the street had been raped and robbed. I decided to analyze the sexual attacks in the area over the past year. There was an assailant committing gunpoint rapes with a silver pistol. He robbed and sodomized them. Some of what he did is too disgusting to talk about. I talked to all the victims and put out a description of the man. I requested other officers to bring to my attention anyone arrested in the area whose yellow sheet indicated a history of sex offenses. This defendant had been arrested for a break-in and his record brought him to my attention. I included a picture of him in a series of pictures, showed them to a number of the victims, and six or seven identified him as the attacker. We arrested him and had a formal line-up. Six women made one hundred percent positive identifications. He was indicted for sex attacks on these women."

The ADA had some problems getting the victims to appear at hearings. "They kept saying, 'Why me, why not someone else,'" according to the police officer. But the ADA would take nothing lower than the top count and 25 years. "This was a situation of multiple rapes and I was very confident for a trial." There was no problem about corroboration. He had raped, sodomized and robbed two women in the same apartment who could, and did, fully corroborate each other's accounts.

The defense attorney, who had explored the possibility of "taint" in the identifications and decided they were solid, said "I might have accepted the offer, but the defendant adamantly refused. I did not push him to plead be-

cause he had little to lose. An extra 5 years in jail." He was convicted. The judge said, "I had some leeway here with the maximum sentence at 30 years. I felt that the full term was justified." He imposed six 25-year sentences, running concurrently with four lesser sentences, and a 5-year sentence to run consecutively. He also imposed a 10-year minimum period of imprisonment. The arresting officer said, "He should get 90 years. This guy was a sickie, a murderer. I'm still trying to link him with the murder."*

Murder and Attempted Murder

Homicide—taking a human life—is murder when the killing is intentional, when it is the result of reckless conduct which created a grave risk of death or when it occurs in the course of committing certain other felonies. Murder is an A felony and conviction may be followed by sentence to life imprisonment. If a homicide is committed under the influence of extreme emotional disturbance or when the assailant only intends injury, the crime is manslaughter (a B felony punishable by up to 25 years in prison).† If a murder victim does not die, despite his assailant's intent to kill, the crime is attempted murder (also a B felony).

Only seven deep sample cases were commenced by arrest on homicide charges (six murders and a manslaughter),‡ and there were only nine attempted homicides. The numbers are small, but the cases do indicate that convictions and felony time are the norms when the charge is murder, and that homicide charges are not dismissed except when the prosecutor makes a considered determination that dismissal is in the interests of justice. On the other hand, the attempted murder cases seem hardly distinguishable, on their facts or their dispositions, from the assault cases discussed in the first section of this chapter.

---

* The maximum sentence on each first degree rape was 25 years; but such sentences cannot be strung together to make a sentence of 90 years (as the police officer wanted) or 150 years (6x25). Section 7.30(1)(c) of the Penal Law provides that the aggregate maximum term, when consecutive sentences are imposed, may not exceed 30 years, where the top charge is a B felony (as it was in this case).

† The B felony is manslaughter in the first degree. When the homicide is the result of recklessness (short of the kind of recklessness that will draw a murder charge), it is manslaughter in the second degree, a C felony punishable by up to 15 years in prison.

‡ One of the seven technically might have been classified with the assaults: the initial arrest charge was assault, since the victim had not yet died. This is one of the rare cases in which the arrest charge was raised as a case moved through the system.

Murder and Manslaughter

Two of the murder charges were dismissed and one was abated by the death of the defendant from an overdose of heroin. One of the dismissals resulted from receipt of a coroner's report stating that the victim (a derelict drunk) had died of tuberculosis and not from injury sustained in his fight with the defendant (another derelict drunk). The reason given for the other dismissal, which might be challenged by some, was related to the prosecution's need for help in securing other, higher priority convictions.

The body of a man was found in a tenement. He had been shot, and blood led to the defendant's apartment. The defendant, a mother of two with no prior record, admitted to the police that she and several other people had conspired to rob the victim, who was known by one of the others to carry large sums of money. He had been invited into her apartment and robbed. The conspirators had been unable to subdue him, however, and one of them finally shot him. Although charged with murder, she furnished the police with the names and addresses of the others, including the triggerman, and testified before the Grand Jury. In exchange for her testimony, she was granted immunity from prosecution, and the murder charge against her was dismissed. Two of these others were quickly found, arrested and prosecuted for the murder.

The detective in charge of the investigation felt she had been let off too lightly. "It was a cold-blooded murder," he said, "and there was absolutely no defense. Maybe she should have been allowed to take a lesser plea, but she definitely should not have been given total immunity. The DA's office works against us—she said she would testify at the trial so she walked free. Now we can't find her or the other man—he still has the gun and the money. She'll help him get away."

The four remaining homicide arrests were disposed of by pleas to manslaughter and felony time sentences, although the most notorious case in the sample had been to trial several times before the plea was entered. This was one of the few cases in which the interviews were contradictory throughout.

The defendant was one of a group of young men charged with the murder of a woman storeowner and the attempted murder of her male partner. The defendants were black, the victims were white. The prosecution viewed it as a racially-motivated crime, committed in the course of a robbery, in which both the robbery and the murder had been planned in advance. The defense viewed it as a racially-motivated prosecution.

The defendant in our sample was convicted, with others, at a jury trial in 1965 and sentenced to life imprisonment. The conviction was reversed on appeal and the case was tried twice more. Both retrials ended with hung juries. The cases were bitterly fought and heavily publicized.

According to one of the defense attorneys, "The DA's *office announced plans for a fourth trial. The* DA's *a vicious beast. These guys had been in the Tombs for eight years. Prosecuting them had become an institution for the office and a vendetta for the* ADA. *The defendants didn't want to go through another trial and were willing to take a plea if they could get time served. Another trial would have meant another hung jury; one of the state's key witnesses has recanted his testimony over and over since the last trial. We asked for an 'Alford Plea'* and they refused. But, in a way, that is what it was. They pled guilty and then we announced to the press that they weren't really guilty. They had to say what the system required so they could get out. It's as simple as that."*

According to the ADA, *who had prepared carefully for the interview, "My reasons for taking the plea at this time were as follows: First, two previous trials had ended in hung juries. Second, the defendants had already been incarcerated for eight years. Third, none of the defendants we were dealing with at this time was the actual killer. Fourth, we learned that the defendants had been rehabilitated; three had jobs and one was continuing his schooling—so, if jail was going to rehabilitate them, that job had already been done. And they had been out on bail in the time since their last hung jury and had not committed any other crimes. Fifth, the recantation by our star witness, though he had repudiated the recantation, would have caused us some problems with the jury. And every time you try a case it gets harder; each time a witness is cross-examined we run into more difficulty. Sixth, we would have had problems getting a unanimous verdict. I felt that the defense had successfully brainwashed jurors by violating the canons of ethics. The public had also got a distorted view of the case through the press—you can't cross-examine publicity. Seventh, we would have had to bring the witnesses back to court to relive the experience again—that would have been particu-*

---

* Under the doctrine of *North Carolina* v. *Alford,* 400 U.S. 25 (1970), a court may permit the entry of a guilty plea by a defendant who maintains his innocence, if the defendant believes that the government's evidence is so strong it would be in his interests to limit his liability by pleading to the reduced charge rather than risk going to trial on the higher charge. It is in the ADA's discretion whether to offer an *Alford* plea, and in the judge's discretion whether to accept it. Many ADAs and judges are reluctant to accept *Alford* pleas.

larly hard on the male victim. Finally, months of court time would have been lost in what was sure to be a very long trial. Our office required a guilty plea because we knew that they were in fact guilty and we had to be sure they were willing to admit their guilt. It was important for us that their guilt be known. Unfortunately, we did not know that they would recant immediately afterwards on television."

The second manslaughter plea was more straightforward. The defendant had been arrested in 1958 for second degree assault. The victim died and the charge was raised to first degree manslaughter, but the defendant was found unfit to stand trial at that time. When he was returned to court as fit to stand trial, in 1973, he was permitted to plead to second degree manslaughter—the C felony carrying a fifteen-year maximum sentence. As he had been locked away for fifteen years already, his sentence was to time served.

The third manslaughter plea disposed of a first degree murder case against a defendant who had previously been arrested for homicide and convicted on other serious charges. The ADA explained the charge reduction and the seven-year prison sentence this way:

"The defendant was drinking in the bar and a heated argument erupted. He claimed the bartender hadn't paid up on a debt. The defendant started to storm out, and the victim made some gratuitous remark. The defendant pulled out a gun and shot him. There was a lot of confusion after that. We had only one witness who could make the identification. It was enough, but it weakened the case. The bar was dark, and the witness made the ID when he was shown just one picture—of the defendant. To do it right there should have been a line-up, or he should have brought 15 pictures for the witness to choose from. There was the shaky ID and a plausible self-defense argument—a jury might have believed the victim had pulled a weapon. I had no question about this defendant's guilt, but there were these evidentiary weaknesses. I figured there was a 60–40 chance of winning a conviction at trial. And also, juries will not convict on first degree murder unless it's a gangland premeditated murder—they hand down first degree manslaughter convictions instead, particularly where the crime is committed in the heat of passion. So, already, you're down to manslaughter one. The question of time [sentence] is important here. Because this guy had a bad record—a homicide arrest, and prison on aggravated assault and weapons charges—I was set on a 10- to 15-year sentence. That would be covered by a second degree manslaughter plea. And he was 47; the older a man gets, the less necessary it becomes to sentence him to a long prison term. In the end, the judge

pushed me down from 10 to 7 years. I wouldn't have compromised those 3 years except I was about to leave the job. The case would have been even weaker if it got transferred to a new ADA."

The judge, who seemed unaware of the ADA's *evidentiary difficulties and his feeling of being "pushed down" to 7 years, explained his view on the sentencing as follows: "There were factors going both ways. He was arrested in the hospital under treatment for a diabetic stroke. I was sentencing a sick man to prison. Again, as mitigating points, the homicide was spontaneous, and he was supporting a wife and young daughter. On the other hand, I thought he should get at least 7 years because of his prior convictions. Besides, as a practical matter, if I'd insisted on 15 years the man wouldn't have pled. That would have contributed to the backlog."*

The last case, also commenced by arrest for first degree murder and disposed of by manslaughter plea, was not plagued by evidentiary problems. The defendant was a 16-year-old drug addict who was sentenced to seven years in prison for shooting an acquaintance during an argument over some money.

The police officer said, "I know everybody says 'I carry a gun for protection,' but I think any kid who carries a gun is out for trouble. He got 7 years? I think he got off lucky. The victim was with a large group—maybe this kid felt threatened, but everybody else was just using fists. He shouldn't have had the gun." The judge said, " I gave a sentence promise of a maximum of 10 years. This was not a murder for profit, it was not planned, and this defendant is not going to get anything from prison. But he had a potential for repeating the crime, and I must act for the community. Letting him walk away from a murder would not help."

At sentencing, the judge said, "Frankly, it's one of these cases where I don't feel that I have the sufficient wisdom to impose sentence. Truly, who does?" A probation report recommended a 7-year prison term and that is what the judge gave him. The transcript shows that the judge then said: "I have children your age which I suppose makes it more difficult to impose a lengthy prison term. . . . The main problem you will have is not being in, but being out, once you're out. I've sentenced young men to prison who come out and make almost incredible efforts at rehabilitation—others just hit the place and fall apart, in again and out again until they finally have enough felonies to make it a life sentence. Under the law you only need three for a life sentence. So I'm asking you to try to do something for yourself. You can come to me for help when you get out, but you have to try."

To our interviewer the judge said, "I love my work but at the same time it makes me sick. I'm going to get out."

Attempted Murder

Two of the nine cases commenced by arrest for attempted murder were dismissed. Three went to trial, where one ended in an acquittal. Four were disposed of by plea—three misdemeanor pleas and a D felony plea. Five of the six sentences were walks, only one was felony time. Six of the nine had no prior record of arrest or conviction.

Although the dismissal rate for this small number of attempted murder cases was not as high as the dismissal rate for the assault cases, the sentences were no heavier. All who pled guilty walked.

The only defendant who got time got felony time (5 to 16 years) was convicted by a jury of first degree robbery and first degree assault. A police officer had been shot and injured in a shoot-out following the robbery, but the attempted murder charge against this defendant was dismissed by the judge before the trial.

"This defendant," said the ADA, "was a member of a group supporting themselves by robbing people who were already breaking the law. They thought this store was a front for a narcotics dealer. When the police responded to an anonymous call, there was a shoot-out. One of the defendants was killed. We had a strong case but not exactly open and shut, as several of the victims could not identify him. But the attempted murder count was dismissed, because all the evidence pointed to the fact that the co-defendant who was killed did the shooting. The issue became whether we could prove the two had agreed to the shoot-out. The judge ruled that, as this defendant was upstairs [with the robbery victims], he could not have acted in concert. I really don't think it mattered too much because convicting him on the first degree robbery count drew the same sentence as a finding of guilty on all the counts."*

An attempted murder charge was also dismissed in the other case ending in conviction at jury trial. But in that case the dismissal occurred much earlier in the process—in the Complaint Room, before the case ever got before a judge.

The complaining witness was a former lover of the defendant. She claimed that she had gone to visit him, that he had become angry when she refused

---

* First degree robbery, like attempted homicide, is a B felony.

to have sex and that he slashed her clothes off with a knife, robbed her and — when she finally screamed — fired several shots at her. The defendant said he had told her he wanted to break it off and she had attacked him. The ADA *did not believe his story but said of the victim: "She admitted to me that the gun was never pointed at her. She never thought her life was in danger. Attempted murder was an overcharge. So were the robbery and sodomy charges. But the charges on assault, unlawful imprisonment and possession of the knife were good. The defendant had to go to trial; he had a job he would lose if he got even a misdemeanor on his record. I thought the incident too serious for misdemeanor plea — it transcended the prior relationship. The complaining witness swayed the jury. She was an intelligent woman, and her demeanor was very important. When she testified that she ran four blocks naked in the middle of winter because she was so afraid — that convinced them."*

The final disposition in that case was a sentence to five years' probation on the conviction of second degree assault.

Another defendant, in the only case carrying the attempted murder label that resulted in serious injury, also received a probation sentence after a guilty plea. That case, too, arose out of what we might now recognize as a typical domestic assault. The defendant, 70 years old, had been drinking heavily and arguing with his wife and her cousin about it. In a rage, he grabbed an old rifle from the closet and fired eight shots. One of his victims was hospitalized for six weeks. Although he was remorseful and although the complainants wanted to withdraw, the ADA insisted on a felony conviction.

"Family cases are always treated differently," said the ADA, *"but the fact that a gun was used in this assault, and the severe injuries, means there was no question of dismissal even if the complainants wanted to withdraw."* But the ADA *was willing to reduce the charge to a D felony assault, and the defendant was sentenced to probation on his guilty plea. The judge and the* ADA *agreed that the result would have been the same if he had gone to trial and been convicted on all charges. "It would have been ridiculous to send a 70-year-old man to jail,"* the ADA *explained. "And he had no prior record — it's an isolated incident in his life — and he needed supervision because of his drinking. Any judge would have given probation."* The judge said, *"He will not do this again. He's no danger to society. And at his age, five years of probation is a very long time and enough of a punishment."*

Assault, Rape, Murder and Attempted Murder

The most important distinguishing factor between deep sample attempted murder and assault cases appears to be the discharge of a firearm: guns were fired (or allegedly fired) in seven of the nine cases.* (Guns were present in only 5 of the 67 assault cases.) Two of the gun-firing cases, initially charged as attempted murder, apparently did not even arise from underlying assaults. Evidence of an intent to cause injury—much less an intent to cause death—is wholly absent from one of these.

A black defendant made a remark to a white woman that provoked a racial dispute. When he and his black companion were surrounded by whites, the defendant pulled a pen gun and fired it into the air. The ADA *considered the case to have been obviously overcharged because of the context and because, though technically a firearm, a pen gun's "accuracy is so bad you can't intend to kill with it." The defendant, a college student with no prior record, pled to an A misdemeanor for possession of the weapon and was given a conditional discharge.*

The case against two co-defendants, who both entered the sample for arrests on attempted murder charges, was dismissed when it became apparent that the gun had been fired by someone else, and there was little to suggest that the gun had been fired *at* anyone.

A noisy party attracted the attention of three police officers patrolling in an unmarked car in the early hours of the morning. The only officer in uniform was in the back seat, out of view from the house. There was heavy drinking going on, and people were going in and out of the party, stopping in groups on the steps outside. As they drove off down the street, the officers heard a shot and, when looking back, saw a man holding a gun that seemed pointed in their direction. They returned the fire. (The arresting officer explained that two police officers had been shot and killed recently.) The three people on the steps ran inside, locking themselves in an upstairs room with others from the party. Police reinforcements were called, and the house was stormed, but the door was finally opened from the inside. Nine persons were charged with resisting arrest, and the three who had been seen on the steps when the shot was fired (including our two co-defendants) were charged with attempted murder. Neither of the two had been seen holding the gun, and neither knew why or in which direction the gun had been fired.

---

* It should be noted, however, that discharge of a firearm in altercations will not automatically lead to an attempted murder charge at arrest. Three assault cases (and the one reckless endangerment case in the assault sample) involved discharge of firearms.

The police officer thought it might have been an overcharge. He said: "Most times if there is a problem [on charging] we will get an ADA *to come to the station. An* ADA *came down in this case and advised charging all three with attempted murder, as the gun may have changed hands after the shot was fired." The* ADA *who handled the cases in court was critical of the charging decision. "At least," he said, "these two cases shouldn't have got past the Complaint Room because the police officers were in there and said only the other man had the gun." When that testimony was repeated at the preliminary hearing the cases were dismissed. (The man who had actually fired the gun pled guilty to reckless endangerment.)*

In the last two attempted homicide cases that did not involve the discharging of guns, the defendants were alleged to have attacked with knives. Neither case involved injury to the victim or an evident intent to kill. One was a domestic squabble which was disposed of, when the common-law wife withdrew her complaint, by plea to a charge of "attempted" resisting arrest (a B misdemeanor) and a conditional discharge. The defendant's lawyer thought the plea was extracted to protect the police against suit by the defendant, who in the course of arrest had received injuries warranting 30 stitches. It was agreed by both the prosecution and the defense that attempted murder was an overcharge. The other knife case was charged as attempted murder because the complaining witness was a police officer and, perhaps, because *he* had discharged his firearm.

The police officer, off-duty and out of uniform, saw two youths fighting in the street—one with a knife in his hand. The officer drew his revolver and approached the pair to break it up. He said he showed his badge and identified himself as a police officer before demanding that the defendant drop the knife. The defendant later claimed that he and his companion had just been fooling around—not fighting—and that he did not know the man approaching, with gun drawn, was a police officer. The officer said that when the youth came at him with the knife, he gave another warning and then fired. The defendant was charged with attempted murder of a police officer and illegal possession of a weapon. The officer was not injured, but the defendant's bullet wounds required three operations on his stomach and four-and-a-half months in a hospital.

Both the officer and the defendant waived immunity and testified before the Grand Jury, which reduced the top charge from attempted murder to attempted assault in the second degree, an E felony. But both the ADA *and the defense viewed the prospect of trial with dismay. After determining that*

Assault, Rape, Murder and Attempted Murder 61

the defendant had a job and was about to marry at the time of the arrest, and that a social worker had taken an interest in the defendant since the incident and secured a place for him in a program, the ADA *offered (and the defendant accepted) a plea to illegal possession of a weapon, an A misdemeanor. Sentencing was left to the judge's discretion. A favorable probation report and the fact that, in the* ADA*'s view, "the defendant had suffered enough" from the wound to learn his lesson, led the judge to place him on probation.*

Summary

The felonies of "pure" personal violence in the deep sample followed a pattern of deterioration similar to that found in the wide sample. Rape charges deteriorated most, homicide charges least. Intermediate levels of deterioration occurred in assault and attempted homicide cases.

A common feature of these crimes was the existence of a prior relationship between victim and defendant: 64% of rape, homicide and attempted homicide defendants and 69% of assault defendants knew the complaining witnesses. Most prior relationships were close—family, lovers, neighbors, and so on—and were a leading factor in dismissals.

When strangers were the victims, dismissal was much less likely. Assault was the only deep sample offense with sufficient stranger cases to warrant generalization. Only 6 of the 21 stranger assaults (29%) ended in dismissal, and none was dismissed because of victim non-cooperation. Nevertheless, conviction in stranger assault cases generally followed a reduction in the charge and sentences imposed were usually light. Only 2 of the 15 defendants found guilty of stranger assaults were convicted of felonies (both lesser felonies than originally charged), and only 4 (27%) did any time (one did felony time). Eleven out of 15 (73%) walked.

In felonies of "pure" violence, the criminal process appears to be generally responsive to the will of the complainant while also considering the consequences of the crime. If a complaining witness becomes reluctant to pursue a case—for whatever reason—it will usually be dropped. On the other hand, if the complaining witness insists on prosecution, the case will usually proceed to a disposition, although the final outcome, including the level of the charge and the sentence, will not be severe unless the injuries are perceived to warrant a severe response.

Within this pattern, the most striking finding of all is the high incidence of prior relationships and the frequency with which those relationships result in dismissal of charges. Another notable finding is the high proportion (43%)

of stranger assault cases that involved assaults against police officers. The interviews suggest that the felony assault charges in a number of cases may be added as protection against a claim of unwarranted use of force by the arresting officers themselves, a practice that some ADAs appear to accept.

Congestion appears to have played only a limited role in deterioration of these cases. It may be that congestion causes prosecutors to take certain cases—such as the two rape charges brought by prostitutes—less seriously than they should. Court congestion might also have had something to do with a prosecutor's readiness to accept a misdemeanor plea before knowing the extent of injuries to the victim in the lye-throwing case. And one plea bargain injurious to the defendant—in a rape case considered to be "terribly weak" by the ADA, who had only spent 20 minutes looking into the case after the 17-year-old defendant had spent 5 months in jail—was clearly the result of congestion. By and large, however, the deterioration of these cases is explained more by the characteristics of the cases themselves, and the participants, than by the characteristics of the criminal process.

3 Robbery

For most citizens, "robbery" conjures up a frightening set of images: street muggings, retail stick-ups and other incidents in which a threatening stranger confronts and demands money from a terrified victim. It is a crime of violence—stealing by force or threat of injury—and because the robber is thought to be a predatory rather than a spontaneous criminal, he may be the archetypal "real" violent felon in the public imagination.

An ordinary robbery in the third degree—forcible stealing—is a D felony punishable by up to 7 years in prison. If the crime is committed in concert with another person, if it involves display of what appears to be a firearm, or if it causes physical injury to victim or bystander, it is robbery in the second degree (a C felony punishable by up to 15 years in prison). First degree robbery, a B felony punishable by up to 25 years in prison, is armed robbery (display or use of a deadly weapon) or robbery resulting in serious injury. The charge at arrest in more than half (28) of the 53 deep sample robbery cases was robbery in the first degree. Twenty-two cases (42%) were charged as second degree robbery, and only 3 (6%) as third degree robbery.

Fact Patterns in Robberies

More than half (60%) of the 53 robbery suspects were alleged to have acted in concert with others. In contrast to defendants in assault cases, only 53% of whom had prior records, almost three-quarters of the robbery suspects (74%) had prior records. Half (51%) of the robbery suspects displayed a deadly weapon or dangerous instrument, compared to 78% of the assault suspects. Sixteen of the 27 robbery weapons were knives, 6 were guns; the rest included a bottle, a vacuum cleaner handle, a screwdriver and a stick. Although injuries resulted in 15 of the cases (28%), the injury was serious enough to require medical attention in only 7 (13%). None of the 6 guns was fired, and no injury resulted in those cases. The amounts stolen from victims ranged from $2 to $300; most were under $50. Surprisingly, given the robber's image as a predatory criminal, prior relationships existed between defendants and victims in 36% of the cases.

A composite picture of the typical robbery suspect shows a youth accused, together with a friend, of threatening a stranger with a knife and demanding cash. He has a record of arrests (though not for robbery), but has never been sent to prison. On this charge, however, he got time after pleading guilty to attempted robbery.

Deterioration of Robbery Arrests

It was shown in the chapter on "Deterioration of Felony Arrests" that a reported robbery is less likely to be cleared by arrest than any other reported violent felony. The low arrest rate (19%) might be expected because robbery seems more likely than other violent felonies to be committed by strangers, and strangers are less likely to be arrested. Stranger robbers—the archetypal "real" felons—may therefore be under-represented in the group of robbers brought to court. Nevertheless, a robbery suspect was more likely than the average defendant in wide sample felony cases to be convicted of a crime (Figure 4), more likely to be convicted of a felony (Figure 5), and more likely to get felony time (Figure 6). Figure 11 shows that the same pattern applies to deep sample robbery arrests.

A slightly higher proportion of deep sample robbery cases ended in conviction than all felony cases together, but felony convictions were three

Figure 11. Dispositional Pattern for Robbery Arrests Compared to All Felony Arrests

(Robbery arrests are 14% of all felony arrests studied.)

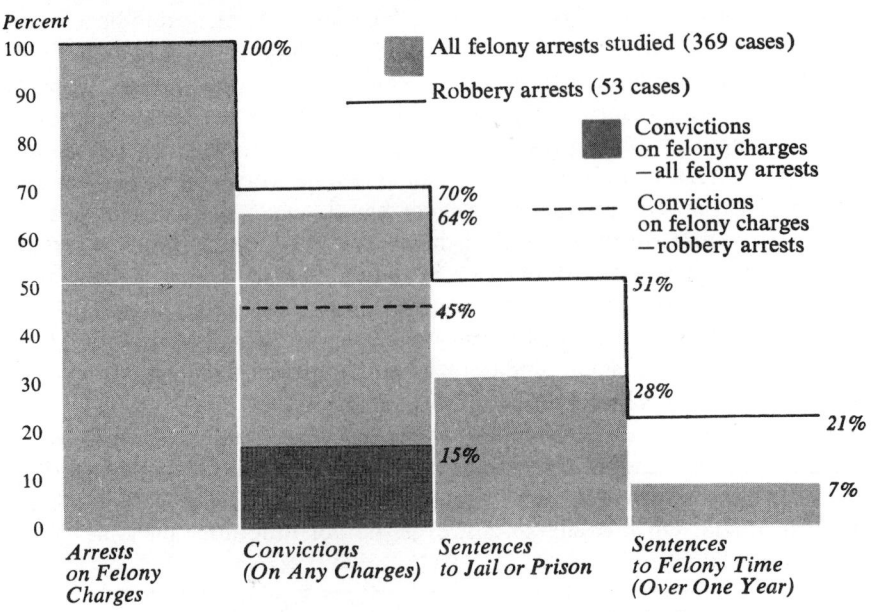

	Arrests on Felony Charges	Convictions (On Any Charges)	Sentences to Jail or Prison	Sentences to Felony Time (Over One Year)
All felony arrests studied (369 cases)	100%	70%	51%	21%
Robbery arrests (53 cases)	100%	64%	28%	7%
Convictions on felony charges—all felony arrests		15%		
Convictions on felony charges—robbery arrests		45%		

Source: Deep Sample Data (1973); Vera Institute Felony Disposition Study.

times more frequent in cases commenced by arrests for robbery than in other cases. Moreover, those convicted were twice as likely to receive prison or jail sentences—and three times as likely to receive felony time sentences—as convicted defendants generally.

The 53 deep sample robberies reached their dispositions by a number of different routes, as displayed in Figure 12, next page.

Only one deep sample robbery case went to trial. The defendant, who had a prison record, was charged with a pocketbook snatch that involved no injury, no weapon and no concerted activity. He turned down the ADA's best offer and waited for trial on the original D felony charge, third degree robbery. He was hoping to avoid another prison sentence by waiting for the ADA's case to collapse. But there were no problems of proof for the prosecution: a police officer was an eyewitness to the crime, there was no prior relationship between defendant and victim, the complainant was cooperative, and the defendant was burdened by a serious prior record. He was convicted as charged and got the maximum, seven years.

The balance of this chapter will explore factors underlying the remaining 52 dispositions: why 30% were dismissed, why all but 2 of the remaining defendants were allowed to plead guilty to reduced charges and why, despite the charge reductions, 28% of these guilty pleas were followed by felony time.

Factors Explaining Dispositions of Robbery Arrests

Two explanatory factors emerged from analysis of the deep sample robbery arrests. A prior relationship between defendant and complainant was found in 36% of the cases. The dispositions in these cases—usually dismissal—appear to have been substantially affected by the prior relationships. In the 64% involving no prior relationship, dispositions are largely comprehensible in terms of the defendant's prior record. Although the statutory gradations of sentences applicable to robbery are tied to the presence of weapons, concerted action or injury, these factors were not strongly associated with the severity of dispositions actually received by the deep sample cases—perhaps because the subsamples in each category were too small.

Prior Relationship Robberies. A significant prior relationship existed in 19 (36%) of the 53 deep sample robbery cases, as shown in Table K, page 67. When the deterioration of felony charges in prior relationships is compared with deterioration in the "stranger" robberies (Figure 13, page 68), it becomes clear that the latter cases get more serious treatment.

Figure 12. The Course to Disposition for Robbery Arrests

Felony Arrests Reaching Disposition in the Criminal Process: 53

- Dismissals: 16
- Acquittals: 0
- Guilty Pleas: 36
  - Guilty Plea — misdemeanor or less: 13
    - Misd. Time: 7
    - No Time: 6
  - Guilty Plea — lesser felony than charged: 21
    - Felony Time: 10
    - Misd. Time: 9
    - No Time: 4
  - Guilty Plea — same felony as charged (or higher): 2
- Trials: 1
  - Conviction — misdemeanor or less: 0
    - Misd. Time: 0
    - No Time: 0
  - Conviction — lesser felony than charged: 0
    - Misd. Time: 0
    - No Time: 0
  - Conviction — same felony as charged (or higher): 1
    - Felony Time: 1

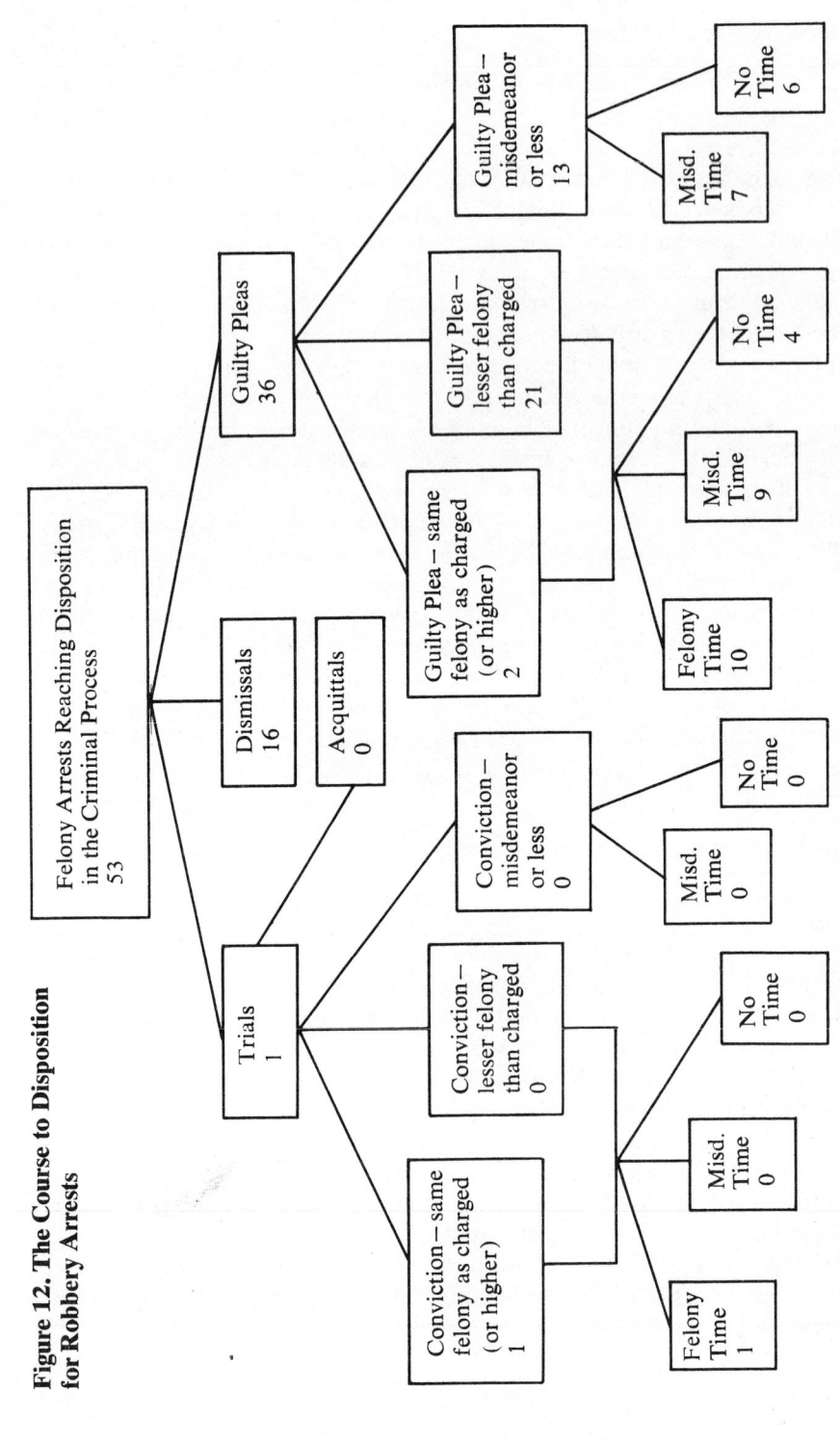

Source: Deep Sample Data (1973); Vera Institute Felony Disposition Study.

Table K: Prior Relationships in Robbery Cases

Family, lovers and former spouses	5
Friends/neighbors	11
Prostitute/client or Prostitute/pimp	2
Other[a]	1
(None)[b]	(34)

Source: Deep Sample Data (1973); Vera Institute Felony Disposition Study.

a. The prior relationship was actually between the defendant's girlfriend and the victim. The defendant, not realizing his girlfriend had given the complainant a key to her apartment, jumped the complainant when he entered the apartment. The complainant broke free, called the police and had the defendant arrested. The mistake was ultimately realized and the case dismissed.

b. In four of these cases, there were prior relationships of a different sort. Defendants were identified by victims in three of these because they lived in or frequented the same area; in the fourth case, the defendant was identified because he had previously been a customer in the store which was robbed. In none of these cases, however, did the defendant expect to be recognized. We have therefore categorized them as "stranger" robberies.

Only about a third of the prior relationship robberies resulted in a conviction of any kind, in contrast to an 88% conviction rate for the stranger cases. All but one of the 24 felony convictions were in stranger cases, and felony time—the result in about a third of the stranger cases—was not imposed in any prior relationship case.* Thus, although the numbers are small, the nexus between prior relationship and disposition is a powerful one.

Many of the prior relationship robbery cases turned out to be personal conflicts—often arising from disputes over money—which found expression in acts conforming in only a technical way to the statutory definition of robbery. In many of these cases, the conflicts were resolved after the arrest, independently of the criminal process. Typically, the result of such a reconciliation was a non-cooperative complaining witness and dismissal of the robbery charge—sometimes to the obvious relief of the ADA.

One such case arose from an argument over money between an intoxicated 59-year-old man and the woman who had been his common-law wife for 15

---

* The sentence imposed for the one felony conviction in a prior relationship case did, however, approach felony time. The defendant, who had a history of mental instability, was arrested for second degree robbery when he attacked his lover with a knife during a fight over money in her apartment. He pled guilty to attempted second degree robbery, an E felony. He had served 318 days in pretrial custody, the victim had not been injured, and he was young and had no prior record, so he was sentenced to "time served."

Figure 13. Deterioration of Prior Relationship Robbery Arrests and Stranger Robbery Arrests

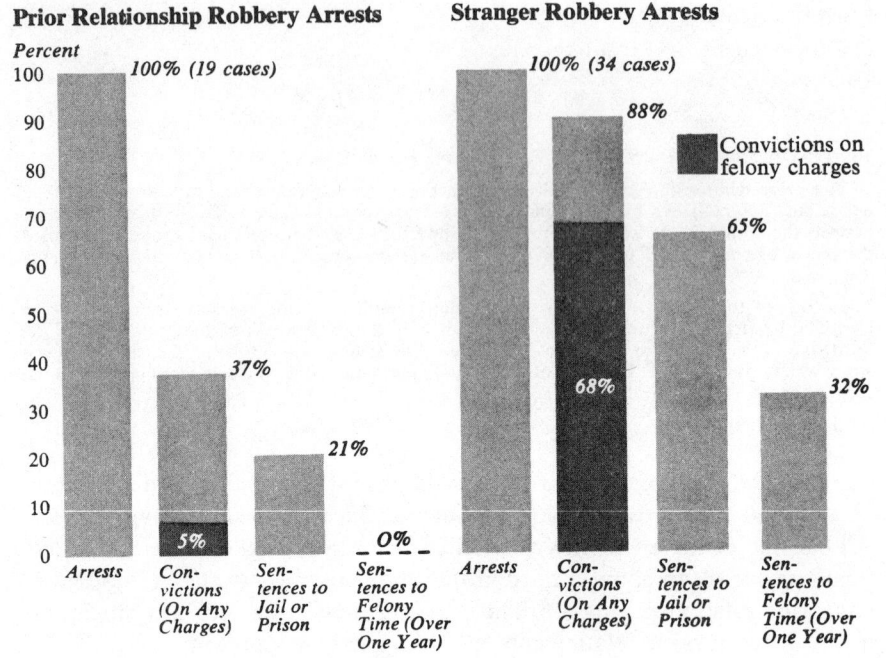

Prior Relationship Robbery Arrests: Arrests 100% (19 cases); Convictions (On Any Charges) 37%; Sentences to Jail or Prison 21%; Sentences to Felony Time (Over One Year) 0%; Convictions on felony charges 5%.

Stranger Robbery Arrests: Arrests 100% (34 cases); Convictions (On Any Charges) 88%; Sentences to Jail or Prison 65%; Sentences to Felony Time (Over One Year) 32%; Convictions on felony charges 68%.

Source: Deep Sample Data (1973); Vera Institute Felony Disposition Study.

years. He struck her and seized $5 and some food stamps. She had him arrested for robbery, went to the hospital where she required 12 stitches, and withdrew the charges a few days later when they reconciled. The police officer had been surprised at her initial insistence on arrest. "Usually with these squabbles we just go in there and try to quiet them down—we separate them and let them cool off. They don't want anyone arrested—just want us to scream at one party."

Dismissal of the robbery charge did not end this case, however. The defendant had offered $20 to the arresting officer on the way to the station, and he pled guilty to an A misdemeanor for that indiscretion. "He thought he could buy a cop—he wasn't the big criminal type, just not very intelligent," said the ADA. His sentence was a conditional discharge, for which the judge *offered the following explanation: "The probation report called for a conditional discharge with a provision that he stay away from the woman. Well, that was ridiculous, they were arm in arm before me at sentencing and she told me he was a damn good provider. Could I as a judge prevent this? I granted the conditional discharge without the provision."*

The ADA in the case above observed that the defendant "wasn't the typical robber," but 9 of the 12 dismissals of robbery charges in prior relationship cases followed in a similar way when the complainant lost interest in pursuing the prosecution.

One dismissal resulted when the "victim" realized his complaint was based on fantasy. The defendant had been arrested for first degree robbery, accused of stealing $45 at knifepoint. This was not an ordinary street mugging. The case interviews revealed that the complainant and the defendant, who had no prior record, were actually "drinking buddies," and that the complainant had misplaced his wallet during an all-night drinking bout.

Generally, although dismissals of robbery cases involving prior relationships were explained in terms of "complainant non-cooperation," the ADAs thought dismissal was in the interests of justice. But there were cases in which dismissal ran against the prosecutor's will, despite his acknowledgement of a prior relationship. One prosecutor observed in general terms that "sometimes there's intimidation, a bribe or a scare to put off the complaining witness. I just don't have time to find out—the drive is just to clear the calendar." The ADA's power to avoid dismissal may in any event be severely circumscribed, despite his power to compel testimony by arrest or detention, because reluctant witnesses make bad witnesses. The following prior relationship robbery, dismissed following a "reconciliation," is illustrative of the problem.

A woman reported to the police that her sister and her sister's boyfriend had taken her purse and $40 after assaulting her (she had a bruised lip) and threatening her baby's life. The sister and her boyfriend were charged with robbery in the first degree.

The victim kept to her story when first interviewed by the ADA, and repeated it in a sworn affidavit. The female defendant (selected in our sample) and her co-defendant remained in custody after arraignment; bail had been set at a very high figure because of the alleged threat to the baby, and because immigration authorities became interested in the boyfriend, who proved to be an illegal immigrant from Uruguay and was eventually deported.

On the hearing date, the complainant told the ADA *she did not want to prosecute her own sister. The* ADA, *to whom "it looked like a good robbery case," and who wanted to press for conviction, tried to put pressure on her to testify: "I told her that if she pulled out her sister could go free, but that she would go to trial (for perjury) because she had sworn to a statement." The threat of prosecution led the complainant to change her story when she testified; the case was dismissed when she swore, in a new statement, that her sister's boyfriend had purchased a baby carriage for her, that she had believed it was a gift and that she had therefore resisted when her sister and the boyfriend demanded reimbursement. She swore it had been a misunderstanding, not a robbery.*

The prosecuting ADA's *immediate superior interviewed the complainant together with the co-defendants before permitting the* ADA *to move for dismissal of the case; he said he had believed her new story. The prosecuting* ADA, *however, thought the new story was "baloney" and that the complainant feared reprisal. The police officer, who had become quite involved during the investigation, was also upset: "I was angry because of the time spent in court and in investigation. This story about the baby carriage was new to me." He too doubted the new story and thought "she could be petrified of her sister yet."*

The possibility of complainant non-cooperation resulting from intimidation is a real one. The high incidence of dismissals in prior relationship felony cases may therefore not be due wholly to extra-judicial resolution of the conflicts, but it is usually impossible to know. For example, intimidation was mentioned as a possible cause of the complainant's refusal to cooperate in a dismissed robbery case in which a prostitute was the victim and her pimp was the defendant. When the prostitute failed to appear for the hearing, the arresting officer suspected intimidation because the pimp had a reputation for terrorizing people. The ADA, on the other hand, thought the original charge in this case had been "trumped-up"—another by-product of the inability of prostitutes to protect their business affairs through ordinary legal process.

"Trumped-up" charges may, of course, grow out of other types of relationships that lack the special circumstances of prostitution. The following robbery case is illustrative.

In the course of an argument with his girlfriend's brother, the defendant smashed a bottle in his face; the injury required seventeen stitches. They had known each other for ten years. "He just picked up whatever was closest to him in the heat of the moment," according to the judge. "Unfortunately it was a bottle. I think he was sorry, and I don't think he expected the bottle to break."

The complainant's admission to the ADA *that his story of a robbery was a fabrication left the defendant still charged with assault. Because he had no prior record and was employed, he was allowed to plead guilty to harassment (a violation) and was fined $25. This is what the data in the preceding chapter on assaults would lead us to expect. The* ADA *said: "This is exactly what would have happened if this case had gone to trial, but this court [Criminal Court] works like a strainer—the stuff that passes through should go to trial, but what sticks here is garbage."*

As this case also illustrates, not all the prior relationship cases commenced by arrest for robbery were disposed of by dismissal. Those that survived dismissal did generally end with "light" dispositions like the fine in the case above, even when there was no reconciliation and the victim cooperated with the prosecution. Another such case arose when a 34-year-old addict was charged with striking his girlfriend and taking her purse in a fight over money. The ADA offered a misdemeanor plea and a conditional discharge even though he believed the girl's story and she wanted to pursue the case. He did not think the case was "triable" as a felony.

"When defendant and complainant know each other the robbery becomes diminished in the jury's eyes," said the ADA. *"It's a dispute and the motive looks like debt collection." The fact that the fight in this case took place in the presence of several witnesses actually weakened the case, from the* ADA's *point of view. He thought a jury would feel that "nobody commits a robbery with others around to witness."*

Thus, leniency was the norm for the 19 prior relationship robbery cases. Seventy-nine percent concluded with outright dismissals or "walks" following pleas of guilty to reduced charges. There were 4 jail sentences—all under a year—and 2 were for "time served."* The third jail sentence was not expressly to "time served," but it was directly attributable to the defendant's pretrial custody.

---

* One of these "time served" sentences, however, was almost felony time—318 days. (See note ‡, page 2, above.) The second was 3 months. The prosecutor in this second case would have dismissed the charges at an early stage as "untriable," had it not been for the defendant's heavy criminal record. The complainant, in the ADA's judgment, would have made a poor witness because, in addition to being the defendant's friend, "his record was as bad as the defendant's."

The defendant, charged with robbing a former girlfriend, was unable to make bail. After the complainant failed twice to appear in court, the defendant agreed to plead to a B misdemeanor (attempted petit larceny) and got a 30-day sentence. The defense counsel said, "If the defendant had been out [of jail] I never would have taken a plea without the complainant present. But if I had requested another adjournment, the defendant would have had to stay in jail for another week or two—past 30 days anyway. So there was no reason for waiting to try to get a dismissal." The prosecutor agreed that the case would eventually have been dismissed if the defendant had not accepted the B misdemeanor.

The last of the four "time" cases among the prior relationship robberies involved a variant of the "time served" pattern and a victim who, although interested in prosecuting the case, kept altering his story in order to avoid public acknowledgement of the nature of his relationship with the defendant.

The robbery arrest was based on the complainant's initial testimony that the defendant and two other men had taken him from a bar, forced him into a nearby empty apartment at knifepoint, beaten him, tied him up and taken his money. The defendant, charged with first degree robbery, did not make bail.

The victim revealed to the ADA, just before the preliminary hearing, that the story had been a fabrication designed to avoid revealing his homosexuality to the police. The ADA asked him for the real story so he could amend the complaint before the preliminary hearing, but the complainant told several different versions. The ADA believed that some crime had been committed, but that the only way to find out whether the charges should be amended or dismissed was to put the victim under oath at the hearing.

At the hearing, the complainant testified that he had met the defendant frequently for drinks on previous occasions and that, on the night of the robbery, the defendant and one other man had invited him to accompany them into a nearby apartment where they continued drinking for a while. The complainant now said that, when the defendant asked for his money, he had voluntarily handed over the $14. Only then, according to this new story, was he tied up and left behind.

Although he did not testify that he was a homosexual or that he expected to have sex with the men to whom he had given the money, this seems to have been sufficiently apparent from his testimony for the ADA to conclude that his story would continue to change as he tried to cover up his own motives. From the prosecution point of view the case was now, at best, a felony assault that stood little chance of conviction at trial. Thus, when the defense attorney offered a plea of guilty to attempted assault in the third degree—a B misdemeanor—the ADA *"felt very lucky to get it. . . . I felt that there had been a crime committed, but having just watched the complainant on the stand, I thought there would be no way to ever prove it to a jury." The defense attorney also indicated his client's willingness to accept the maximum sentence—90 days. The judge agreed to this disposition because he too thought an assault had been committed, because he knew from the defense attorney that the defendant was already facing 30 days on an unrelated conviction, and because he was told by the* ADA *that the defendant had a hefty prior record. The 90-day sentence was to be served concurrently, so this defendant really got 60 days.*

The judge, the ADA *and the defense attorney all agreed that if the defendant had not pled guilty to the B misdemeanor, he would have had a good chance of acquittal on the only proper charge—third degree assault, an A misdemeanor. According to the defense attorney, he tried to convince his client to demand a trial where the complainant's testimony could be pulled apart, but the defendant refused when he realized he could finish the matter with no more than 60 days. He admitted to his lawyer that he had struck the complainant and tied him up, and he feared a certain 12-month sentence (because of his prior record) if he were to go to trial on the A misdemeanor and the victim's story were to hold together.*

Stranger Robberies. Convictions were obtained in most (88%) of the 34 deep sample robbery cases that involved no prior relationship between defendant and victim. None of the stranger robbers was acquitted and only 4 (12%) won dismissals. Two of the 4 dismissals were attributable to nonappearing complainants who could not be traced by the police.* The third dismissal occurred when the co-defendant of the defendant in our sample went to trial and was acquitted. The last of the 4 stranger robbery dismissals was an "adjournment in contemplation of dismissal." Leniency in this case was attributed to the defendant's lack of any prior record and to his successful involvement in a rehabilitative program at the time of sentencing. Continuation in the program was the condition required for ultimate dismissal of the charge.

In the 30 stranger cases resulting in convictions, the influence of prior

---

* In one case, ironically, police inability to locate the complainant was a by-product of the robbery: the complainant's welfare check had been taken, he was evicted when he did not pay the rent, and he left no forwarding address.

Table L: Sentences Following Arrests for Stranger Robberies, by Defendants' Arrest Records

	Walk	Misdemeanor Time	Felony Time
Prior Arrests (N = 24)	2 (8%)	12 (50%)	10 (42%)
No Prior Arrests (N = 6)	5 (83%)	—	1 (17%)

Source: Deep Sample Data (1973); Vera Institute Felony Disposition Study.

criminal record was apparent. Table L shows sentences according to defendants' arrest records.

Again, though the numbers are small, the message is too clear to be discounted. A convicted stranger robber with no record had only one in 6 chances of being sentenced to time, while the chances rose to 9 in 10 (22 out of 24) for those with prior arrests. Convicted stranger robbers with prior arrests also had a good chance (42%) of getting felony time.

Deviations from these apparent norms occurred in only three cases: two robbers with prior arrest records walked and one robber without a record got time. No rational explanation emerged for the three-year sentence imposed upon the defendant who had no criminal record: he got, according to his lawyer, "a raw deal":

"Ninety-nine percent of all other judges would have given him probation." There had been no sentence promise, and the defense lawyer thought the judge would think the "taste of jail" that the defendant had received during his pretrial custody was enough. But according to his lawyer, the judge decided to give the defendant time as an example to other muggers.*

Both defendants who walked despite previous records had been incarcerated prior to disposition. One had spent about 6 months in pretrial detention before being sentenced to 3 years probation. The other, who was 19 years old, had just spent 22 months in prison on another offense. Since the robbery had actually preceded the other offense, the judge saw no point in imprisoning him further, despite the fact that the robbery had been a brutal one.

---

* It was rare, in interviews following deep sample cases, for anyone to suggest that the judge's sentence was influenced by the timing of the defendant's decision to plead. The defense lawyer in this case did suggest that the defendant's withholding of his plea at arraignment may have influenced the judge. But other defendants, who delayed pleading as long or longer, did not suffer the same fate.

Evidentiary Problems. We have noted the prosecutor's difficulty in proving charges, and his readiness to dismiss charges, when there is a non-cooperating complaining witness in a prior relationship case. Lack of complainant cooperation can also plague stranger cases and lead a prosecutor to settle for lenient dispositions. For example, one would have expected more than a 15-day sentence for the stranger-robber who was grabbed on the spot by a store detective after snatching a purse from an out-of-towner shopping at Macy's. When the woman, who returned to her home city, did not show up to testify, the defendant was allowed to plead guilty to public intoxication; for that he got a 15-day sentence.

In other cases, a prosecutor may believe that chances for conviction at trial will be seriously undermined by the victim's character, no matter how great the cooperation. The ADA had solid evidence against two sampled defendants charged jointly with threatening a victim with a screwdriver and stealing nine dollars and his watch. One might expect heavy sentences for this, apparently a stereotypical "street" mugging. The case was marred, however, by the victim's long history of drug addiction and criminality. The ADA felt he could not afford to risk his chances for a conviction on a jury's reaction to his only witness, so he allowed the defendants to plead to two lesser felonies. One received a six-month sentence and the other a term of up to four years.

This kind of evidentiary difficulty is illustrated even more dramatically in the following case.

A drug addict, attempting to snatch a woman's handbag, went berserk when she resisted and stabbed her half a dozen times. A passing police officer, who saw her staggering and bleeding, caught the defendant, still nearby, holding the knife. It was a "high quality" arrest for a robbery in the second degree or higher, punishable by up to at least 15 years. The defendant had a prison record for robberies, but he was allowed to plead guilty to third degree robbery and was sentenced to 4 years, although the maximum sentence, even on this C felony conviction, could have been as high as 7 years.

When interviewed, the ADA at first said that such an "air-tight" case against such "a bad type of guy" was "worth 15 years." The defense attorney estimated that, if it had gone to trial, it would have been worth 10 years. The ADA pointed to court congestion as an explanation for the surprising leniency: "Right now we are giving away the court house, when you give 4 years on a robbery like that."

But when the ADA *led the interviewer through the file on this case, a different reason for deterioration of the charge was revealed. The file contained a letter, from the* ADA *who had presented the case to the Grand Jury for indictment, saying that the victim was a "terrible witness" who made speeches in a thick foreign accent about how the defendant and others of his race (black) should get the electric chair. "She cannot be interrupted or be made to answer questions," the first* ADA *had written. The* ADA *who had accepted the plea acknowledged that the weakness of this complainant's testimony as evidence at trial was at least as important as court congestion in his decision to negotiate the plea.**

Archetypal Robberies

The deep sample did include robberies matching the archetype. In addition to the case immediately above, in which a stranger robber with a prison record for previous robberies stabbed a woman during a purse snatch, drawing a four-year sentence, two other cases are relevant:

- A woman reported to the police that she had been robbed by two men armed with both a gun and machete. She had a gash on the hand, but did not need medical attention. Her assailants were quickly spotted and arrested; the machete, the gun (a stolen police officer's weapon) and the victim's check were found in the car. The arresting officer said, "It was a clear case. No problems—both the defendants had long records." The ADA said, "There was no serious injury, so I was ready to go down one degree. The highest charge [at arrest] was the B felony [first degree robbery], so I offered a C felony plea which would, in fact, 'cover' ['fit,' by definition, a robbery with] the assault and the gun. But I was not going to go any lower." The

---

* The evidentiary problem arising from the complainant's testimony explains the offer of a plea to the lesser felony, but it does not explain the sentence. We were unable to interview the judge in this case, but the defense attorney pointed out that the judge had deferred sentencing three times, finally handing down the four-year term six months after the plea and a year after the incident. During those months the defendant had finally secured his release on bail and entered a drug rehabilitation program. The defendant, according to his lawyer, had been badly shaken by the violence he had displayed in the robbery. ("I went crazy. I really think I could have killed that woman," he had told the lawyer.) The defendant had in fact done well in the program and had stayed out of trouble. The judge apparently indicated at the deferment of sentencing that he wanted to see how well the defendant progressed. In the defense attorney's view, the crime would have ended with a ten-year sentence if it had gone to trial, but even less than the four-year sentence if the defendant's rehabilitation had been taken into account by a different, more generous, judge.

judge agreed: "I made a promise of seven years maximum at the plea. And I ended up giving him six years, based on his record." The ADA said, "The plea was best; it avoided a long trial and he got a proper sentence. There is always a risk of acquittal in a trial."

- Two young men with long prison records hid in the lobby of an apartment building. When a 68-year-old female tenant walked in, they grabbed her handbag and pushed her around, hurting her. The ADA said, "I think it's worse to attack women. Women get special protection on these sorts of crimes." The two were caught almost at the scene of the crime. "The evidence was overwhelming," according to the ADA. "We had her testimony, the hospital reports to corroborate the injury, and it would have been hopeless for them to testify at a trial—their records were too long. I offered them both pleas to the charge on the indictment." The indictment charge was second degree robbery, a C felony with a fifteen-year maximum term. There was no weapon, nor injury serious enough to make out a first degree robbery charge at arrest or in the Grand Jury. "One took the plea first time around and drew seven years," the ADA continued, "and the other [the defendant in our sample] faced the possibility of a life sentence as a repeated felon." The judge, however, felt that the special sentence provision was not necessary: "It's hard to conceive of a case where the punishment available for a crime would not be enough. I didn't really think of using [the persistent felony offender sentence] in this case." "We put a top of ten years on his sentence," said the ADA, "and he pled on the day the case was on for trial. He was offered virtually nothing for his plea because of his record." The defendant, according to his lawyer, had been out of prison for only three days when he committed this robbery. The judge sentenced him to eight years in prison.

All three of these defendants received felony convictions and felony time on felony charges. They robbed strangers, they hurt their victims, and they had records. In the two latter cases, the sentences were more than the minimum but substantially less than the fifteen-year maximum allowed by statute for their crimes, second degree robbery. And in both cases, the sentence was negotiated as part of the plea bargain.

Summary

Explanations for the bulk of the dispositions in this robbery sample are reasonably straightforward:

- Thirty percent were dismissed. But three-quarters of the dismissals occurred in prior relationship cases. Some of these robbery charges were "trumped-up"; in some that were technically robberies, the prosecutor was left without a case by the withdrawal of the complainant; and in others, the complainant was so unsavory that the case was not really "triable."

- Although the incidence of prior relationships in robberies was higher than might be expected for the archetypal predatory crime, the majority of defendants (64%) were accused of robbing strangers. And only 4 of these stranger cases (12%) were dismissed. Two dismissals were attributable to complainant non-appearance, and one followed from a co-defendant's acquittal at trial. Only the fourth, an adjournment in contemplation of dismissal for a defendant who was progressing well in a diversion program, might seem an inappropriate exercise of prosecutional and judicial discretion; but this defendant was young and had never been arrested before.

- Thus, 88% of the stranger robbers were convicted and 77% of these were felony convictions. Three-fourths (77%) of the convicted stranger robbers went to jail or prison. Their sentences were largely explained by prior criminal record, or the lack of it: 92% of sentences for those with a prior record were "time" (and 42% were felony time). The two with prior records who walked had actually served time prior to sentence. On the other hand, 83% of convicted stranger robbers with clean prior records walked. The only defendant who got time despite a clean record was sentenced to a 3-year term as a warning to others, rather than because he was thought to be a truly dangerous felon.

- Heavier terms of imprisonment might have been imposed on some stranger robbers, who managed to avoid felony time by pleading to lesser offenses, if the "triability" of the prosecutors' cases had not been weakened by the complainants' lack of interest or unsavory character.

- Although deep sample robbery cases got more serious treatment by the criminal process than charges of assault (and as we shall see, other crimes less serious than robbery), few (13%) of these defendants were responsible for inflicting serious injuries and few (11%) had threatened their victims with guns. These data, together with the suprisingly high incidence of prior relationships, suggest that people arrested on robbery charges are not representative of the felons committing robbery in the streets. The few clear cases of predatory robbery against strangers were, however, punished severely.

Although this overall picture of sampled robbery arrests appears to be one of proportionality, there were several defendants whose convictions and sentences seemed products of court congestion, with its attendant delays and extended pretrial custody. Pretrial custody figured prominently in each of the 4 prior relationship robbery cases that ended with jail sentences. The defendants in these cases may not have been wholly innocent of crime in the incidents leading to these arrests, but justice may not have been fully served either. One defendant, arrested for robbery despite the police officer's uncertainty about what, if anything, he had done, pled guilty to attempted petit larceny (a B misdemeanor) and got a 30-day jail sentence because it was not worth waiting even longer in jail for the dismissal that was sure to follow from the complainant's non-cooperation. The defendant charged with robbing his girlfriend in her apartment, who waited 318 days in jail before pleading guilty to a E felony and being sentenced to "time served," may in fact have committed a crime. But the prior relationship would have reduced the likelihood of his conviction at trial and, in any case, extended pretrial jailing was not the most responsible way to dispose of a charge of violent crime against a defendant with a history of mental instability.

One stranger robbery case stands out as a poignant, particularly worrisome example of the potentially damaging effects of pretrial delay.

Twenty-four years old, practically blind, and lacking any prior record, this defendant was apprehended by a civilian police photographer who claimed he saw the defendant trying to snatch a woman's pocketbook on the street. According to the defendant, he had approached and lightly touched the woman because he thought he recognized her. When he got close enough to her for his poor eyesight to reveal her as a stranger, she screamed. He saw no reason to flee (although another man who was with him did flee), because he had done nothing wrong.

When the police arrived, the civilian who had held the defendant (he had made over 100 citizen's arrests, according to the defense lawyer—more like 50, according to the ADA), told the arresting officer that he had seen the defendant pulling on the woman's pocketbook. According to the defense counsel, this man also told the police he had heard (from 90 feet away) the defendant's companion say, "Give us your pocketbook or we'll kill the baby." The woman, however, was not at all sure she heard this statement. The arresting officer was not sure who was telling the truth and arrested the defendant for robbery in the second degree (because of the "concerted action"). The ADA believed that the woman had been genuinely terrified, and that there probably was an attempted purse-snatching, although he thought the defen dant's companion at the time—who was not found and arrested—was probably the primary actor.

The defendant initially refused a B misdemeanor plea. A trial resulted in a hung jury. During the trial, the defendant had been put in jail for a few days because he came in late for court once. The ADA rejected defense attempts to get an ACD, saying he "couldn't do it because as a matter of fact we had a case." Eventually the defendant entered a plea to a B misdemeanor because, his lawyer explained, "he didn't want to go back to jail and could no longer afford the cost of subway tokens to get to court."

4 Burglary

Burglaries accounted for over one-third of all felonies reported to the police in New York City in 1971. There were 178,175 reported in the four major boroughs. Surveys show that victims report about 65% of burglaries to the police, so as many as 274,000 burglaries may actually have been committed during the year. While not a violent "street crime," burglary nevertheless creates much of the same kind of fear, outrage, and anger in the average citizen. For many individuals, the home (or business) is an extension of the person, and the thought of its invasion by a prowling stranger arouses basic self-protective instincts. In addition, when an intruder breaks into a home or business, there is danger that he will encounter the rightful occupant and that violence will erupt from the confrontation.

Under New York Penal Law, entering or remaining in a building or in enclosed real property with intent to commit a crime constitutes burglary. The intrusion is technically burglary if there is intent to commit any crime—it does not have to be theft.* Simple (third degree) burglary is a D felony carrying a maximum of 7 years in prison. It rises to the second degree, a C felony punishable by imprisonment for up to 15 years, if the burglar (or a co-burglar) is armed with a deadly weapon, displays what appears to be a firearm, causes physical injury to an innocent party or uses or threatens to use a dangerous instrument. First degree burglary, a B felony carrying a 25-year maximum sentence, arises when the premises are a dwelling, the burglary occurs at night, and the firearm is loaded.

Burglary is more commonly committed and more often reported than felonious asssault or robbery, but the clearance rate of burglaries reported to the police is lower.† Even though, on average, two reported burglaries were cleared for every burglary arrest, it seems unlikely that the 15,559 suspects arrested in the four major boroughs for this crime in 1971 were representative of those responsible for the 178,175 burglaries reported in the same boroughs.

The lower clearance and arrest rates might be explained by a lack of face-to-face contact in most burglaries. In assault, attempted murder, rape and rob-

---

* If the intrusion is not with an ulterior criminal purpose, only criminal trespass is committed. Criminal trespass can be a D felony if the trespasser possesses a deadly weapon. Otherwise, criminal trespass is an A misdemeanor if the trespass is in a dwelling, or B misdemeanor if it is in a building or enclosed (fenced) real property. As we shall see, guilty pleas to criminal trespass, either the A or B misdemeanor, frequently dispose of burglary arrests.

† The 1971 clearance rate for reported burglaries was 16%; for assaults, 39%; for robberies, 25%.

bery, the victim has at least seen the perpetrator once. But the "real," professional burglar will make his getaway before the crime is discovered, and the police acknowledge that the chances of finding and linking him with that crime are slim. Thus, the courts are likely to be processing a minority of burglars unlucky or incompetent enough to be caught, or who are already known to their victims.

Fact Patterns in Burglaries

The first degree burglar, the dreaded armed night prowler, does not appear very often in court—at least not as often as he appears in the popular imagination, rummaging around strangers' apartments. None of the deep sample was charged with first degree burglary, and only 5% of burglary suspects in the wide sample were so charged. Most of the deep sample burglary cases were initially charged in the second degree (60%); the rest (40%) entered the criminal process as third degree burglaries.*

Burglaries that make their way into the criminal process are probably not representative of all burglaries. The strongest evidence of this is the presence of a prior relationship between defendant and victim in 17 (39%) of the 44 deep sample cases. Although this figure is lower than the incidence of prior relationships in the violent felonies discussed in previous chapters, it is surprising (given the stereotype) to find *any* prior relationships in burglary cases.

To the extent that there was a "typical" burglary in the deep sample, it was burglary of an unoccupied commercial establishment at night by a suspect with a prior criminal record. Twenty of the 44 deep sample burglary cases involved unoccupied commercial establishments (14 stores, 4 factories, a grocery marketing center and a hospital). Only one of these 20 defendants was apprehended as a result of a fingerprint match, and this did not occur until one and a half years after the burglary, when he was processed on an arrest for a different crime. The others arrested for commercial burglaries were apprehended at or close to the scene of the crime (entering, inside, leaving, or in the immediate vicinity with the "loot"), often after setting off a burglar alarm. All but 2 of the commercial burglars had prior criminal records, and in most cases an intent to steal appeared clear from the facts.

The 24 deep sample residential burglaries do not yield a type so easily. The most surprising aspect of these cases is the prior relationship between burglar and victim in 63% (15 of 24). Of the 9 residential burglaries committed by

---

* In contrast to these deep sample figures, 5% of the wide sample burglaries were initially charged in the first degree, 17% were initially charged in the second degree, and the remainder (78%) were all charged in the third degree.

Burglary

strangers, it appears in 4 that there was no *intent* to commit a crime on the premises—the element which distinguishes burglary from the criminal trespass misdemeanor. Half (8) of the 15 defendants charged with residential burglary of people known to them had no prior arrest record. This contrasts markedly with the commercial and the stranger/residential burglars, of whom only 10% and 11%, respectively, had no prior arrest record.

The value of goods stolen was low, in both residential and commercial burglaries. It clearly exceeded $500 in only 2 cases. Only one case involved an injury or the use of a weapon, but a prior relationship (marriage) was involved in that case, and the knife wound was superficial.

Deterioration of Burglary Arrests

A graphic comparison of the dispositional pattern for deep sample burglary cases with that for all felonies (Figure 14), indicates few differences. Appre-

Figure 14. Dispositional Pattern for Burglary Arrests Compared to All Felony Arrests

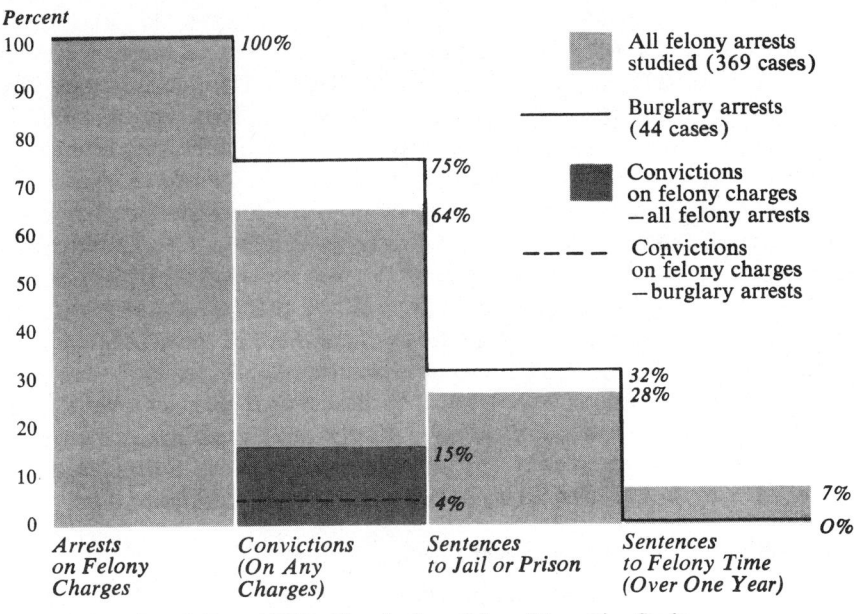

(Burglary arrests are 12% of all felony arrests studied.)

- All felony arrests studied (369 cases)
- Burglary arrests (44 cases)
- Convictions on felony charges — all felony arrests
- Convictions on felony charges — burglary arrests

	Arrests on Felony Charges	Convictions (On Any Charges)	Sentences to Jail or Prison	Sentences to Felony Time (Over One Year)
All felony arrests	100%	75%	32%	7%
Burglary arrests	100%	64%	28%	0%
Convictions on felony — all		15%		
Convictions on felony — burglary		4%		

Source: Deep Sample Data (1973); Vera Institute Felony Disposition Study.

hended burglars were more likely to be convicted, but less likely to be convicted of a felony and given felony time, than other apprehended felons.

A comparison of the dispositional pattern of burglary cases with robbery (page 64) suggests that the court perceived the deep sample burglary cases to be less serious than the deep sample robbery cases. If arrested, a burglary suspect was a little more likely to be convicted than a robbery suspect (75% compared to 70%) but much less likely to be convicted of a felony. The rate of felony convictions was 10 times greater in the robbery cases (45%) than the burglary cases (5%). Further, a burglary arrest was less likely than a robbery arrest to be disposed of by sentence to jail or prison, and there were *no* felony time sentences in the deep sample burglary dispositions, while a fifth of the robbery cases ended with felony time.

The 44 deep sample burglary cases reached disposition by the routes indicated in Figure 15.

Only one burglary arrest was disposed of by trial. In that case, a nighttime residential burglary by a stranger, the defendant was apprehended a block from the scene of his crime, but he claimed that he intended only to take a lawn chair (worth $25) from the victim's front porch. The jury believed his story, acquitted him of burglary and convicted him of petit larceny (a B misdemeanor). He was conditionally discharged.

Eleven cases (25%) were dismissed. A high proportion of burglary charges surviving dismissal were reduced: 94% of undismissed burglary charges were reduced to misdemeanors or less, compared to 35% among undismissed deep sample cases commenced by arrest for robbery. It should be noted, however, that over half the deep sample robbery arrests were originally charged in the first degree—a B felony—while the majority of deep sample burglary cases were originally charged in the second degree—a C felony. Charge reductions were therefore likely to hit the misdemeanor range more swiftly in the burglary cases. Only 2 pleas of guilty were made to felony charges, and they were the only felony convictions. No one got felony time. Five of the 14 sentenced to misdemeanor time were addicts who were sentenced to NACC.

Nevertheless, recurring factors found in the sampled burglary arrests, independent of the crime class of the original charge, may explain why the typical disposition was a guilty plea to a misdemeanor or violation followed by a sentence that was slightly more likely to be a walk than misdemeanor time.

Factors Explaining Dispositions of Burglary Arrests

Prior relationships, when found in the deep sample burglary cases, had a powerful influence over disposition—leading most often to dismissal, as they did in

Figure 15. The Course to Disposition for Burglary Arrests

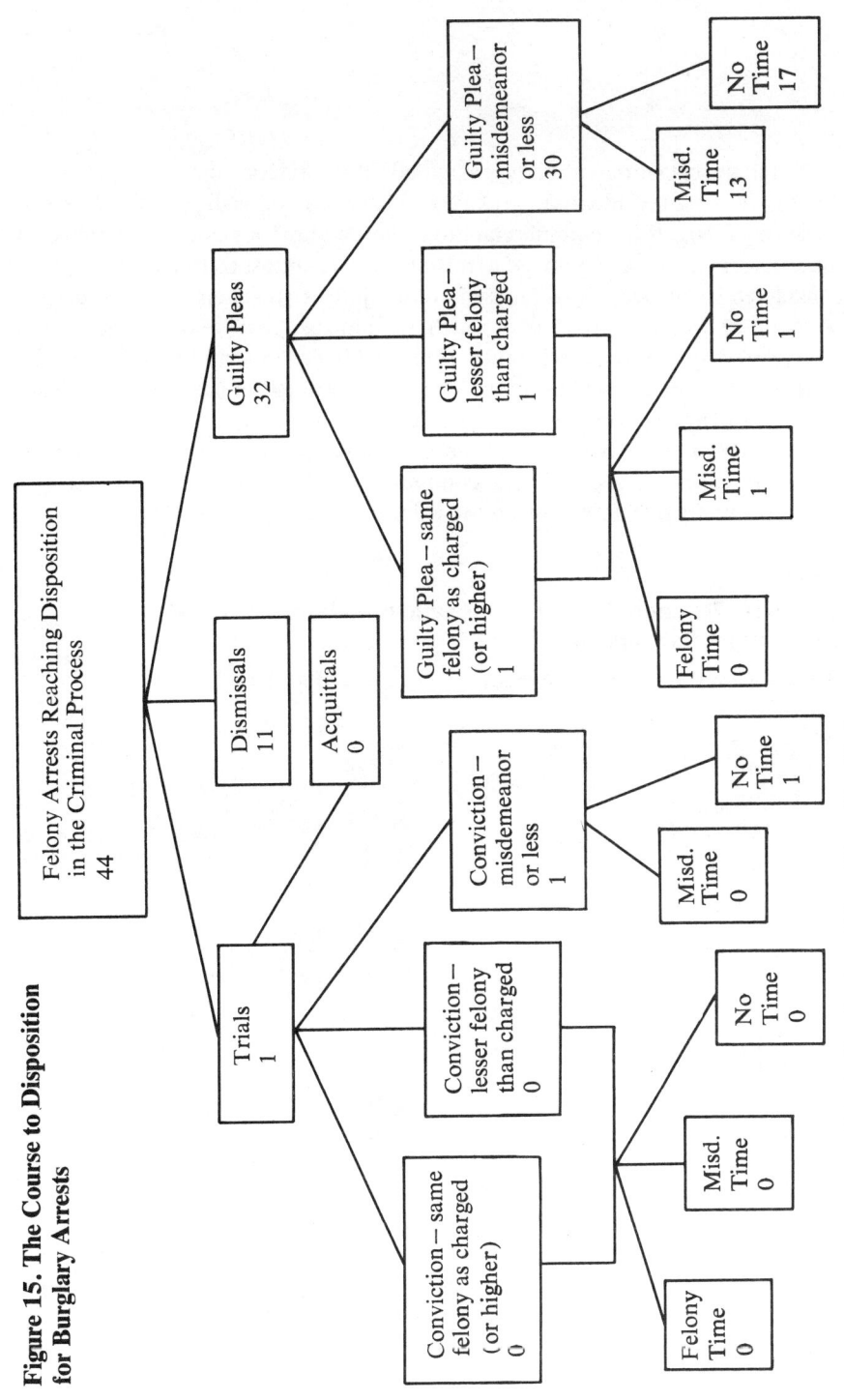

- Felony Arrests Reaching Disposition in the Criminal Process: 44
  - Dismissals: 11
  - Acquittals: 0
  - Trials: 1
    - Conviction — same felony as charged (or higher): 0
      - Felony Time: 0
      - Misd. Time: 0
      - No Time: 0
    - Conviction — lesser felony than charged: 0
    - Conviction — misdemeanor or less: 1
      - Misd. Time: 0
      - No Time: 1
  - Guilty Pleas: 32
    - Guilty Plea — same felony as charged (or higher): 1
      - Felony Time: 0
      - Misd. Time: 1
      - No Time: 1
    - Guilty Plea — lesser felony than charged: 1
    - Guilty Plea — misdemeanor or less: 30
      - Misd. Time: 13
      - No Time: 17

Source: Deep Sample Data (1973); Vera Institute Felony Disposition Study.

other felony categories already examined. Prior relationships figured in 15 (63%) of the 24 residential burglaries and accounted for the dismissal of 8 of these cases. Nighttime commercial burglaries, comprising about two-thirds of the stranger cases, were reduced to misdemeanors almost routinely. They were considered by prosecutors, defense counsel, judges and even police officers to be nuisance crimes not worthy of much attention as "real" felonies (at least in a congested system), because they rarely offer an opportunity for violence. Whether the commercial burglar gets time, following what is typically a misdemeanor conviction, seems to depend on whether he has a prior record.

Prior Relationship Burglaries. Figure 16 shows that almost half the prior relationship cases were dismissed, compared with only 11% of the stranger cases. And only one defendant in the prior relationship cases (6%) got time,

Figure 16. Deterioration of Prior Relationship Burglary Arrests and Stranger Burglary Arrests

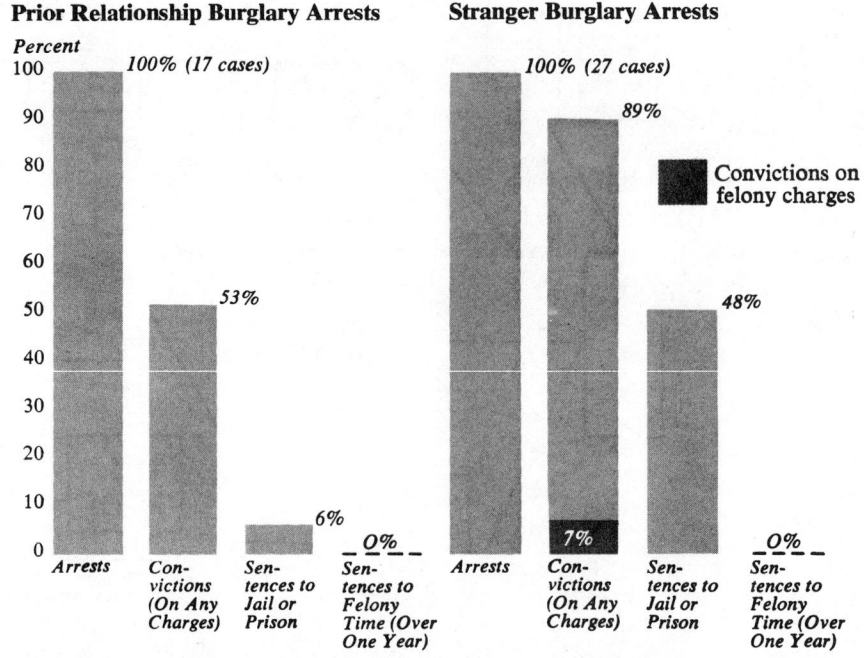

Source: Deep Sample Data (1973); Vera Institute Felony Disposition Study.

Table M: Prior Relationships in Burglary Cases

Lovers, spouses, or former spouses or lovers	5
In-laws and relatives	2
Friends, neighbors and acquaintances	7
Employment or landlord-tenant	3
(None)	(27)

Source: Deep Sample Data (1973); Vera Institute Felony Disposition Study.

compared with almost half the stranger defendants.

The variety of prior relationships is indicated in Table M. Four of the five prior lover or husband/wife relationship cases resulted in dismissal. Both cases involving more distant family relationships were dismissed, as were two that involved friends. All but one of these eight dismissals resulted from complainant non-cooperation.*

In most of the prior relationship burglary cases, whether resulting in dismissal or conviction, there was no dispute about what the defendant had done, but the prior relationships significantly colored the implications of those acts. The following cases are illustrative.

- A man was arrested when the landlord saw him removing cabinets from an apartment building. The defendant, who had a long history of burglaries, was at first not believed when he told the police that his sister-in-law had rented the apartment and had asked him to fix the cabinets. The case was dismissed when the landlord checked his records and found that the apartment had in fact been rented to the defendant's sister-in-law six days before the alleged burglary.

- A man with no prior record had returned to retrieve some property from premises where he used to live while his former landlord was away. The landlord said some of the property taken was his own, and he had the defendant arrested for burglary. The ADA explained the leniency of his plea offer (disorderly conduct and a conditional discharge) in this way: "If the case went to

---

* In the one case where the complainant persisted, both the DA and judge thought she was lying. The defendant, a middle-class 30-year-old man with no criminal record, was accused of breaking into his separated wife's apartment. He said he had been let in by one of his children whom he had come to visit. She said he broke in and attacked her with a bowie knife. She had superficial cuts, but her testimony at preliminary hearing was contradictory. The case was adjourned in contemplation of dismissal and ultimately dismissed.

the Grand Jury, and they heard that the defendant lived in the building for three or so years, and that the defendant was returning to get his property which had been locked away, then they'd say this case belongs in landlord-tenant court and not in Criminal Court."

- An undersized young man with a history of psychiatric troubles but no criminal record went one night to visit old neighbors. He found they were not at home and became upset. He climbed through their basement window and took several worthless objects, including old record albums and a moth-eaten fur coat. The victims cared only that he get psychiatric help, feeling that jail was not the answer to his problems. The charge was reduced to attempted petit larceny, the defendant pled guilty, and he was conditionally discharged. The DA, who refused to dismiss the case despite the complainants' reluctance to testify, stated, "In Brooklyn, nighttime residential burglaries are treated severely. This case would have been sent to the Supreme Court [for processing as a felony] if there hadn't been the prior relationship."

- An elderly white woman living in a black neighborhood remonstrated several black children for throwing rocks at her window. She received a midnight visit from their two mothers who, intoxicated and belligerent, pushed her front door open and entered to confront her. They were charged initially with burglary (because they entered the premises with the intent, it seems, to commit assault) and assault, but the Grand Jury sent the case back to Criminal Court where the defendants pled to criminal trespass and were discharged on condition that they not bother the complainant again. Neither the sampled defendant nor the other mother involved in this case had prior criminal records.

- A group of day laborers was found at 11 P.M. standing on a loading platform, inside the fenced-in area of the Hunts Point open market. They all worked there during the market's open hours, and they disclaimed criminal intent. No goods were taken. The owners didn't want to prosecute, and the policeman described it as a "garbage case." The ADA said, "I think you could assume some criminal intent, and unless they had a credible story they probably would have been convicted of criminal trespass, third degree, at a trial. But there was definitely no burglary—I guess police officers just like to make felony arrests. I offered them a violation [criminal trespass, fourth degree], and they were given conditional discharges. They would have been sentenced to 'time served' except one of them [not in the sample] had been out on bail, and it would have been too much paperwork to give them different sentences." Defense counsel agreed there had been a technical trespass, but doubted criminal intent would be shown. He advised the sampled defendant to accept the plea because of his prior record and because he had already been in jail overnight, unable to put up $50 cash bail.*

In only 3 of the 17 prior relationship burglaries did the primary motive appear to be economic gain. In one case—a burglary motivated by the co-defendant's need for cash to meet drug and gambling debts—the complainant was grandfather of the defendant and father of the co-defendant (who was not in our sample). The co-defendant had a long record, and the ADA wanted a conviction, but he predictably dismissed the case against both defendants when the complainant absolutely refused to cooperate. In the 2 other economically motivated prior relationship burglaries, misdemeanor convictions were obtained. One of these was followed by the only "time" disposition among the prior relationship cases.

The defendant and a companion were caught by the complainant—a man with whom they had previously shot up drugs—in the act of burgling his apartment. They were held at bay by his dog until the police arrived. As the case wore on, the complainant began to show signs of reluctance, but the defendant had a history of narcotics arrests, and the ADA *didn't want the case dismissed. The* ADA *finally offered a plea to criminal trespass. It was accepted, and the defendant was sentenced to* NACC. *The* ADA *thought "the judge did the right thing. It was a junkie case, in every sense of the word."*

Lack of conventional criminality in most of the prior relationship cases is underscored when the prior criminal records of the defendants in these cases are compared with the prior records of defendants in the stranger cases. Almost half (8) of the 17 defendants in prior relationship burglary cases had no prior arrests, in contrast to 3 of the 24 defendants in stranger burglary cases. And while defendants in prior relationship cases generally received more favorable dispositions than those in the stranger cases, they received even lighter treatment if they had no prior record. Of the 8 defendants in prior relationship cases who had no prior criminal record, 5 had their cases dismissed, and the 3 who were convicted all walked. Of the 9 in prior relationship cases who had arrest records, only 3 had their cases dismissed; 5 walked and one got time.

Stranger Burglaries of Commercial Premises. Nighttime commercial bur-

---

* One other case involved an employee who, like this one, was arrested for being inside his employer's premises with no "loot" but with no permission to be there at the time. He also pled to criminal trespass—but he pled to the misdemeanor, not the violation—and walked. These were the only two commercial burglary cases involving prior relationships.

glaries were usually reduced to misdemeanors. This was reported to be official policy in some boroughs and appeared to be the unofficial operating principle throughout the system, even though other factors were often cited in interviews as contributing to charge reductions. The policy may itself be a prosecutorial reaction to court congestion and to the need to allocate scarce prosecutorial resources to the more dangerous felonies. As one ADA said of a nighttime grocery store burglary, "There are too many major crimes in this city to regard this as a serious offense."*

Jail sentences, following reduction of the burglary charge to a misdemeanor, were given to 9 of the 17 defendants in stranger nighttime commercial burglary cases. Three of the 9 were sentenced to NACC, and the other 6 got jail sentences of between 60 days and 9 months. Eight of the 9 had prior records.

Only one commercial burglary, involving a defendant who had two similar charges against him, ended in a plea to a felony (attempted burglary, an E felony). The judge in this case, who had been an ADA, thought the case "simply does not belong in Supreme Court. I don't think this case was worth the trouble of the indictment." He thought it should have ended with a plea to an A misdemeanor in the lower court, but he did not treat it as trivial either: he sentenced the defendant, who had been in pretrial custody for almost a year, to five years' probation. His theory was that this way he could exercise more control over the defendant (via the threat of probation revocation) than he could by handing down a three-year prison sentence. A three-year term, he felt, would have been the longest conscionable on the facts of the case, but he feared that the defendant's long pretrial custody would have made him eligible for almost immediate release on parole from such a sentence.

Two of the eight remaining stranger commercial cases were dismissed, and the other six were disposed of by misdemeanor pleas and walks. These dismissals and walks were explained by a variety of factors, primarily the evidentiary weakness of the cases and certain mitigating characteristics of some of the defendants. Both dismissals occurred in cases with non-cooperating stranger victims. One dismissal involved the only case in the sample arising from a match of a defendant's fingerprints with prints found at a burglary, although in this case the burglary had occurred a year and a half earlier.† The only evidence

---

* His attitude might be different in an uncongested system. But the judge handling the same case said, "I just don't think that breaking into a grocery store is worth a felony. I would have given him no more than one year even if this case were tried in a trial system."

† The defendant was already in the court system, on a weapons charge, when his prints were matched and this burglary charge was brought against him. Curiously, he had

for the prosecution was the prints, as the complainant had not seen the person who burgled his store and was not interested in a prosecution after so much time had passed. The prosecutor did not believe he could prove this case, particularly after the lapse of time, on the prints alone. The ADA who handled the other stranger commercial burglary ending in dismissal believed that the complainant refused to proceed in that case because he had been intimidated by the defendant or his brothers.

In one of the six stranger commercial cases where plea to a misdemeanor or violation was followed by a walk, the defendant's intent to commit a crime on the premises was far from clear and would have been difficult to prove.

One night someone broke the gate to a factory, and sometime during the night $2,000 was stolen from the premises. The defendant was arrested inside the factory at about 1 A.M., but a few moments earlier there had been 40 other persons wandering around. The Legal Aid attorney thought he was likely to be convicted and get time—perhaps misdemeanor time—if he went to trial, but the defendant refused the ADA's first offer of an E felony. At that point the ADA first learned about the others not arrested, and about the defendant's rather minor role. He accepted a plea to an A misdemeanor, and the judge sentenced the defendant to 3 years' probation. The ADA said, "It was not a house, just a factory. There were 40 kids in there, and he's the only one who got caught—no stolen goods or money on him. It was not a real burglary. It was a joke." No promise was made regarding sentence before the plea in this case, but the ADA was not interested in the defendant's getting time. He was 19 years old and "he's got only one [previous] arrest, which is still pending. His co-defendant on that one was acquitted."

The judge did not really consider a heavier sentence on the plea: "He was found just wandering around, looking far from sinister, and it wouldn't have been fair to punish the one who wasn't quick enough to get out when 40 others were equally guilty. Anyway, jail is appropriate only for violent cases or for thieves. This was trespass, no more, and he had already been 10 weeks in custody; any more time would have been damaging—and unjust."

The five remaining walks in stranger commercial burglary cases appeared attributable primarily to the defendants' characteristics. One of these defendants had no record at all and was found with a companion in the rear of a burned-out store with some old carpeting that the owner had already taken up, appar-

---

been through the system on two previous occasions, after the burglary, without his prints having been matched.

ently with the intent of throwing it away. The lack of prior record in this case was reinforced by the triviality of the crime. According to the police officer, "It was a question of two neighbors getting an easy opportunity to get some carpeting. They were simply opportunists—not criminals."

Two of the walks are harder to understand because the defendants had long records. After their arrests, however, both had enrolled in drug treatment programs, in which they were doing well. Each was given a "last chance" to avoid prison, perhaps in part because the ADAs did not know if the prosecution cases could be pulled together after the long delay following arrest in both cases.* The fourth of the five walks occurred in the case of a defendant with a record of mental and alcohol problems and of confinement in mental and penal institutions. He had been apprehended while trying to break into a store with an axe. He was drunk and may have been hallucinating at the time of the attempted burglary; he later claimed to have no recollection of the incident. After several months in pretrial custody he pled guilty to a misdemeanor and was placed in a special probation program on the condition that he participate in therapy for his alcoholism.

The final walk in a stranger commercial burglary was similarly attributable to the defendant's special status. The crime was a perfectly straightforward factory burglary, but the defendant was given a conditional discharge because he was a narcotics informant.

The Legal Aid attorney noted that "most informants have carte blanche to commit small crimes as long as they keep turning in dealers." According to the ADA, the complainant agreed wholeheartedly with the charge reduction and sentence promise because the defendant was "doing a job for us on the street."

Stranger Burglaries of Residential Premises. Burglary of a residence by a prowling stranger is the archetypal non-violent felony. Fear of it causes us to put double locks on doors and bars on windows, and makes our hair stand on end when we wake to strange noises in the night. There is no prosecutorial policy to reduce burglary charges to misdemeanors in these cases, as there is when the premises are commercial. Nevertheless, the nine defendants in deep sample stranger residential burglaries appear to have received lenient treatment. Of the nine, one defendant's case was dismissed, four pled guilty to misdemeanors and walked, one was convicted of a misdemeanor at trial and walked,

---

* One prosecution was delayed because a co-defendant had absconded and the ADA was hoping he would turn up so that, if a trial were necessary, it would be a joint one. No explanation emerges from the interviews for the long delay in the other case.

and two others pled to misdemeanors and got misdemeanor time. Only one of the nine pled to a felony charge, and he was sentenced to a year in prison.

None of these nine stranger residential burglars came close to the archetypal night prowler. Not only was none armed, but there were also genuine ambiguities in the factual situations behind several of the arrests. For instance:

- One defendant, who was very drunk, passed out in front of a house and fell in through the window as it broke. He pled guilty to criminal mischief, a B misdemeanor, and was discharged on condition that he attend Alcoholics Anonymous. "There was definitely no burglary involved," according to the ADA who handled the case.

- A 42-year-old man with no criminal record was seen taking pipes out of an abandoned building. He claimed to have bought the rights, from the prior owner, to everything that remained. His story could not be checked because the prior owner had abandoned the neighborhood as well as his fixtures. The defendant pled to criminal trespass and was fined $100, although the ADA (who thought "this was nowhere near a felony") had been prepared to adjourn the case in contemplation of dismissal if his offer of a walk for a misdemeanor plea had not been accepted.

One of the other stranger residential burglars who walked was never connected with a burglary at all: he was simply caught near the complainant's residence with burglary tools and was conditionally discharged after pleading guilty to their possession.

In the one stranger residential burglary case that was dismissed, the disposition was attributed in part to the complainant's refusal to cooperate. The defendant in that case, and a co-defendant not in our sample, had been observed by a tenant trying to open doors in a run-down apartment house. The arresting officer said:

"I don't believe they were really trying to burglarize any apartment, but I charged it because the facts were there. I think that they were trying to get into a vacant apartment, of which there were many in that building, to [shoot] some of their drugs." (Drugs were in fact found on the co-defendant, who pled guilty to their possession.)

The sample was not totally devoid of traditional residential burglars, albeit unarmed and operating in the daytime. Three defendants fit this mold. One was convicted of a lesser felony and was sentenced to a year in jail (a day short of felony time). The second, an addict, was sentenced to NACC after he obtained a reduction of the charge to a misdemeanor because the complaining witness was moving to Ohio (taking his testimony with him). The third pled to a misdemeanor and received a conditional discharge—one of the more perplexing penalties in the sample when the facts and interviews are scrutinized.

The complainant, a 16-year-old boy, saw a burglar leaving his apartment building with his T.V. The burglar threw down the set and ran. The boy jotted down the license of the getaway car, which was traced to the defendant. The boy picked the defendant's photo out of a group of pictures shown to him by the police officer. Later, after he identified the defendant again at a line-up, he began to be less certain that this was the man he had seen.

The defendant offered several alibis. One after the other, they were investigated and proved false. He insisted on his innocence, however, and his Legal Aid lawyer readied the case for trial, despite his concern that the defendant would be convicted when his prior record (14 arrests, with convictions and time on burglary charges) came out on cross-examination. At the same time, the ADA *was "sure" that the boy's identification testimony—his only evidence —would "fall apart under cross-examination, and he would say he didn't know whether this guy was in fact the burglar."*

A jury was selected but, when the defendant was three hours late for court on the second day, the judge remanded him to jail for five days. The Legal Aid lawyer said that at the next court appearance the defendant wanted to plead to an A misdemeanor. "He didn't think he'd get a fair trial. He'd rather spend a year in jail than risk it." The ADA *did offer the A misdemeanor even at that late stage, explaining, "I thought he'd still get a year in jail on the plea." The defendant took the plea.*

But the judge conditionally discharged the man, explaining, "I put him inside when he came late. I'm tough and I don't like any defendant running my court. But I think I may have jeopardized his chance of getting a fair trial. He was an innocent victim of mistaken identity. His son looked exactly like him, and I think the police got the wrong man. He would have been acquitted if he'd gone to trial, but he was afraid—yes, because of his prior record but I think also because, after the five days in jail, he thought he wouldn't get a fair trial or that I would be harsh at sentencing if he were convicted. I accepted the Alford plea,* but I feel very bad for how I conducted this case."

---

* See note * on page 54.

Summary

The deterioration of burglary arrests was striking, given the stereotype of an armed night prowler breaking into apartments. But no case in the sample fits the stereotype—none was even charged as first degree burglary. This, in part, accounts for the greater deterioration of burglary arrests than of robbery arrests, most of which were initially charged in the first degree; 94% of the convictions in burglary cases were for misdemeanors, compared to only 35% of the convictions in robbery cases. But other factors were also at work.

A surprising 39% of the cases commenced by burglary arrest involved prior relationships, and almost half these were dismissed. Half of the defendants in prior relationship cases had no prior criminal record. Most (63%) of the residential burglaries—the ones most likely to be treated as dangerous felonies—involved prior relationships and lacked aspects of serious criminality.

On the other hand, 61% of the burglaries did *not* involve prior relationships: 89% of these defendants had prior records, and only 11% of these cases were dismissed. The great bulk of the stranger burglaries were nighttime break-ins of unoccupied commercial premises. Judges and prosecutors consider these crimes "nuisances" rather than felonies, and it was the policy in several prosecutors' offices routinely to reduce them to misdemeanors. Although commercial burglaries generally share two characteristics which are usually associated with severe sentences—they are committed against strangers, and the defendants have prior arrest records—commercial burglaries rarely result in prison sentences, because they are acknowledged to present little risk of violence.

Congestion is almost certainly an important reason why commercial burglaries—the most common for which felony arrests are made—are not treated as felonies by the ADAs or judges. The policy is not condoned by statute but is the product of priorities which place greater weight on crimes of violence or potential violence. While there might be general agreement with a policy to concentrate on the violent felonies, perhaps not everyone would agree that sentences for nighttime burglaries of unoccupied commercial premises—particularly by repeat offenders—should be limited to no more than a year in jail. The judge who remarked that he "would have given no more than one year even if [such a] case were tried in a trial system" might in fact change his mind if the system was less congested.

5 Grand Larceny

Grand larceny is the "pure" property felony.* Larceny is the taking or withholding of property from its rightful owner, with an intent to deprive him of it or to deprive him of its use. Unlike burglary, which involves intrusion upon premises and the risk of confrontation, and unlike robbery, which, by definition, requires the use or threat of force, larceny entails little risk of personal violence.

Grand larceny arises when the property taken is worth more than $250, when the property is taken by extortion, or when the theft is of public records, credit cards or secret or dangerous material. If extortion is involved, grand larceny is a C felony punishable by up to 15 years in prison. (None of the 63 deep sample cases discussed in this chapter were commenced by arrest for the C felony.) Otherwise, grand larceny is a D felony (punishable by up to 7 years in prison) when the property is worth more than $1,500, or an E felony (punishable by up to 4 years in prison) when the property is worth between $250 and $1,500. If the property taken is not worth $250, the crime is petit larceny, an A misdemeanor punishable by up to a year in jail.

If an automobile is taken, the charge is usually grand larceny (auto). If the value of the car is less than $250, conviction cannot be for a greater offense than petit larceny, the A misdemeanor, or "unauthorized use of a motor vehicle," also an A misdemeanor. "Unauthorized use," which is usually added to the grand larceny charge in auto theft cases, presents fewer evidentiary problems to the prosecutor; unlike larceny, it does not require proof of the de-

---

* Forgery and criminal possession of stolen property, which might also be considered "pure" property crimes, are not discussed separately in this monograph.

Forgeries are omitted altogether. Sixty-nine percent of the deep sample felony arrests for forgery were for offenses that would be better described as "victimless" than as "property" crimes: they involved alteration of documents such as drivers' licenses. As one judge said of such a felony charge:

"It's like 'driving without a license.' The defendant just penciled in his name. This should not be given felony treatment, and we usually reduce these sorts of things to violations and give a fine."

Criminal possession of stolen property was rarely encountered, except as an alternative charge to second degree grand larceny. In many of these cases, the larceny was inferred from the suspect's possession of recently stolen goods and could not be proved independently. The few arrests in the sample for which criminal possession of stolen property was the top charge are treated, in this chapter, as if the arrest charge had been grand larceny. As there were no C felony grand larceny charges in the sample, the criminal possession charge (a D felony, in the first degree) carried the same range of penalties and scope for reduction as the top grand larceny charges (D felonies as well). Both felonies have their misdemeanor counterparts when the property is worth less than $250.

fendant's intent to steal the car but simply knowledge that the owner has not consented to his use of it.

Fact Patterns in Grand Larcenies

Twenty of the 63 deep sample grand larceny cases (32%) involved a prior relationship between the defendant and the owner of the property that was stolen. However, 43 of the grand larceny cases were auto thefts, of which only 9 (21%) involved prior relationships. Among the 20 non-auto cases, 11 (55%) involved prior relationships.

Just over half (52%) of the defendants had prior criminal records; 45% of the defendants in prior relationship cases and 56% of those in stranger cases had been arrested at least once before. The value of the goods taken ranged from $3.50 (in a case that had clearly been overcharged as a felony) to $50,000 in the case of a defendant (never convicted before) who got felony time. Only 17 cases (27%) appeared free of evidentiary problems; the rest were plagued by non-cooperative complainants, doubts about whether the property was worth more than $250, doubts about the legality of the search, or doubts about whether the defendant actually stole, intended to keep or even had the property in his possession.

To the extent that a typical grand larceny case can be constructed from the deep sample data, it started with a grand larceny (auto) charge against a young man with prior arrests for the same crime and prior misdemeanor convictions for petit larceny or unauthorized use of a motor vehicle. Typically, there were doubts about whether the car he was arrested in was worth more than $250, whether he had been the one who first took it from the owner, whether he knew it was a stolen car, and whether he intended to keep it for more than a joyride. Typically, he pled guilty to unauthorized use once again, was fined and walked.

Deterioration of Grand Larceny Arrests

Like burglary, grand larceny accounted for almost a third of all reported felonies in 1971. The larceny and burglary arrest rates (11% and 9%) and clearance rates (13% and 16%) are also similar. In the deep sample, deterioration of the grand larceny cases was marginally greater than deterioration of burglary cases.

Figure 17 (next page) compares the conviction and sentencing rates for grand larceny arrests to those for all felony arrests.

Although conviction was as likely in grand larceny cases as in all other cases commenced by felony arrests, conviction of a felony and a sentence to

Figure 17. Dispositional Pattern for Grand Larceny Arrests Compared to All Felony Arrests

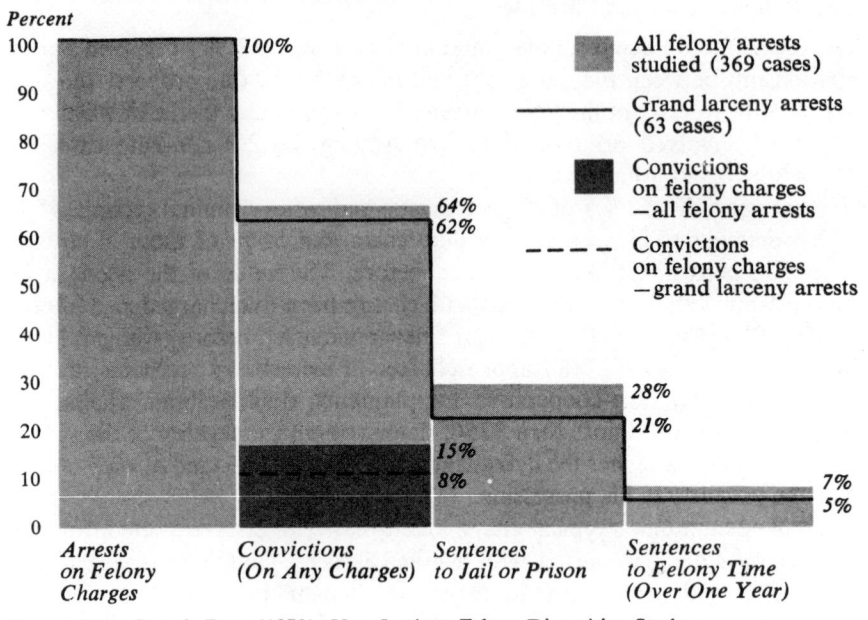

(Grand larceny arrests are 17% of all felony arrests studied.)

▬	All felony arrests studied (369 cases)
────	Grand larceny arrests (63 cases)
■	Convictions on felony charges — all felony arrests
─ ─ ─ ─	Convictions on felony charges — grand larceny arrests

Arrests on Felony Charges: 100%
Convictions (On Any Charges): 64% / 62%; 15% / 8%
Sentences to Jail or Prison: 28% / 21%
Sentences to Felony Time (Over One Year): 7% / 5%

Source: Deep Sample Data (1973); Vera Institute Felony Disposition Study.

prison or jail were less likely. The proportion of defendants arrested for grand larceny who were sentenced to felony time was similar to the proportion for all felony arrests.

The deep sample grand larceny arrests proceeded to their dispositions along the routes shown in Figure 18.

As in assault, robbery and burglary cases, trial was the abnormal path to disposition for deep sample cases commenced by grand larceny arrest, although 8% (5 cases) *were* disposed at trial, a higher incidence than for the other felonies. The most common path to disposition was by guilty plea to a misdemeanor charge (80% of the convictions were by such pleas) followed by a walk (73% of those who pled guilty to misdemeanor charges walked). Some explanations for the dispositional pattern emerge from analysis of the facts and interviews in the deep sample cases.

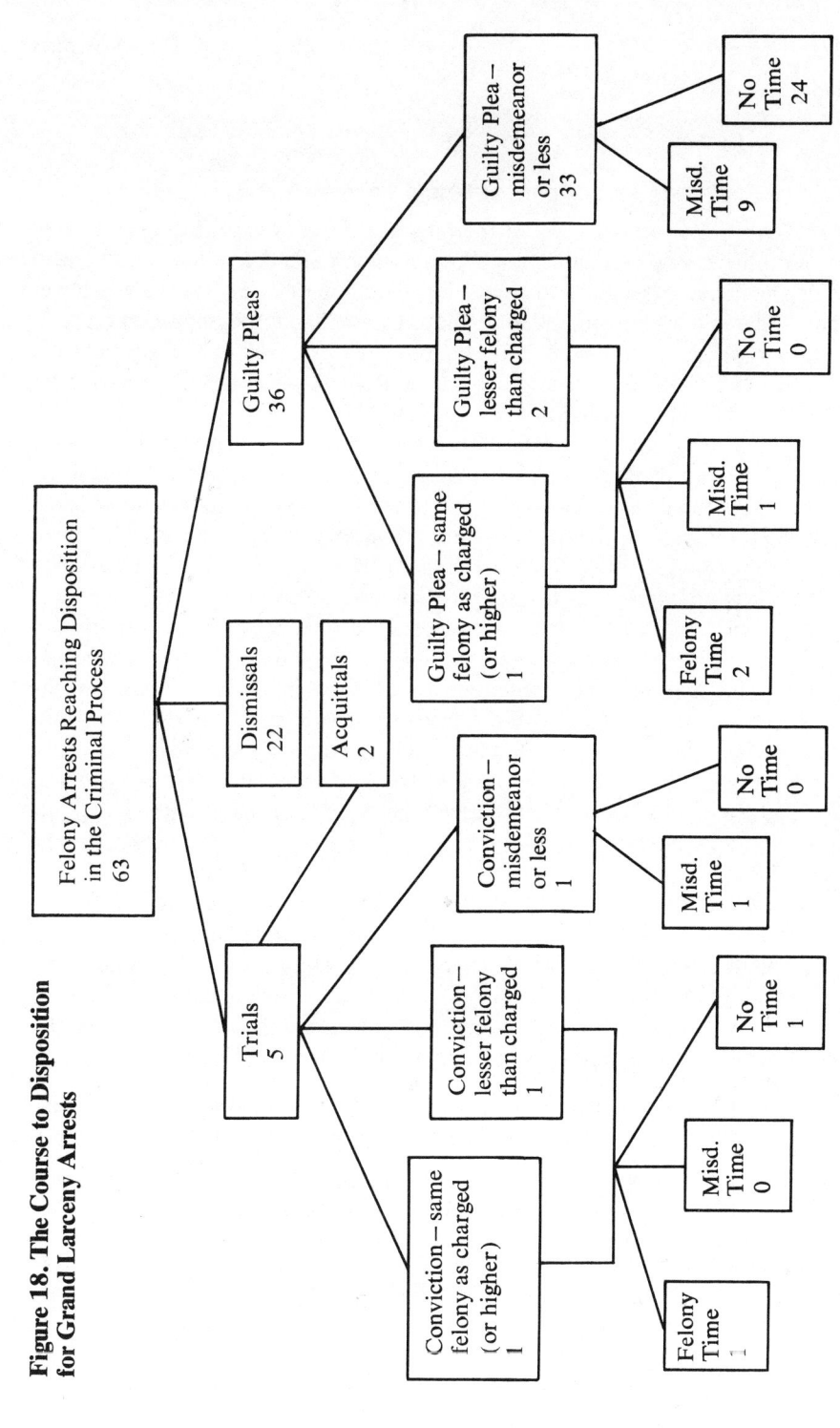

Figure 18. The Course to Disposition for Grand Larceny Arrests

```
Felony Arrests Reaching Disposition in the Criminal Process
63
├── Dismissals 22
├── Acquittals 2
├── Trials 5
│   ├── Conviction — same felony as charged (or higher) 1
│   │   ├── Felony Time 1
│   │   └── Misd. Time 0
│   ├── Conviction — lesser felony than charged 1
│   │   ├── Misd. Time 1
│   │   └── No Time 1
│   └── Conviction — misdemeanor or less 1
│       ├── Misd. Time 1
│       └── No Time 0
└── Guilty Pleas 36
    ├── Guilty Plea — same felony as charged (or higher) 1
    │   ├── Felony Time 2
    │   └── Misd. Time 1
    ├── Guilty Plea — lesser felony than charged 2
    │   └── No Time 0
    └── Guilty Plea — misdemeanor or less 33
        ├── Misd. Time 9
        └── No Time 24
```

Source: Deep Sample Data (1973); Vera Institute Felony Disposition Study.

Factors Explaining Dispositions of Grand Larceny Arrests

Auto Theft. Two-thirds (43) of the 63 grand larceny cases began as arrests for auto theft. Prior relationships between victim and defendant were present in 9. The incidence of prior relationships in auto theft cases (21%) was lower than in the felonies considered in previous chapters, but the impact on disposition continued to be strong: three-quarters (25 of 34) of the stranger car cases ended in conviction, whereas convictions disposed of only one-quarter (2 of 9) of the prior relationship car cases.*

Thus, seven prior relationship car cases and nine stranger car cases were dismissed. Two of the prior relationship car cases were dismissed when the owners said the arrest had been a "mistake" and that the defendants—one a neighbor, the other a friend—had permission to use their cars. A third prior relationship case ended with an acquittal at trial when the defendant testified he had jumped into the car to get away from the complaining witness who was trying to kill him; he had a stab wound to support his story. In the four remaining cases, in which the prior relationships were commercial, dismissal seems to have been the product of different forces. One ended in dismissal despite the complainant's insistence that the case be prosecuted. The defendant, a cabbie, had lost the keys to his cab and called the company to report it. He gave the wrong address and, when the tow truck couldn't find the cab, he was arrested for grand larceny. The judge who dismissed the charges said: "He did nothing except maybe drink on the job; that shouldn't be punished by the court."

Another of the dismissed commercial cases involved a car rental agency employee whose job was to drive cars from one airport to another. He had a friend with him one night when he was transporting his last car. They took a detour into the Bronx, where he let his friend borrow the car for an errand. The friend was arrested for grand larceny (the arrest in our sample), but the agency agreed with the judge's assessment of the case:

---

* One of the two prior relationship car cases ending in conviction involved a car rental agency employee. He borrowed a car for the night from one of his employer's locations. He had no intent to steal it and was convicted of resisting arrest, not car theft. He was fined $150 on the misdemeanor plea. In the other prior relationship case, the defendant worked in a garage and was a passenger when another garage employee took a car on a joyride that ended in an accident. The case against the sampled defendant was not considered serious by anyone interviewed, and he pled guilty to petit larceny. Because he had a prior record, he was placed on probation for three years.

"It was my view that the employee was the prime mover and [the rental agency] should be satisfied with a trial against that one. . . . But the ACD was the best course here—this fellow has no prior record and he is a student."

The last two commercial case dismissals began with straightforward rentals from the same agency. In one, the customer kept the car beyond the agreed time, claimed he had notified the agency of his change in plans, and readily paid the extra amount due. In the other, the customer lent the car to his nephew, who was arrested when the car did not get back to the agency on time. When the uncle corroborated the boy's story in court and it became evident that a misunderstanding was at the root of the incident, the agency withdrew its complaint.

These prior relationship dismissals occurred in weak cases, against defendants with no prior criminal record or with only minor records.* The pattern was similar in stranger car cases disposed of by dismissal.

Four of the nine stranger defendants whose cases were dismissed had merely been riding as passengers in the cars. One was a hitchhiker, picked up only minutes before the police stopped the car and found, through a routine check to the computer, that it had been stolen. In the other three cases, the passengers may have known the cars were stolen but claimed otherwise, and their claims were corroborated when the drivers "took the rap."

A fifth stranger case ended in dismissal when the defendant, a cab driver, produced receipts to show he had rented the vehicle. The ADA also accepted the story of a sixth defendant, who claimed he was just trying to move a ten-year-old car off the road after finding it abandoned; he had no record, was a solid citizen, and the circumstances supported his story. Dismissal disposed of a seventh stranger car case because the defendant, who claimed he had not known the car was stolen when he bought it, helped the police trace the man who had sold it to him. The judge dismissed the charges against the eighth stranger car thief despite the fact that he had been caught stealing the car and had a prior prison record; the defendant had enrolled in a drug treatment program, and the judge had received positive reports for nine months.

The last dismissal of a defendant arrested for theft of a stranger's car highlights a recurrent evidentiary problem: when a suspect is not actually observed stealing the car, the prosecution usually lacks evidence to prove either that he actually stole it or knew it had been stolen.

---

* Sixty percent of the defendants whose cases were dismissed (including both prior relationship and stranger cases) had no prior criminal record.

"I stopped the car for a routine check and found from the computer that it had been reported stolen for three months," said the police officer. "The driver's uncle came in, voluntarily, and said he'd bought the car. He had paid almost the going price for it, and he had even paid the sales tax. I had to arrest him, but he gave me one-hundred-percent cooperation on the investigation." The car, a two-year-old Buick, was worth $3,500. The defendant had paid $3,300 for it to a man he met in a bar. The ADA *thought the defendant, 64 years old with no record, should have known better than to try to get a bargain on the street, but said, "There was no question of getting a plea here; I moved for an* ACD. *The man lost enough—the car, the lawyer's fee and the $3,300."*

If the defendant in this last of the dismissed stranger car cases had paid less for the car, he might have been convicted. The following case, in which the defendant also claimed innocent purchase of a stolen car, is illustrative.

"This car [a two-year-old BMW*] goes for $4,000," said the police officer. "He had a bill of sale for $800. He knew it was stolen; had he paid $3,500 or $3,800, it might have been honest." The grand larceny, initially charged as a D felony because the car was valued at more than $1,500, was reduced to unauthorized use of a motor vehicle, an A misdemeanor, and the defendant was conditionally discharged and fined $250 on his guilty plea. The* ADA *felt a reduction was necessary because the defendant's lack of any prior record and his bill of sale made for "real shortcomings at trial—I could lose it all if the jury believed him." The police officer thought the jury might believe him, because the car was of foreign make and its value would not be widely known, and because the defendant had only been in the country for two years and might not be expected to know the value.* The* ADA *thought the conditional discharge was an appropriate disposition, but he felt the fine was unnecessary: "He had already lost $800 and the car."*

The value of the car can affect dispositions in another way, simply because the felony charge depends on value exceeding $250. The result in the following case—a misdemeanor plea and a 5-month jail sentence—apparently turned on the difficulty of proving that the stolen car was worth $250.

A police officer observed the defendant for half an hour as he checked each car on the street. He unlocked one car, got in and left it. He then opened another, got in and started it. When the officer made the arrest, he found a Gen-

---

* The car and the defendant did not have the same country of origin.

eral Motors master key in the defendant's possession. The car's owner, a fireman, had witnessed the incident too and was prepared to testify.

The ADA and Legal Aid lawyer agreed that it was an "open and shut case," and they agreed with the arresting officer that the defendant, who had a prior record of arrests for car theft, was "a professional car thief" or "part of a ring." According to the ADA, this was just the sort of case in which the felony charge is justified and in which prosecution policy is to refuse reduction of charges for a plea. "Joyriding is routinely reduced to the A misdemeanor," he said, "and the felony charge is reserved for the real auto thief. So this was not considered a minor case, given that he had the master key—and his record."

But this ad hoc prosecutorial policy conflicted with another rule of thumb described by the ADA: "In New York City, it is considered only a misdemeanor, for all practical purposes, to steal a car if the value is under $500. The real problem here was the value of the car—it was a '64 Chevy, and it wasn't worth more than $250. We couldn't have gone to the Grand Jury on that." He offered a plea to unauthorized use—the A misdemeanor—and a five-month sentence.

The interviews suggest that the five-month sentence was the result of the ADA's insistence on the defendant doing some time because he was not really just a joyrider, and the fact that the defendant had already been in jail, unable to make bail, for three months when he entered his plea for the promised sentence. Both the ADA and Legal Aid attorney thought the defendant would have been convicted of the A misdemeanor and sentenced to nine months in jail if the case had been tried. There is, however, a hint that the prosecutor's decision was influenced by more than the presumed difficulty of proving that the car was of felony value. He also said, "I wanted a plea, to get rid of the case. The A misdemeanor was my goal. Auto cases like this are not heinous. Unless there's some violence with it, it is routinely reduced."

Certainly, the reduction of grand larceny charges appears routine in the bulk of these deep sample stranger car theft cases. Twenty-one of the 25 convictions were by plea to misdemeanors or violations.* Eight of these pleas were

---

* The other four convictions in stranger car cases were reached as follows: One misdemeanor conviction, followed by a ten-month jail sentence, was by trial in a case where the charge had been reduced to a misdemeanor in the Complaint Room. The defendant, who had a prison record for car thefts and stood to have parole revoked if convicted on this new charge, thought there was nothing to be gained by a guilty plea. The three remaining convictions were for felonies. Two were pleas to E felonies after arrests for D felonies, one by a drug addict sentenced to NACC for theft of a new and valuable car, and the other by a bank robber who stole an almost new car while on (continued on page 104)

followed by jail sentences, 4 by probation, 4 by fines and 5 by conditional discharges. Seven of the 8 defendants who were sentenced to time on their misdemeanor pleas had prior records; the eighth, although lacking a prior record, attempted to take an almost new Cadillac, was arrested when chased from the scene by a police officer, had a co-defendant who was caught with goods stolen from the car and, perhaps most important, had spent 25 days in jail before pleading to the misdemeanor charge for a 30-day sentence.

The sampled arrests for grand larceny (auto) do not bear out conventional wisdom, which holds that this crime is largely the province of the compulsive joyrider. Many were joyriders, but almost half (47%) of the defendants had never before been arrested and only 32% had been previously arrested for a similar or related offense. A record of multiple car thefts was infrequent; only 5 of the 43 car case defendants had been arrested for more than two. One case highlights the difficulty the criminal process faces in disposing properly of the defendant who just cannot keep his hands off others' cars.

"It was a policeman's intuition," said the arresting officer. "I don't think the car had any tail lights. . . . Something drew my attention to it, and we pulled it over. The driver couldn't produce the registration. I asked for a check on it and the car was wanted. I didn't have anything to link him to the theft, but he was pretty cooperative—he gave us all the information we would need to process the arrest. He had a long sheet—17 arrests." In fact, the 27-year-old defendant had been arrested for car theft as recently as 3 months earlier—his seventeenth auto theft arrest in 6 years. He was convicted of unauthorized use of that motor vehicle and sentenced to 9 months in jail. Before he went to jail on that charge, however, he had taken another car, pled guilty and served the jail sentences concurrently. Two weeks after his release from those sentences, he was arrested for the car theft that brought him into the deep sample.

"All the arrests were for grand larceny (auto)," said the judge. "This guy must have an obsession with it. He's either very sick, or he doesn't give a damn. I don't believe people don't give a damn. Yet, if you put him away, when he gets out there's going to be more ways and means to commit more and greater crimes." The defendant pled guilty to unauthorized use of a motor vehicle. No sentence was promised, and the defendant must have expected to do another

---

bail for federal bank robbery charges and received a three-year prison sentence concurrent with the sentence on the federal charges. The third felony conviction followed a trial on a D felony charge of criminal possession of stolen property. The defendant, a sixty-year-old man with no prior record, insisted on his innocence, claiming the car was a gift from his son. But the son had a record of arrests for auto theft, and the jury believed the father knew his car had been stolen. He was put on probation.

turn in jail. But the judge received a report that he had been accepted into a residential drug treatment program and, convinced that jail would make no dent in this man's behavior, the judge discharged him with the condition that he reside with the program. "Not that I'm an optimist, but I've seen too often a person, not expected to succeed, succeed and do what's right. You've got to have faith." Unfortunately, the defendant absconded ten hours after arriving at the program.

It might have been possible to obtain a felony conviction in this case, but the difficulties are typical. The car was a 9-year-old Chevrolet, and the ADA could expect difficulty proving, even with expert testimony, that its value was over the felony line. He would also have difficulty proving larceny because this defendant—like all but 3 in the 43 car cases—was not observed actually stealing the car and could raise at trial one of the common themes of people caught in stolen cars: "I borrowed it from an acquaintance; I was just taking it for a spin; I bought it from a man I've never seen before"; and so on. In this case, however, the defendant's credibility would have been seriously damaged by his prior record.

It is difficult to tell whether congestion and scarcity of prosecutorial resources discourages prosecutors from attempting to prove felony cases against such defendants, or whether there is a wholly independent ground (perhaps the one reflected in the Penal Law provision for a separate crime of "unauthorized use") to support the almost automatic reduction to misdemeanor charges. The view that pervades the interviews was best summed up by a Bronx judge in another auto case:

"This is only worth a misdemeanor plea. It's not a felony situation. In the whole scheme of justice, I think we should be concerned about the crimes of violence."

Other Larcenies. Dispositions in the 20 grand larceny cases involving other kinds of property were not very different from dispositions in the car theft cases, as Table N, page 106, shows. The only difference appearing on the surface is that the convicted defendant in a car case is somewhat more likely to get a taste of jail and a little less likely to walk than the convicted defendant in a case involving another kind of property.

Prior relationships figured in 11 (55%) of the non-car grand larcenies. Five of these were dismissed, 5 ended in guilty pleas to misdemeanors and walks, and one—an insurance fraud—ended at trial with conviction for the E felony initially charged and a 3-year prison sentence. This was the only prior

Table N: Dispositions in Grand Larceny Cases, by Nature of Property Taken

Property Taken	Ac- quittals	Dis- missals	Convic- tions	Sentences Walks	Mis- demeanor Time	Felony Time
Cars (N=43)	1	15	27	17	9	1
Other (N=20)	1	7	12	9	1	2

Source: Deep Sample Data (1973); Vera Institute Felony Disposition Study.

relationship non-car case to end in time. The 9 strangers fared almost as well, however. One was acquitted, the cases against 2 were dismissed, 4 pled guilty to misdemeanors or less and walked, one pled guilty to a misdemeanor and was sentenced to 30 days, and one—a con man—entered a plea to the E felony initially charged and was sentenced to prison for 3 years.

The range of prior relationships in non-car larcenies is displayed in Table O. Each of the 5 dismissals in prior relationship cases resulted from failure of the complaining witness to press charges. The failure of the prostitute's client to show at court is no surprise, but it is surprising that she was charged with grand larceny when his complaint alleged that she took only $3.50 from his trousers. Another dismissed grand larceny complaint arose when an 83-year-old woman accused her 43-year-old neighbor of keeping the proceeds of a check made out to her. The defendant, who had been handling the woman's financial affairs, had been given the check to deposit in the bank and had thought he was to keep a commission. The charge was withdrawn when they straightened out the terms of their agreement.

The third dismissal involved a defendant who broke windows in his brother-in-law's home. They had been feuding for years and the brother-in-law had

Table O: Nature of Prior Relationships in Non-Car Grand Larceny Cases

Theft by Employee from Employer (or Employer's Customer)	6
Theft from Neighbor or In-law	2
Theft by Prostitute from Client	1
Theft by Welfare Recipient from Welfare Agency	1
Theft by Customer from his Bank	1
(No Prior Relationship)	(9)

Source: Deep Sample Data (1973), Vera Institute Felony Disposition Study.

accused the defendant of extortion when he broke the windows in anger. The judge adjourned the case in contemplation of dismissal when restitution was made. In the fourth dismissal, a bank accused one of its customers of grand larceny when he overdrew his firm's account by $6,000. The case was dismissed when he deposited the missing funds and the bank withdrew its complaint. The final dismissal involved an alleged theft of merchandise by employees at a lingerie shop. The sampled defendant and a co-defendant took home 600 items when, according to the shopkeeper, they had been told they could take a few items for their wives. The case was dismissed because the complainant refused to come to court—in fact, he had re-employed the defendant.

Employees caught stealing from their employers cannot, however, count on avoiding conviction. Five of the six charged with such larcenies were convicted, including the two co-defendants who entered our sample in the following case.

"The practice of employees stealing material from the Long Island Railroad Yard was evidently very common," said the judge, "and the LIRR *apparently thought these stunts had gotten out of hand. They put the yard under surveillance and these two men, along with four or five others, were seen putting crates in their cars. They were arrested. There was some problem with the search, but I indicated I thought it was* O.K.*"* All the men had worked for fifteen or more years with the railroad, and all were close to retirement age and pensions.

The search turned up cans of tuna and a lawnmower. The ADA *said, "Tuna is not a catastrophic crime. I really doubt any jury would convict them for that. And the defendants had witnesses to the effect that for years employees had picked up things left on the track." The Legal Aid attorney was flabbergasted at the felony charge—"for fish! It should have been a misdemeanor and* ACD'd*. I have to assume the railroad leaned on the* ADA *to make an example of these men."*

The men were fired and lost their pension rights after a railroad hearing; they then pled guilty to criminal possession of stolen property, at the A misdemeanor level, and the judge gave each a conditional discharge and a $500 fine. The judge explained his sentence this way: "These were older men with families and therefore not suitable for probation—they had been around long enough not to need any guidance. Neither of them had a record, so I saw no reason to punish them further—they had already lost their jobs—but I fined them to show that the law meant business."

In a third case arising from theft by an employee, the ADA obtained a misdemeanor plea, despite the employer's loss of interest in the case when the employee, who had embezzled a series of small sums totaling $250, made restitution. After the defendant had admitted his guilt, entered a guilty plea to petit larceny and been put on probation, the complainant offered to re-employ him.

In another case, involving a delivery boy accused of taking an envelope containing $2,000 from a drawer in a shop where he had made a Christmas delivery, the Supreme Court ADA explained his acceptance of a misdemeanor plea and promise of conditional discharge this way:

"I felt this was a weak case. Only the complainant as a witness, and she didn't see him take the envelope. There was no direct evidence—just that the money was there before the defendant arrived and no longer there after he left. Often, when we know a defendant is guilty but are not sure of winning the case, we take what we can rather than lose all the marbles at trial. Anyway, I figured that this defendant would be placed on probation if he were convicted after trial, because of his age (23) and that, at most, he had only one prior—an old one. I discussed the case with the complaining witness to get her feeling. She only wanted her money back and was not interested in seeing him go to jail. I considered either grand larceny, third degree, with probation or, if restitution would be made, an A misdemeanor and conditional discharge. That's what he ultimately took. She wanted the restitution, and I couldn't give him the conditional discharge without reducing it to a misdemeanor. But it could have been handled in Criminal Court—not up here. I feel there is an inherent problem in the way our courts work because the people in Criminal Court are new and don't have enough experience to evaluate what a case is worth at trial—they should have been able to reduce this for the disposition it got."

At this point in the interview, the ADA was informed that the arresting officer had told us of a second witness—a customer in the store—who claimed to have seen the defendant actually remove the envelope from the drawer. The ADA examined the Grand Jury minutes, found the testimony and was embarrassed.

"Oh, my God! I didn't see that when I took the plea. You're right; what a jerk I am. Scratch everything I've said in the last 25 minutes. With this, the case is even triable. He would have been convicted of a D felony. But still, it wouldn't have changed the disposition much. The restitution was what was wanted, and he had already got a job in Florida [where the family had moved after the arrest] and made a new start. Even if I'd offered him only the one step down [the D felony], I would have let him go at that."

The last of the six thefts from employers went to trial. An insurance agent, who had just been acquitted on similar charges in another county, overconfidently chose trial and was convicted of defrauding his employer of $20,000–$50,000. He had no prior convictions on his record, but it seems that at sentencing the judge took into account the charges of which he had just been acquitted. He was given a three-year prison term.

A welfare fraud case, the last of the prior relationship non-car larcenies, involved a lesser sum—$635—and was not regarded as "serious" by any of those interviewed about it. A welfare client drew public assistance in that amount while illegally working on the side. She admitted her guilt, made restitution and was given a conditional discharge on a plea to attempted petit larceny, a B misdemeanor.

The charges against another welfare recipient were clearly of the "stranger" variety, but her equally lenient disposition was expressly shaped by the view that the attempted theft was "an act of desperation, not a felony." She had been caught trying to cash a stolen welfare check for $361, made out to someone else. The judge believed that she needed the money for her children and put her on probation after she pled guilty to attempted grand larceny, an A misdemeanor.

Two other stranger cases reached similar dispositions—pleas to misdemeanors and probation. One began with a felony arrest for criminal possession of stolen property, a set of hi-fi speakers. A burglary charge was added to the case after arrest but later dropped when the defendant pled guilty to a misdemeanor-level criminal possession charge. The speakers were worth less than $250, and the prosecutor would have had difficulty connecting the defendant with the burglary. The other case was a purse-snatch which lacked the element of violence or threat necessary for a robbery charge. The complaining witness disappeared, the police officer's identification testimony was shaky, and the ADA settled for a plea to attempted grand larceny and probation. The defendant, who was an addict with no prior arrests, voluntarily committed himself to NACC for treatment.

One stranger grand larceny arrest was disposed of with a plea to disorderly conduct (a violation) and a conditional discharge. The defendant had been seen throwing an empty billfold into a refuse bin, but he had not been seen taking it. In fact, the complaining witness did not know if it had been stolen or just mislaid. The evidentiary problems made felony conviction impossible, and the case would probably have been dismissed had it not been for the defendant's prior record of convictions.

Dismissal was the result in another stranger case in which evidentiary problems were equally daunting. A construction worker was arrested for grand larceny for taking a jackhammer off a worksite. The equipment turned out to be worth less than $250, no one had actually seen him remove it, and an investigation failed to turn up anyone claiming to own it. The final dismissal of a stranger grand larceny case involved a purse-snatch from a plainclothes policewoman. There were no evidentiary problems, but the defendant was found to be mentally unfit to stand trial.

Not all the arrests for stranger grand larcenies were "junk" cases, however. One defendant was caught with seven stolen credit cards in his possession. He had a prior record, including prison sentences, and although he could have been tried for felonious possession of stolen property, he was allowed to plead guilty to "attempted possession of stolen property," an A misdemeanor, and was sentenced to only thirty days in jail. There were evidentiary problems (he had not used the credit cards, and there was no proof that he had actually stolen them), but there was little danger that the defendant would get away with the sorts of excuses that plague prosecutors in the car theft cases. He could not very well maintain, for example, that he had "borrowed" the credit cards from a friend. The ADA's explanation for reducing the charge from an E felony and for promising a thirty-day sentence seems weak:

"The possession of stolen credit cards is really petit larceny.* Credit cards are used to buy small things. I would have offered him the same plea later, when he would have gotten ninety days—I gave him the lower time to expedite the case. He pled at arraignment—that way we don't have to bring in the cop and the witnesses later on. This case has to be looked at in reverse, from the Supreme Court angle first, and worked back. Should we try this in Supreme Court? Even with the defendant's record, the answer is no. I wouldn't consider sending it to the Grand Jury; even though it would indict, we would not want to proceed on it. It is just not a serious crime."

The defense attorney called it "a great disposition. Originally the ADA asked for more than thirty days; we hammered this down because the plea was at an early stage. The defendant was unemployed and had no resources; the chances of release on recognizance or making bail were minimal, so if the case were delayed he would spend the time in jail. We are dealing here with a defendant with a long record. He had lots of experience with the courts and knew what he wanted."

---

* This must mean that the ADA does not believe it *should* be treated as a felony. It is an E felony under the statute. (New York Penal Law, § 165.45.)

Again, it cannot be clear from the deep sample data whether a defendant like this one should have been prosecuted more vigorously. It seems likely, however, that in cases such as this, where evidentiary problems do not appear to rule out a felony conviction, congestion explains the pressured plea bargaining and the casual handling and rapid deterioration of the charge.

The interviews in the last of the stranger non-car larceny cases provide confirmation that some participants in the system do not regard these as serious cases. The defendant, a 35-year-old con man with 21 previous arrests for similar offenses, pled guilty to the E felony as charged and was sentenced to 3 years in prison. The ADA who had handled the case at the Grand Jury stage, when our interviewer told him of the disposition, remarked: "The judge gave him 3 years for a con game? Incredible!" The case serves as an illustration of the complexity of the dispositional process and the possibility of conflict between competing system goals.

The defendant was arrested after the complaining witness identified him from a collection of 5,000 mugshots. She claimed he had shown her a lot of money, told her he was a preacher from Africa and did not trust banks, promised her a hefty commission if she would act as his banker, held her hand on the way to her bank where she was to prove her liquidity, and finally switched an empty packet for the packet she had produced containing $600 from her account. He was arrested two years later and charged with E felony grand larceny. There were two other cases, arising from similar incidents at about the same time, pending against him. His total take had been $2,750.

The defendant agreed to a deal worked out by the ADA and defense attorney to cover all three cases—a plea of guilty to the felony charge, one year in jail, and complete restitution. The ADA favored the deal because complaining witnesses in such cases are "generally idiots," the identifications were shaky, the complaining witness in the sampled case was reluctant to come to court and retell her embarrassing story in public, and the defendant had stayed out of trouble ("retired," as the defense attorney put it) in the two years since these incidents. The judge, however, refused to sanction the arrangement unless the ADA's superior would recommend it; the request to that quarter was refused. "The ADA was now talking three years on a plea," said the defense attorney. "I said 'forget it' because I knew the defendant would get only three years if convicted at trial—even though the maximum is four—and that the sentences would be made concurrent. We had nothing to lose. And we almost won the one they took to trial first—the complaining witness was so bad on the stand." But that case ended in conviction and a three-year sentence, and the judge in the sampled case accepted the E felony plea and imposed a concurrent three-year sentence.

This appears to be a favorable disposition for the People—felony time on felony conviction of a confirmed predatory felon—but the defense attorney's view is at least thought-provoking.

"The DA's office was thoroughly silly about this.* They wasted four days for the trial and all the time and money involved. My client got three years—but no restitution has been made. This really turns out to be a bad deal for the People, and it's really hard on the victims."

Summary

Grand larceny, like burglary of unoccupied commercial premises, is a "pure" property crime, lacking the potential for violence that might incline prosecutors toward pressing for felony convictions and judges toward imposing felony time. The deterioration of arrests for grand larceny therefore is due in large measure to the view that this crime is something less than a felony in most cases. That attitude can be overcome if the larceny is believed to be part of a professional criminal operation (for example, a car theft ring) or if it occurs on a grand scale (for example, the con artist or the insurance defrauder).

The deterioration of felony arrests for grand larceny was accelerated by the existence of prior relationships in 32% of the cases, by evidentiary problems in most of the rest, and by the relatively low incidence of prior criminal records among defendants. Seventy-three percent of the cases presented evidentiary problems (non-cooperating complainants, doubts about the property being worth more than $250, doubts about the legality of the search that turned up the stolen property, doubts about whether the defendant ever stole, intended to keep or ever even possessed the property in question). Thirty-five percent of the cases were dismissed; 80% of the convictions were by plea to misdemeanors; and 73% of those who pled to misdemeanors walked.

Grand larceny (auto) was the charge in the majority (68%) of the cases. Prior relationships do not account for the deterioration in this category; only 21% involved prior relationships, the lowest incidence among the victim fel-

---

* In fairness to the DA's office, it should be pointed out that the rejected deal worked out for this case would have disposed of a robbery charge as well; this had been added to the grand larceny charge when the complaining witness said the defendant pulled a gun on her after she realized he had switched the packets. No one believed her, and it was ignored when the case was finally disposed of, but it might have influenced the ADA's superior when he was asked to approve the deal for restitution.

onies. There were many evidentiary problems in auto cases, however. Only 3 of the defendants in those cases were actually seen taking the autos. In addition, there would have been difficulties in almost all cases in proving the defendant intended to do more than use the auto without authority (an A misdemeanor), and many of the cars were old enough for doubts to be raised about valuing them at more than $250.

The factors shaping the dispositional pattern of arrests for grand larceny (auto) emerged from the sample with considerable clarity, and have the flavor of policy:

- Virtually no one will be prosecuted for the felony if the car is not worth more than $500;

- Unless the defendant is believed to be a professional car thief or part of a ring, he will be allowed to plead guilty to a misdemeanor no matter what the value of the car;

- The compulsive joyrider is usually given a taste of jail in the hope that he will soon grow up.

Although prior relationships were relatively rare in grand larceny (auto) cases, they had the expected effect—7 of the 9 cases were dismissed. The relationships tended to be commercial in nature, and the complaint was likely to be withdrawn after restitution was made. Generally, dismissal of grand larceny (auto) charges occurred—in stranger as well as prior relationship cases—when the evidence was weak and the defendants had no prior criminal record or only a minor record.

More than half (55%) of the non-car grand larceny cases did arise from prior relationships, and half of these prior relationship cases were dismissed because of complainant non-cooperation. The generally lenient pattern of sentences for those who were convicted—usually by plea to a misdemeanor—was a product of mitigating circumstances or evidentiary problems unique to each case. Two felony time sentences were imposed, both upon professional criminals whose thefts were substantial. (The only other felony time sentence was imposed in a car theft case in which the defendant, who took a new and valuable car while on bail for federal bank robbery charges, was to serve the grand larceny sentence concurrently with the federal sentence.)

Like the policy of routine reduction of burglary charges to misdemeanors when the target is an unoccupied commercial establishment, the *ad hoc* policies governing grand larceny prosecutions seem the product of priority-setting in a congested system. While not obviously irrational, the policy has the effect of virtually ensuring that auto theft will not be treated as a felony. It could be argued that this would not be the case if the system was less congested, so that prosecutors could give proper attention to the violent felonies and still devote time to litigation of less serious issues, such as the value of a 1964 Chevrolet or the credibility of a defendant's story about having innocently borrowed or bought a stolen car.

The *ad hoc* policy disfavoring felony prosecution of grand larceny (auto) charges, unlike the policy regarding burglary of unoccupied commercial premises, does have some support in statute. The Penal Law provision of a separate misdemeanor—unauthorized use—does lend some legitimacy to the prevailing view that these cases are "only worth a misdemeanor plea." There is, however, no statutory sanction for the prosecutors' view that $500 is a more sensible level to separate felonies from misdemeanors.

On the other hand, exacting misdemeanor pleas from the railroad workers who had already lost their jobs and pensions "to show that the law meant business," and from the petty embezzler who was offered his job back, might still be considered excessive when compared to the general pattern of dispositions for larceny cases. Prosecutorial interest in securing some kind of conviction may have overridden justice in these cases.

6 Criminal Possession of Dangerous Weapons: Guns

Illegal possession of a gun is a "victimless" crime, in the sense that there is rarely a complaining witness to report it to the police or to testify in court. (When a gun is used against a victim, the top charge will be assault or higher.) As with other felonies in this category, the "arrest rate" and "clearance rate" for criminal possession of weapons are high—but most reports are simultaneous with a police officer's discovery of the weapon and arrest of a suspect for the crime. We have chosen gun possession arrests as illustrative of "victimless" felonies, because a speech by the New York City Police Commissioner regarding deterioration in the processing of gun possession arrests prompted this study (see page xi, above). Furthermore, gun possession may be a prelude to more serious felonies; guns were responsible for 50% of the murders and were used (though not necessarily fired) in 32% of the armed robberies reported to the police in 1974.*

New York City imposes the tightest restrictions in the country on the ownership and carrying of firearms.† Yet it was estimated in 1973 that one million New Yorkers owned them—the great majority illegally. Only about 100,000 handguns (not counting those belonging to police) were registered in 1974, including those belonging to 28,000 civilians who were licensed to carry them outside homes and business premises. In addition, some 130,000 New Yorkers were licensed to own long guns.‡ In 1974, the Police Department confiscated some 15,000 guns that were possessed illegally.

In New York, the possession of unlicensed handguns and certain other concealable weapons is a crime with a complicated sentencing structure. It is a D felony to possess an unlicensed handgun (for example, a pistol or a sawed-off shotgun) if ammunition to fit the gun is also possessed, whether or not the gun is loaded when it is found. If the gun is in the defendant's home or place of business, or if he does not possess ammunition for the gun, the offense is only an A misdemeanor. These A misdemeanors will rise back to the D felony level, how-

---

* New York City Police Department Statistical Report, Complaints and Arrests, 1974.
† A license to own a long gun can be obtained after a background check on the applicant, but the applicant need make no showing of "need" for the gun. Registration of handguns and licenses to carry them are much more tightly controlled. To register a handgun, the owner must first produce an ownership license issued by the police only after a screening which disqualifies applicants with criminal records or histories of alcoholism, drug abuse or mental disorder. If the owner of a registered handgun wishes to carry it legally outside his own premises, he needs still another license that is issued only on his showing of a "need" to do so.
‡ License Division of New York Police Department and New York City Firearms Control Board, 1974.

ever, if the defendant has previously been convicted of any felony or misdemeanor. Possession of an imitation pistol and most knives* is no crime at all unless an intent to use the weapon unlawfully can be proved; if criminal intent is proved, possession of the weapon is an A misdemeanor. That misdemeanor will also rise to the D felony level if the defendant has previously been convicted of any felony or misdemeanor. Only D felony arrests for possession of guns will be discussed in detail in this chapter.

Fact Patterns in Gun Possession Cases

Thirty-four cases in the deep sample were commenced by arrest for felonious possession of a weapon. In 6 of the 34 deep sample cases, the weapon was not a gun, leaving 28 gun cases for analysis in this chapter.†

---

* Possession of a gravity knife, switchblade, cane sword, billy club, sand club, blackjack, metal knuckles, sling shot or any other dangerous or deadly instrument is an A misdemeanor which rises to a D felony if the possessor has previously been convicted of a crime.

† In four cases, the weapon was a knife, in one it was a broken bottle and in one it was a molotov cocktail.

Four of the six were disposed of by guilty pleas to misdemeanors or lesser offenses. In one of the four, the weapon was a conventional knife but there was no evidence suggesting criminal intent. The defendant, who had been drunk and waving the knife about in the street, pled guilty to public intoxication and was conditionally discharged. Another, who pled guilty to disorderly conduct, had been arrested for urinating in the street. The knife found when she was searched was not a gravity knife or switchblade, and there was no evidence suggesting she intended to use it criminally. The third misdemeanor plea arose from the arrest of a boy thought to have thrown a molotov cocktail at a police officer, an E felony. His clean prior record and the difficulty of showing intent to attack the police, led the ADA to settle for a plea to reckless endangerment and a probation sentence. This defendant had been arrested for attacking his former lover with a broken soda bottle. The bottle was never recovered to be used in evidence and the weapon charge was dismissed. Despite the prior relationship, his numerous prior convictions ensured that this defendant would do some time on his plea of guilty to third degree assault.

One of the knife cases ended in dismissal when the knife proved not to be a gravity knife and there was no evidence of an intent to use it criminally.

The last of the knife cases ended in an E felony plea and probation, although the weapon charge was dismissed. The defendant, arrested on the police officer's belief that the knife on the front seat of his car was a gravity knife, offered the officer a bribe to let him go. (He was driving his girlfriend to the hospital.) He pled guilty to attempted bribery. Ironically, the knife was not a gravity knife and there was no evidence of criminal intent. Even if there had been, he could not have been convicted of a felony because he had no previous record.

All but two of the guns were real, and all but one of the real guns were loaded when seized. The unloaded gun was found by a search of a suitcase in which fitting ammunition was also found. Only one gun was found in a defendant's home. Prior relationships figured clearly in only two cases; a prior relationship may have been present and may have influenced the disposition in a third, but the data are not clear in that case. Nevertheless, only eight felony convictions were obtained, and only two were to the D felony originally charged. The remaining felony convictions were by plea to the purely hypothetical E felony of "attempted" criminal possession of a gun. But the sample was riddled with evidentiary problems peculiar to the "victimless" crimes of possession. The most important factor in shaping disposition of these cases was the defendant's prior record or lack of it.

Deterioration of Gun Possession Arrests

The pattern of deterioration of arrests for possession of handguns is similar to that of felony arrests generally, as shown in Figure 19 on the next page. The principal difference between gun cases and other felonies is that conviction (and felony conviction) is more likely in the gun cases, which means that sentences given to those who are convicted are comparatively lenient. Figure 20, page 119, shows how these cases reached their dispositions.

Once again, trial is the rare path to disposition. Only one of the 28 cases followed this route. The defendant in that case was convicted of the D felony with which he had been charged and sentenced to 3 years in prison.

Only seven months earlier he had been arrested on a weapon charge, and he had previous convictions in juvenile court for assault, maiming and disorderly conduct. The arresting officers said they became suspicious when a car in which the defendant and others were riding cruised slowly up and down the street. When they approached, according to their story, a gun was in "plain view" on the front seat. They arrested the group, searched the car, and confiscated several other weapons and ammunition. The ADA's *doubts about the officers' story—that the gun was in plain view, justifying the arrest and subsequent search—were resolved when the judge denied a motion to suppress the evidence on constitutional grounds.*

From then on, according to the ADA, *"it was a good and easy case to prepare. We just had the officers as witnesses. The case was ready to go at any time. Nothing funny; the jury would either believe or it wouldn't. I knew the defendant wouldn't take the stand [to rebut the presumption that he possessed any gun found in a car he was occupying] because of his prior record—he had*

Figure 19. Dispositional Pattern for Handgun Possession Arrests Compared to All Felony Arrests

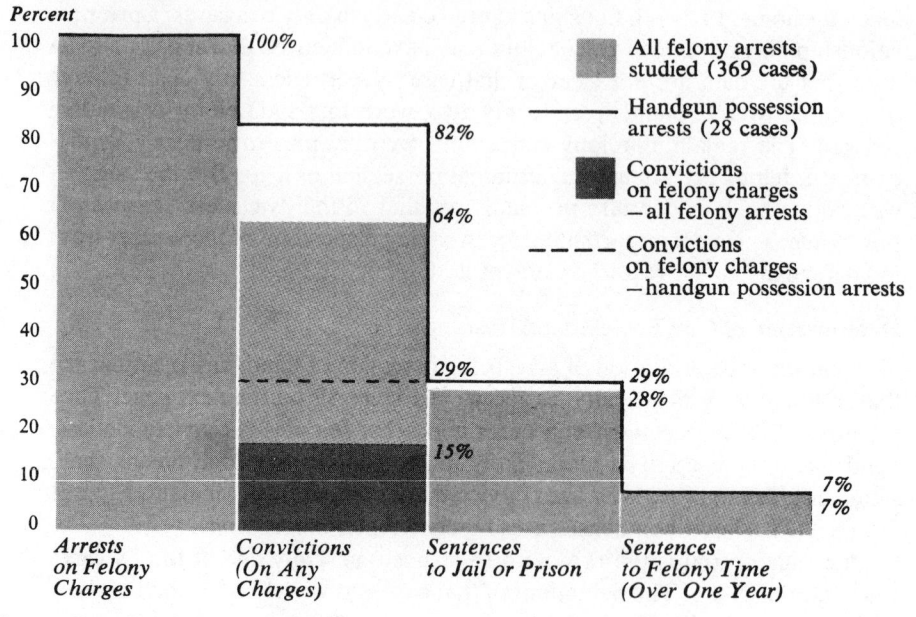

(Handgun possession arrests are 8% of all felony arrests studied.)

[Bar chart showing:
- Arrests on Felony Charges: 100% (both)
- Convictions (On Any Charges): 82% all felony arrests, 64% handgun possession; felony convictions 29% all, 15% handgun
- Sentences to Jail or Prison: 29% all, 28% handgun
- Sentences to Felony Time (Over One Year): 7% all, 7% handgun

Legend:
- All felony arrests studied (369 cases)
- Handgun possession arrests (28 cases)
- Convictions on felony charges — all felony arrests
- Convictions on felony charges — handgun possession arrests]

Source: Deep Sample Data (1973); Vera Institute Felony Disposition Study.

a prison sentence for a vicious assault in which he severed the victim's hand. And he had let it slip to the officer that they were a stick-up team that held up junkies because junkies couldn't turn them in." The judge gave the sentence recommended by the probation report—three years.

Comparatively few—5 of the 28 cases—were dismissed, and the typical course to disposition was a misdemeanor plea and a walk. Walks also disposed of 5 of the 7 pleas of guilty to felony charges.

Thus, the deterioration of felony arrests for handgun possession is broadly consistent with the data produced in 1972 by the New York City Police Commissioner (page xi, above). The deep sample cases will be examined more closely, however, for evidence bearing upon the Commissioner's conclusion that the court system must bear "the giant share of the blame for the ... rise in crime."

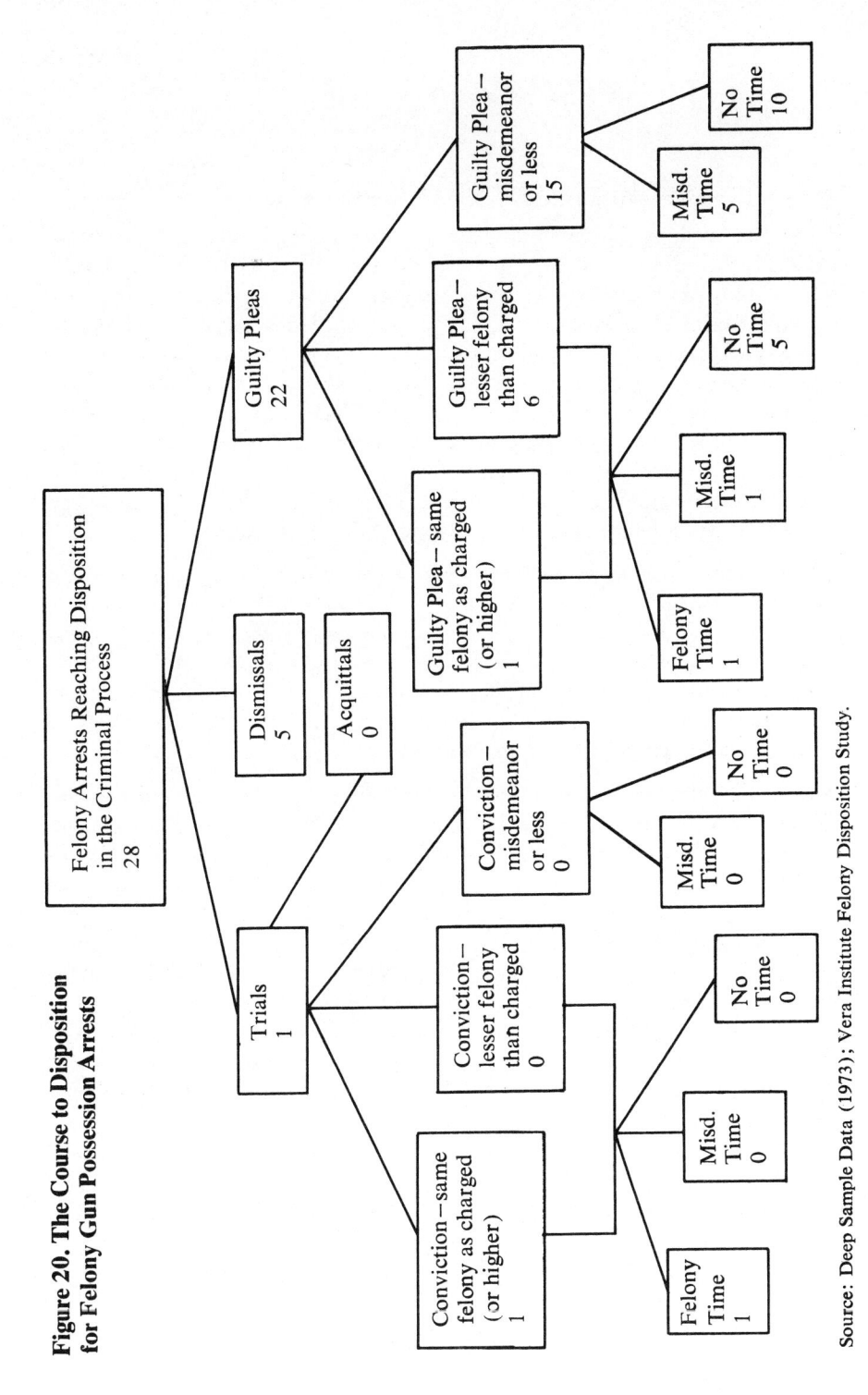

Figure 20. The Course to Disposition for Felony Gun Possession Arrests

- Felony Arrests Reaching Disposition in the Criminal Process: 28
  - Dismissals: 5
  - Acquittals: 0
  - Trials: 1
    - Conviction — same felony as charged (or higher): 1
      - Felony Time: 1
      - Misd. Time: 0
    - Conviction — lesser felony than charged: 0
      - No Time: 0
    - Conviction — misdemeanor or less: 0
      - Misd. Time: 0
      - No Time: 0
  - Guilty Pleas: 22
    - Guilty Plea — same as charged felony (or higher): 1
      - Felony Time: 1
      - Misd. Time: 1
    - Guilty Plea — lesser felony than charged: 6
      - No Time: 5
    - Guilty Plea — misdemeanor or less: 15
      - Misd. Time: 5
      - No Time: 10

Source: Deep Sample Data (1973); Vera Institute Felony Disposition Study.

Factors Explaining Dispositions of Gun Possession Cases

Prior relationships and non-cooperating complaining witnesses are understandably scarce among the gun possession cases, but one case serves to illustrate that the prior relationship factor can play a role in the disposition of even victimless crimes. A woman reported to the police that her husband had an unregistered gun. When the police searched him and his closets and drawers, however, they found nothing. They did find a loaded gun in the trunk of a car registered in the wife's name, which was opened with her keys. Because the car was unoccupied at the time the gun was found, the ADA's case rested upon the wife's testimony that the gun belonged to her husband.* She never appeared in court to testify against her husband, and although the case was not dismissed outright, it was adjourned in contemplation of dismissal (ACD).

The ADA *said: "An* ACD, *from our point of view, is better in some ways than a dismissal—though it will be the same in the end—because we are holding something over his head. He knows he won't get leniency next time." This statement is surprising in view of another remark by the same* ADA: *"The case should have been dismissed in the Complaint Room. If I'd heard the story there, that's what I would have done. I think it was a bad case. There was no evidence of that gun being anyplace near the defendant."*

Possession offenses—whether they involve guns or other contraband—are plagued by evidentiary problems arising either from the search that turns up the contraband or from the difficulty of proving possession when the contraband is not discovered by searching the defendant or his premises. The "search" problem typically involves the following question: if the gun was not "in plain view" of the police officer and was discovered without the defendant's consent by a search of his person, car or premises, did the officer have sufficient cause under Fourth Amendment standards to make his search "reasonable"? The "possession" problem typically poses the following question, as in the case mentioned above: if the gun was not discovered by search, is there sufficient evidence linking the defendant to the gun to show that he possessed it?

Four of the five dismissals resulted from "possession" problems, and they illustrate the variations in which this evidentiary difficulty presents itself. The possession problem that led to dismissal in the case above—the gun was found

---

* Section 265.15(3) of the Penal Law creates a presumption of possession "by all persons occupying [an] automobile at the time" when a gun is found in it. In this case, neither the husband nor the wife was in the car.

in a place to which more than one person had legitimate access—is compounded when the place is public. A judge explained the difficulty as follows, in a case commenced by arrest for possession of a loaded revolver:

"The two policemen said they heard a 'metallic sound' in the darkness as they approached the defendant and another man on a street at midnight. Allegedly, one cop flashed a light on the gutter several feet from the men and located the gun. I decided to dismiss at the preliminary hearing. As far as I could see, there was more than reasonable doubt as to whether either of these defendants actually possessed the gun. I did not believe there were any chances of conviction. I probed the officer carefully: the area was rubbish-strewn—there were lots of cans and bottles lying around. The sound might have been caused by a can in the street or any number of things. And it was pitch dark at the time. I did not believe that the officer, hearing a metallic sound some fifteen or twenty feet away, could immediately find the object with his flashlight. If the officer had testified that he saw one of the defendants drop the gun, or even that he saw the gun in flight, I would probably have accepted it. But this gun was just as likely lying in the gutter when the cops reached the scene. That is, if the gun was there at all—I thought the police version was a bit fabricated."

The ADA was furious: *"This defendant had a long record and had done time at least once—that's why I was pushing for the felony. And there was no point to a lesser charge here—possession was the essence of either the felony or a misdemeanor. But this judge went far beyond the bounds of discretion; the sufficiency and credibility of the evidence should have been left to the jury. It would have been OK for him to dismiss a case where the cop finds a gun on the street and then arrests someone standing fifteen feet away—then there's no real link. But here the officer could testify to the metallic sound and the gun was close to the defendants."*

"I don't blame the ADA," said the judge. *"He should have been angry. If he wasn't, he should not be in the DA's office. But I was within my power to dismiss this case; the evidentiary weakness justified it, and a judge has to play jury sometimes. That's what these hearings are for."*

In another of the dismissals, however, the ADA believed the possession problem was insurmountable.

During a fight near a precinct house, someone yelled to the police, "The guy in the car has a gun." The police searched the car and arrested the two occupants when they found a loaded gun under the seat. When they found the owner of the car standing nearby, he, too, was arrested and charged with possession of *the gun (he is the defendant in our sample). The statutory presumption of possession by all persons who are occupying a car in which a gun is found (see note*, page 120, above) did not apply to this defendant, and there was no other evidence suggesting that he had ever handled the gun or knew of its existence. Dismissal was likely, according to the ADA, even before a witness was found who told the police that he had seen one of the two occupants of the car throw the gun under the seat.*

In the final dismissal attributed to a "possession" problem, neither the gun nor the witness who had reported the crime could be found.

"We got a radio call that there had been a fight on the street," said the arresting officer, "and that there was a man with a gun. We had a description of the man and his car, and we found someone who fitted. He said, yes, he had been in a fight with some drunk over a parking place. We placed him under arrest and searched the car. But there wasn't any gun. And the complaining witness never showed or made contact with us again. We check out every gun call, but this will happen nine times out of ten on a radio call—and it's we, the police, who turn out to be the bad guys. This complainant probably just wanted the defendant locked up for his own satisfaction."*

The police officer went to court three times. The ADA said: "This defendant had a bad rap sheet—a number of felonious assaults, two grand larcenies—but it was impossible to get any sort of conviction out of this case without the gun or without a complaining witness to testify that he had it. It all had to be thrown out. It was an administrative decision—the case had been on the calendar for two months and three hearings. Even if the defendant had wanted to plead guilty, he couldn't have done it technically because the complaint hadn't been sworn to. But the witness gave the wrong telephone number, the wrong address —everything. The officer was never going to find him."

In the fifth case disposed of by dismissal, there were no evidentiary problems, the prosecution case was strong, and the defendant had a record of convictions. Both the ADA and the judge wanted the charges dismissed, however, after hearing the defendant's story.

---

* There are several suggestions in the interviews that this is another prior relationship case or, at least, that the call was made to the police by the man with whom the defendant had the fight. The police officer said, "The defendant said the complaining witness was drunk." The ADA said: "This whole case depended on the complaining witness's testimony — many times, in these sorts of complaints, the complaining witnesses have longer records than the defendants."

"I was in the patrol car," said the arresting officer, *"when I saw this defendant walking along with what appeared to be a gun bulging from his back pocket. I asked him what it was and got an evasive response and then a refusal to explain. I went for his pocket and found the loaded gun. At that point he explained that he was a maintenance worker at Shea Stadium; he'd found the gun there and was taking it to the precinct just up the street. And he was walking in that direction. But I arrested him for the felony—he had no license, he hadn't gone through the right procedures to turn in a gun, and he had a record from way back."*

The officer was right in thinking that—whatever the story—the man was technically guilty, but the Legal Aid attorney, the ADA, the officer and the judge all agreed at arraignment that the man, who was 44 years old, had been working steadily at Shea Stadium for more than ten years and had been out of trouble for almost twenty, was telling the truth. The judge said, "I'm very stringent on weapons charges. If I'd had the slightest doubt, I wouldn't have dismissed the case; weapons charges are too serious. I just couldn't see any criminal intent here. And we don't have court time to waste on obvious mistakes like this." Said the ADA: "I was sorry we had taken it that far—it was a nothing case. There was really no evidence of any crime."

In 7 of the 15 gun cases disposed of by plea to misdemeanor charges, evidentiary problems go a long way toward explaining the deterioration. Two of these had "possession" problems similar to the ones that led to the dismissals discussed above. In one, involving a defendant with no prior record, the loaded gun was found in a paper bag on a toilet seat in a public bathroom in the presence of others. The ADA settled for a plea to loitering and a conditional discharge. In the other case, the defendant and another man were the only two passengers in a subway car where a paper bag containing a loaded gun was found. This case might have ended in dismissal, except that the defendant, who had numerous previous convictions, was unable to make bail and eventually pled to a misdemeanor weapon charge for time served (about 10 months).

All five of the cases presenting clear "search" problems ended with misdemeanor pleas; two were disposed of by conditional discharges, one by probation, and two by misdemeanor time sentences. A six-month sentence went to a defendant who was arrested following a search triggered by an unidentified passer-by. The defendant was standing on the street with a group of men when the passer-by told the police officer that one of the group had a gun. The ADA offered an A misdemeanor because of his doubts about the legality of the search; the judge promised that, if the probation report recommended time, the maximum sentence would be six months. Six months was imposed when the report revealed, for the first time, an extensive out-of-state record.

A one-year misdemeanor sentence in another case is harder to explain. There, too, the felony charge was dropped because of a search problem, but there seems little to support a jail sentence.

A 23-year-old college student, with no prior record, was arrested for possession of a loaded gun. The officer said the defendant, a cab driver, had reached out of his parked cab and placed his gun at the curb as the officer approached. He made the arrest for the gun, which was in plain view, and then found misdemeanor quantities of marijuana and cocaine on the defendant when he searched. The Supreme Court ADA, after reading the case papers, was prepared to offer an E felony: "In Supreme Court we will reduce a case only one count for the plea. The defense didn't want to accept it so we were proceeding to jury selection. It was then that I spoke with the officer and I knew something was wrong—the story was incredible. So I dropped my plea offer to an A misdemeanor."

The ADA said it had been the judge who suggested the thorough interview with the arresting officer, because in another case earlier that day the same officer had told the same incredible story: "First he sees the gun, then he searches pursuant to the arrest, then he finds the drugs. The gun charge," explained the ADA, "would never hold up."

The ADA offered to drop the gun charge for pleas of guilty to the two misdemeanor drug charges: "In effect, he was asked to plead to the part of the indictment that would have held up at trial.* I normally wouldn't want to bring a case like this to trial because we tie up the part for a week on a minor offense. There was no discussion as to sentencing, but I thought there was a strong possibility he would get jail time."

The jail sentence—one year—seems heavy for a first offender pleading guilty to possession of small quantities of marijuana and cocaine. The probation report recommended probation, if the judge concluded the defendant was not a seller of drugs. The irony is that the judge seems to have taken the gun possession charge into account when passing sentence, despite the fact that the prosecutor did not believe the weapon arrest had been properly made or, therefore, that the search producing evidence for either the gun or the drug charges could be supported. The judge was not available for interview, but his law clerk explained: "I see no motion to suppress in this case—there's nothing to

---

* The ADA did not explain why the drug charges would hold up at trial if the bad search that made the gun inadmissible was also the search that produced the drugs.

suggest that the ADA *thought the officer's testimony was incredible. The judge took the weapon charge into consideration. And the probation report said he wasn't an addict, so he must have possessed the drugs for sale. It also said he was a youth worker—that shows he was gainfully employed and committed to improving his station in life, but it also indicates his danger to the community, walking around with drugs on him. And, as a student, he's becoming a useful citizen, but it also means he should know better. I think making the two one-year sentences concurrent was lenient."*

The defense lawyer was unavailable for interview, so we do not know why no motion to suppress was made in this case, or whether the lawyer reasonably expected a walk once the gun charge was out of the case.

The prosecutor in another case had similar doubts about the legality of the search that produced a loaded gun, and he was satisfied with a three-year probation sentence on the misdemeanor plea.

"The search was weak. They first arrested him because they thought he matched a description of a man wanted for a shooting. But the shooting had been in the Bronx and the defendant was driving in Manhattan, the defendant's clothing didn't match the description, and I thought it was very questionable whether we could survive a motion to suppress. And the A misdemeanor seemed sufficient—the defendant had only one prior arrest six years before."

The deep sample dispositions and interviews suggest that the "exclusionary rule,"* by which evidence may be suppressed if constitutional protections against unreasonable search are violated, works rather differently than many may assume. Whether or not the rule deters the police from making questionable searches, it does not seem to produce dismissals in cases brought into the criminal process in which the searches are probably illegal and the evidence could be suppressed. Not one of the gun cases was dismissed following a suc-

---

* The "exclusionary rule," designed by the Supreme Court to give substance to the Fourth Amendment's prohibition of unreasonable searches and seizures, provides that when a search does not satisfy the constitutional standards of reasonableness, the "fruits" of the search must be suppressed and not used in evidence. As exclusion of the unlawfully seized evidence would mean acquittal at trial for many defendants accused of crimes of possession, when there is no complaining witness's testimony for the prosecutor to fall back upon, it was thought that the "exclusionary rule" would deter police officers from making unlawful searches. (See *Mapp* v. *Ohio,* 367 U.S. 643 (1961).) This rationale assumes, of course, that the law enforcement interest is the securing of convictions rather than the discovery and confiscation of dangerous contraband. The deep sample data suggest that this assumption may be mistaken.

cessful motion to suppress illegally seized evidence; in the few cases in which such a motion was made, it was denied. Instead, the risk of losing a suppression motion seemed in several cases to have so weakened the prosecutor's chances of conviction that he settled for a misdemeanor conviction and a walk. The guns, of course, were removed from circulation by the police at the time of arrest—and that, after all, may be the main objective.

The following case, in which a defendant with a prior record and a loaded gun in his car pled guilty to a misdemeanor weapon charge and was conditionally discharged, illustrates the complexity introduced into a case by "search problems."

"A man on a motorcycle said there was a guy around the corner in a car who pointed a gun at him. They'd had an argument," said the arresting officer. The complainant rode off, never to be seen again, and the officer drove around the corner to find the defendant pulling out from the curb. "We stopped him and arrested him for having a court officer's shield on the dashboard. He said he'd borrowed the car." The defendant was taken to the station on the charge of impersonating a court officer, but it was dropped when it became clear he had not done so. After the car was brought to the station house it was searched—the gun was then found in it.

As there had been no lawful arrest, there had been no reasonable ground for searching the car. "This was an exceptionally weak case," said the ADA. *"There was a definite search and seizure problem, but it was never cleared up. Ordinarily, I would not go below an E felony on a gun case, but a motion to suppress at trial here might well have meant outright dismissal. So I waited for them to offer a plea." The defense attorney believed "it was better to take a plea instead of risking having a motion to suppress denied and having to go to trial. It was unlikely that this motion would have been denied, but there's always a risk involved, and the defendant would have had no defense at a trial."*

"He asked for an A misdemeanor," said the ADA, *"and under the circumstances of the arrest—there were no witnesses—I accepted. There was no discussion of sentence, but this guy had only an old A misdemeanor conviction on his record, and a conditional discharge was the best all around solution—at least we have something on him for the next six months."*

The judge agreed to the disposition, saying, "In a trial it might have been dismissed; there was no defense, but the ADA *was having search and seizure problems. With the conditional discharge we have some control over him if he gets into any kind of trouble. But there was no need for more, or for special conditions. He was a working family man, no real record, and his family depended on his income."*

Although all parties seemed in agreement about the disposition of this case, some concern was expressed about the waste of time and court resources. The felony arrest charge survived Complaint Room, Criminal Court Arraignment, Preliminary Hearing and Grand Jury; it was reduced and disposed of at a Supreme Court Pretrial Conference after 219 days in the criminal process. In the judge's words, "This case, like so many cases in Supreme Court, could have been worked out in the lower court. These don't belong up here."

The final misdemeanor plea and walk (another conditional discharge) in the five "search problem" gun cases can be traced to the judge's certainty that the defendant's parole would be revoked anyway and that he would, in effect, do time for possession of the gun. He had already spent 145 days in custody waiting for disposition of the gun charge and for a parole revocation hearing.

In 8 cases in which misdemeanor pleas were accepted despite the lack of "possession" or "search" problems, prior record played a major role in the final outcome. In one of these, the loaded gun was found among the 62-year-old defendant's possessions, after he was arrested for a violation—propositioning a plainclothes policewoman posing as a prostitute in Times Square. The ADA offered this explanation for accepting a misdemeanor plea and promising a $500 fine, despite his office's policy against reduction from felony charges in gun cases:

"First, he had a very old record [serious charges, but all between 1933 and 1950] which involved mostly acquittals and dismissals, so we consider that he really doesn't have any record at all. Secondly, he's an older man and has been steadily employed for 15 years. It didn't seem proper to give him a felony conviction on this. His being arrested and the compromising situation would serve as embarrassment and punishment enough. And it would have been difficult at trial, with the defendant probably gaining a good deal of jury sympathy."

Two of the cases that lacked search or possession problems, but were disposed by pleas to misdemeanors (or less), were overcharged as felonies in the first place. One was a prior relationship case. The police were called into a family dispute in which the defendant had threatened an in-law. The defendant's unregistered gun was loaded, but it was in his home and he had no prior felony or misdemeanor convictions. These facts do not satisfy the Penal Law requirements for a felony gun possession charge. The defendant pled guilty to the property (misdemeanor) gun charge and was fined $75. In the other overcharged case, the gun was loaded but it was only a starter pistol. Again, possession was not a felony under the statute because the defendant had no prior convictions. In addition, criminal intent (necessary to make possession of a starter pistol even a misdemeanor) would have been difficult to prove on the facts of the case. He pled guilty to disorderly conduct, a violation, and was fined $50. In contrast, the one other defendant arrested for possession of a starter pistol was sentenced to 5 months in jail. The factors underlying the different disposition seem to have been that he had prior convictions and that the gun charge had been added on top of an E-level grand larceny charge; his plea was to petit larceny.*

Two defendants, who were conditionally discharged upon pleas to misdemeanor gun possession charges, were from out of state, just passing through New York, and were thought to be ignorant of the Penal Law provisions. Neither had any prior record. One was a soldier whose gun was discovered in a routine airport search of luggage. He might not have been prosecuted at all, except that he was AWOL at the time, and the walk was conditional upon his returning to the Army.

In the last of the misdemeanor pleas, the gun was loaded but the charge reduction and lenient sentence (a conditional discharge) were explained by the defendant's lack of prior arrests or convictions. He was "a family man and a city employee," and the fact that he would lose his city job if he was convicted of a felony was given weight in reduction of an otherwise solid technical felony possession case. This case also provides evidence for the proposition that in a city with such a large number of weapons, it is not only "people of criminal intent," to borrow Commissioner Murphy's phrase, who are illegally armed. In any case, it is doubtful that a jury would be willing to convict an obvious non-criminal like this man on felony charges.

Seven cases were strong enough for the prosecutor to hold out for a felony plea. Despite the strength of the prosecution's case,† 5 of these 7 felony pleas

---

* The gun possession was not related to the larceny, and it would have presented problems to prove a criminal intent in possessing the gun—a prerequisite to making the possession a felony by reason of his prior convictions. He was first arrested for stealing a wallet, and only when he was searched was the starter pistol found.

† In one case there had been a "search problem," but the judge denied a motion to suppress. The ADA held the view that the motion ought to have succeeded; the judge, inexplicably, thought "it is the duty of the ADA to dismiss it if the search was questionable. It's his responsibility. Titles don't matter—he's a lawyer as much as a judge is." As it was his office's policy not to reduce gun charges to misdemeanors in Supreme (continued on page 130)

were followed by walks. None who walked had a substantial criminal record. The following case is illustrative.

An off-duty police officer buying gasoline noticed that the attendant was carrying a gun and arrested him. The defendant had been arrested only once—20 years before—and that charge had been dismissed. He had been steadily employed for 20 years, supporting a family. He pled guilty to attempted possession of the gun (an E felony) and was given five years' probation. Neither the judge nor the prosecutor saw a point in putting him in jail.

The conviction charge—"attempted" possession—is nonsense, but there would seem little to be gained by forcing such a case to trial and conviction on the D felony when the defendant does not appear to be a dangerous felon. Thus, a similar E felony plea was devised, and followed by probation, for a man with no prior arrests who had actually fired his gun—into the air on an impulse, with no hint of criminal or malicious intent.

One of the five who walked following a felony plea had several prior convictions, but the offenses were minor. He was arrested as a passenger in a stolen automobile. A search of his pockets, pursuant to the arrest, turned up a loaded gun. Though he walked with a sentence to probation, his liberty was conditional upon participation in a drug program. His troubles seemed to stem from drug abuse, so he was dealt with as sick rather than dangerous.

The two defendants with serious prior records who pled guilty to felonies got time. In one case the charge was knocked down one step (to the hypothetical "attempted" possession E felony) by an ADA who was surprised to find himself with a strong case. ("Based on the testimony presented by the officers," he said, "I would have granted the motion to dismiss."*) The ADA

---

* "Just from hearing the officers talking to each other," said the ADA, "it became obvious that the only just ruling would be to grant the motion. The judge denied it because it's hard to call the police officers liars. This officer was an inherently unbelievable character, and his story was impossible. You have to have a hearing first in a case like this, because there is a good possibility that the judge will dismiss the case. Judges seldom will dismiss a case, even with valid questions of the search and seizure, where there are one or two officers testifying who would be made liars. They take the search question into consideration for sentencing purposes instead." The judge, inexplicably, expressed the view that although the police officer's testimony was "not very convincing, I felt I could not dismiss the case. I thought it was a question for the jury to resolve, whether the police officer was telling the truth about the search or not." The judge said he had promised the one-year maximum "because of the search problems," but stated he would not have gone any lower to secure the plea "because of the prior conviction."

wanted a felony conviction and time because "the People are always even more uptight with a gun case than with a drug case," and because this defendant had previous felony convictions and a prison record for a violent crime. He was not surprised, however, when the judge agreed to promise no more than a year. "The only reason he went that low was the search and seizure problem. There was a good chance—50-50—of acquittal if they made the motion again at trial." The other defendant with a serious prior record entered a guilty plea to the same felony as charged. There was no search problem in this case: he was arrested while drunkenly waving his loaded revolver about in the street. The probation report was negative, and he got the three-year sentence it recommended to cover the gun felony and an outstanding assault charge.

The overall importance of the defendant's criminal record in shaping the disposition of gun possession felony arrests is apparent even if evidentiary problems are ignored. Table P displays the sentences for all the gun case defendants who were convicted of something, by the nature of their prior records.

The numbers are small, but the association between prior convictions and time sentences on the current charge is strong. Twelve of the 14 walks went to defendants who had never before been convicted; 8 of the 10 with prior convictions got time. Four of the 5 who walked with arrest records had only very old or only misdemeanor arrests. The one defendant who got time despite a clean record was the cab driver who pled to two misdemeanor drug offenses.

It is not surprising that prior convictions—or their absence—are so powerfully associated with disposition. The assumption built into the statutory scheme for classifying and setting maximum sentences in weapon offenses is that possession is a serious matter because it is potentially dangerous. The potential danger is likely to be even greater when the possessor has, by previous convictions, already demonstrated criminal propensities.

Summary

When an illegally possessed gun is used in a criminal way, arrest will bring the defendant into the criminal process with a more serious top charge (for example, homicide, rape, robbery, burglary or assault). Nevertheless, most of the ADAs and judges interviewed about the disposition of deep sample gun cases indicated that they viewed the possession charge as serious because of the

---

Court, this ADA used the "attempted" possession E felony for a plea offer. The defendant, who had never been arrested before, was put on probation. The ADA thought that the judge probably took the search issue into account at sentencing, as well as the lack of prior record.

Table P: Sentences in Gun Possession Cases, by Prior Criminal Record

	Walk	Time [a]
No Prior Record	7	1
Record of Arrests	5	–
Record of Convictions	2	8

Source: Deep Sample Data (1973); Vera Institute Felony Disposition Study.

a. For the purposes of this table, the defendant who was conditionally discharged because he was known by the judge to face a year in jail for parole violation on the gun possession and because he had already done 154 days in pretrial custody, is considered to have been sentenced to time. Similarly, the defendant who was sentenced to probation after ten months in pretrial custody is considered to have been sentenced to time.

violent crime that is associated with guns and because of office policy and public pressure to resist charge reduction in cases involving guns. Thus, deterioration of these arrests, which fits the pattern of deterioration in felony arrests generally, does not appear to represent callousness towards the public interest. There are few deep sample cases in which—when the facts of the situations and the evidentiary obstacles to felony conviction are explored—it could be said that the disposition was clearly too lenient or that the courthouse was "bargained away." The cases in which conviction was possible and in which there was also a suggestion of the potential for more serious harm seem to have been singled out for more severe dispositions. The defendant who fired his gun into the air in a vacant lot was evidencing a potential for causing harm, despite his lack of malice or criminal intent. He did 154 days in detention before being conditionally discharged on his misdemeanor plea, and he will do felony time because of the parole revocation triggered by his conviction for possessing the gun. The drunk with a record of assaults who was waving his loaded gun about in the street got felony time on a felony conviction. And the defendant with a juvenile record, whom the ADA believed was about to commit an armed robbery with a gun found in the car he and his friends were using to "case" the street, was convicted of a felony at trial and drew felony time.

Even in an uncongested system, in which every case could be taken to trial as originally charged, many of the remaining cases would have deteriorated because:

- The defendant's lack of prior record or his possession of the gun in his own premises warranted only a misdemeanor charge under the terms of the Penal Law;

- The sympathy of the jury could easily have been won by the defendant's obvious lack of criminal intent in arming himself in a city where so many go forth armed, and by his otherwise responsible behavior towards family or community;

- The prosecutor would have had difficulty persuading a jury that the defendant actually possessed the gun if it was not discovered by searching him;

- If the gun was discovered by search, the prosecutor would have lost a defense motion to suppress the evidence (or the conviction would have been reversed on appeal) because the search did not meet constitutional requirements.

In any event, it is difficult, from the deep sample data, to support former Police Commissioner Murphy's suggestion that leniency by judges and callous plea bargaining by ADAs in gun cases are responsible for large numbers of "people of criminal intent carry[ing] handguns in New York City" or for a rise in crime. To the contrary, even in the face of serious evidentiary problems in gun possession cases, the police and courts seem to perform efficiently what may, after all, be their primary mission—removing illegal weapons from circulation.

7 Reflections on the Study

This has been a study of the processing of felony arrests by the New York City Criminal Courts. We have looked in particular at those cases that have been processed all the way through to final disposition—or three-fourths of all the cases. We have examined what happens to original charges as these cases are adjudicated in court, and then looked at rates of conviction and at sentencing patterns.

Our findings have been unexpected, at least in part. We did expect charge deterioration, as Commissioner Murphy's statistics indicated we might, and we found it. We also found a system dominated by plea-bargaining, in which only 2.6% of the cases ended in trial. And we found, somewhat to our surprise, that the charge reductions and dismissals were often explicable, according to the participants in the system, by factors other than congestion and the pressure congestion creates to dispose of cases quickly through pleas rather than trial. Depending on the perspective of the reader, this reliance on plea-bargaining to dispose of cases may be damaging to the defendant, on one hand, or to the victim and the public, on the other. And, indeed, there were cases in which a defendant who pled guilty and was sentenced to jail would probably have been acquitted had the case gone to trial. There was also the reverse situation, in which a conviction after trial would probably have ended in a heavier sentence than the one negotiated by the defense lawyer, prosecutor and judge. In general, however, we found dispositions proportional to the seriousness of the offenses, the length of the defendants' criminal records, and the closeness of their relationships to the victims. Thus the system was proportional in its outcome, although not in its process.

It must be remembered that we saw the system through the eyes of participants who explained their actions in specific cases. We recognize that it may have been only natural for them to portray a system that proceeds with integrity and consistency. It may be, too, that congestion was not mentioned more frequently as an explanation for deterioration because it so pervades the system that judges, lawyers and police officers no longer recognize it as a discrete influence. Despite this caveat, we found sufficient agreement among the participants as to the facts of given cases to persuade us that dispositions of felony arrests were generally in accord with the individual acts that provoked the arrests and with the character of the defendants (primarily determined by their prior criminal records).

It must be emphasized again that we have been looking not at all felony crimes in New York City, nor at the total population of felons, but at those persons actually charged with felonies whose cases were disposed of in the adult criminal courts. We know these accounted for about three-fourths of all felony arrests, and that felony arrests, in turn, represented about one-fifth of all felonies reported. We are thus dealing with that relatively small proportion of potentially guilty felons who are caught in the police net, accused in court, and, in this study, have their cases carried through to final disposition.

There is no doubt that the deterioration of these felony arrests once they get to court, as revealed in our data and confirming Commissioner Murphy's data, indeed seems alarming:

- 43% of the cases commenced by felony arrest and disposed of in the Criminal Court were dismissed;

- 98% of the cases that ended in conviction were disposed of by guilty pleas rather than trial;

- 74% of the guilty pleas were to misdemeanors or lesser offenses;

- 50% of the guilty pleas were followed by "walks," 41% by sentences to less than a year in prison;

- Only 9% of the guilty pleas were followed by felony time sentences;*

- Only 2.6% of cases were disposed of by trial.†

What are we to make of these figures? Are serious criminals "getting away with it" in the adult criminal court system and being turned loose or being given inappropriately light sentences? Our probe suggests that this is not the case, and that we may arrive at a different conclusion: Where crimes are serious, evidence is strong, and victims are willing to prosecute, felons with previous criminal histories ended up with relatively heavy sentences. One is thus tempted to conclude that if criminals are "getting away with it," they may be getting away with it more on the streets than in the courtroom.

There are other groups of defendants, however, not included in our figures, who *may* be getting away with it—both on the streets *and* in the court room. In those cases where the defendants failed to appear in court (about 6%) we did not have the dispositions of the cases because the de-

---

* These are wide sample data. Deep sample data paralleled these figures closely except that fewer deep sample cases (34%) resulted in dismissal, and more (57%) of those who pled guilty were given walks.

† The data from the wide sample trial cases showed more trials ending in acquittal than conviction. However, aggregate statistics indicate that trials are more likely to end in conviction than in acquittal.

fendants were still at large. Nor do our figures include the 12% of defendants under 16 years of age, who were more likely to be arrested for robbery and burglary than other crimes. We do not know what happened to these juveniles, although from other studies we can guess that they are less likely to be incarcerated than adults. Of course, a study of the reasons for the disposition of juvenile arrests could help answer these questions.

The reason why so many cases that come into the system as felonies are not prosecuted as charged is, we now know, that a high precentage of them, in every crime category from murder to burglary, involve victims with whom the suspect has had prior, often close, relations. Logically, suspects who are known to their victims are more likely to be caught than strangers because they can be identified more easily by the complainants. And this very fact of a previous personal relationship often leads a complainant to be reluctant to pursue prosecution through adjudication. The study found that tempers had cooled, time had passed, informal efforts at mediation or restitution might have worked, or, in some instances, the defendant had intimidated the complainant.

The study found an obvious but often overlooked reality: criminal conduct is often the explosive spillover from ruptured personal relations among neighbors, friends and former spouses. Cases in which the victim and defendant were known to each other constituted 83% of rape arrests, 69% of assault arrests, 36% of robbery arrests, and 39% of burglary arrests. The reluctance of the complainants in these cases to pursue prosecution (often because they were reconciled with the defendants or in some cases because they feared the defendants) accounted for a larger proportion of the high rate of dismissal than any other factor. Of course, this kind of "familial" crime is still crime, and its victims often as strongly aggrieved as the victims of stranger crime. But there can be no doubt that the relatively close defendant-victim relationship is responsible for much of the case deterioration in court. And although this deterioration may be rational from the perspective of the decision makers, it may not be rational or desirable in all cases from the perspective of injured wives, tenants and neighbors.

It also has an effect on the sentences ultimately imposed in those cases that survive the adjudicating process. Judges and prosecutors, and in some instances police officers, were outspoken in their reluctance to prosecute as full-scale felonies some cases that erupted from quarrels between friends or lovers. (An exception was found in the assault category, where long-standing personal conflicts were more likely to result in serious injury than spur-of-the-moment stranger assaults.) Sometimes the prosecutor argued that a jury would never convict in such a case; sometimes the judge felt that it would serve no purpose to imprison the defendant and possibly disrupt the relationship permanently, or to penalize heavily what was clearly an unpremeditated over-reaction to a personal grievance—especially if the injury was minor or the crime unlikely to recur. Thus, where prior relationship cases survived dismissal, they generally received lighter dispositions than stranger cases.

Our penal laws make no mention of the prior relationship factor. This study does not purport to resolve the question of whether the high fallout of personal relationship crimes is to society's good or detriment; nor does it indicate what happens after the victim and defendant leave the courthouse and go home. Do prior relationship assaults return to the courts as prior relationship homicides, or do the individuals live happily ever after? How often do assaults on family members within the home escalate to assaults on strangers in the streets? Clearly there is a need for research in these areas.

The other major factor that appeared in this study in every crime category as a determinant of both conviction and sentence was prior record. Overall, 84% of convicted defendants who had any kind of prior adult criminal records were sent to prison, compared to 22% of those with no prior records. The impact of prior criminal record escalated with the gravity of the record (for example, arrest only, conviction only or prison time). Thirty-nine percent of the sample had no adult criminal records and were accordingly given more lenient treatment than those with records.

But how many of these defendants had juvenile records? And how many were merely caught for the first time? Is prior adult record a valid factor on which to base a conviction or sentencing decision? If someone has committed a crime, why should it matter, except perhaps in the duration of the sentence, that he had not been involved with the law before? Does the frequently articulated justification that a first offender should be given a "break" make sense, or as some critics of the system suggest, would it be a greater deterrent to vest penalties automatically on conviction, regardless of record?

Many judges and prosecutors interviewed in this study hesitated to send a first offender, particularly a young one, to prison because they believed he would not be rehabilitated and, indeed, might be corrupted and exploited. Although current statutes make some provisions for prior record (for example, youthful offender status may be accorded a defendant between the ages of 16 and 19 if he has no prior felony conviction), there is no New York law that restricts harshness of sentence for all first offenders. Yet the presence or absence of prior records dictates what happens to a large percentage of cases. In a fast-moving system, this presence or absence of a prior record is an obvious and easily available guidepost for making decisions, and future studies might concentrate on first offender treatment in case processing: How many are genuine first offenders as opposed to first-time-caught offenders? How many had serious records as juveniles? If first offenders are not formally diverted from the system, would first offender status be legitimized as cause for dismissing, offering a plea, or putting someone on probation? If the answer to the latter question is yes, then we can expect continued high attrition rates.

Prior relations and prior record as factors in the disposition of cases create unexpected complexities. For example, residential burglaries are considered, in the Penal Law, more serious than commercial burglaries. But prior relationships were more common among the residential burglaries, and the residential burglars were also less likely to have criminal records. The net result was that commercial burglars were more likely to draw time than residential burglars.

Dismissals and pleas to reduced charges that were not attributed to prior relations or prior record often grew from overcharging at arrest or from evidentiary obstacles to conviction. Overcharging was particularly evident in the attempted murder, handgun possession and grand larceny cases. In some cases, felony charges appeared to be levelled against defendants, guilty at most of resisting arrest or harassment, to "cover" use of force by arresting officers. But more generally, overcharging involved levying the highest permissable charge to set the stage for negotiation of a plea to an offense that would, in the police view, be appropriate to the circumstances.

It has been suggested that the remedy for congested courts is to end plea bargaining and mandate minimum sentences, but our study indicates that the present pattern is proportionate to the seriousness of the offense and prior record of the offender. The public may not wish to punish family or neighborhood squabbles in the same way as cold-blooded stranger street crimes. And it would not be practical for a legislature, on one hand, to prescribe a range of different sanctions for every combination of circumstances that leads to a robbery crime, or, on the other hand, to obliterate all differences and require a 15-year sentence for all robberies.

One plea bargaining reform is that proposed nine years ago by the President's Commission on Law Enforcement and Administration of Justice: "If a negotiated agreement to plead guilty is reached, care should be taken by prosecutor and defense counsel to state explicitly all its terms. . . . Upon the plea of guilty in open court the terms of the agreement should be fully stated on the record and, in serious or complicated cases, reduced to writing."*

A similar reform may be appropriate in the area of sentencing; the reasons for a sentence should be explicitly stated. To reduce sentencing disparities and to make the judge accountable to the defendant, complainant and community, sentencing guidelines could be formulated. Such guidelines could take into account the nature of the offense, the criminal history of the defendant, and the relation of the defendant and the victim. If a judge were to depart from the guidelines—to give either a more or a less harsh sentence than the guidelines called for—he would have to state his reasons.

Although the statistics show enormous rates of charge reduction, the need for quick dispositions and the lack of an open system may in fact be leading to sanctions against persons who are not guilty. The study uncovered cases in which the judge and prosecutor believed the defendant was in fact innocent or could not be convicted at a trial, or had reasonable doubt about his guilt, but nevertheless found a guilty plea to a minor offense followed by a walk to be appropriate so as to resolve the doubt and end the case.

Perhaps the most troublesome question raised, but not answered, by the study was whether the 100,000 felonies that resulted in arrest in New York City in 1971 were typical of the 500,000 felonies that were reported and the one million or so that were committed. We suspect the answer is no. The reasons can be drawn from the deep sample and include the high incidence of prior relationships in all categories but weapons; the absence of even one nighttime armed burglar in the deep sample; the fact that 38% of robbers and burglars were identified by victims who already knew them; the fact that 30% of reported armed robberies but only 9% of the deep robbery sample involved guns; and the fact that one-half of the stranger assaults in the deep sample were the result of altercations with policemen. All of this seems to suggest that the adult criminal justice system may not be catching in its net the kind of criminal citizens worry about most—the violent stranger.

If further study supports the finding that arrests for serious felonies are weighted toward those involving prior relationships between victim and defendant—arrests that forecast heavy rates of attrition—then our perception of how the system should work might change. If police are not arresting the more serious felons, perhaps the answer is to develop and test further measures the police have been experimenting with, such as the use of decoy

---

* "The Challenge of Crime in a Free Society," U.S. Government Printing Office, Washington, D.C., 1967.

policemen (and women) and other preventive patrol strategies. Such efforts might help shift the distribution of arrests toward the predatory stranger crimes.

For those prior relationship cases that remain in the system—and in which the complainant does not want to pursue prosecution—alternatives to court processing such as mediation and conflict resolution could be introduced. A number of experiments are demonstrating the promise of conflict mediation as an alternative to court processing. In New York City, a Dispute Center created by the Institute for Mediation and Conflict Resolution offers mediation and arbitration as alternatives to arrest and criminal court processing for selected offenses ranging from harassment to assault. Similar projects in Boston and Columbus, Ohio, handle court- and prosecutor-referred cases. And a recent task force report to the American Bar Association has recommended that the ABA support the development of "neighborhood justice centers" that would make available mediation and arbitration services.* Experiments are also underway on mechanisms that provide compensation for the injured in lieu of retribution. Alternatives such as conflict resolution—given the numbers of cases they might affect—could make a substantial impact on congestion in the criminal courts. If felony prosecution is not always the answer to felony arrests, neither in many cases is outright dismissal.

This monograph posed the question: Are serious felons getting away with it? The answer is that some do, because they do not get caught—at least on serious charges free of evidentiary difficulties. And many felons who *are* caught are not the ones we fear and dread—the ones the law is meant to incapacitate and punish.

Like most studies, this one has served mainly to spotlight the complexity of individual decisions and to suggest that there are no easy targets for citizens' ire or frustration. Unquestionably, the criminal court process could be improved if more experienced prosecutors were given greater decision-making authority earlier in the process, so they could screen out cases that are eventually going to be dismissed anyway, reduce charges that do not need Grand Jury and Supreme Court attention, and give first attention to assuring speedy trial for the vicious crimes that remain.

Further investigations could help illuminate some of the areas not probed deeply or at all in this study. One would be to look at the adjudication of

---

* American Bar Association, *Report of Pound Conference Follow-up Task Force*, August 1975, p. 1.

felony arrests in Family Court, so as to learn more about the disposition of juvenile cases. Another would be to examine the disposition of felony arrests in a non-congested court system in another city. Still another would be to investigate the criminal behavior patterns of defendants known to their victims, to see whether and how much these people also engage in "stranger" crime.

Although this study enables us to arrive at some tentative explanations as to what happens to felony arrests once they get to court, and why, we have barely begun to understand what is really happening inside our criminal justice system.

Epilogue: 1980

The 1970s saw almost constant change in the administration of justice in New York City; nowhere was change as evident as in the processing of felony arrests. Given this systemwide tightening up, it should be asked whether, at the beginning of the 1980s, our 1973 "deep sample" data still illuminate the pattern of dispositions reached in felony arrest cases.

The question is not easy to answer, but an attempt is appropriate as we republish the monograph without revision. Only replication of the deep sample research could tell us for sure whether the dismissals, pleas to lesser charges and sentences occurring in felony arrest cases today reflect a mix of prior relationships, evidentiary obstacles and prosecution policies similar to the mix found in 1973. But there is a more simple way to test for continuing relevance of our old deep sample data: If the dispositional pattern has remained the same over the years, the kinds of behavior and patterns of underlying circumstances giving rise to felony arrests are likely not to have changed. (We would expect this to be so, because we found the dispositional pattern to be best explained, not by characteristics of the process but by combinations of underlying behavior and circumstances in the individual cases.) Therefore, we can test whether the data from the 1973 deep sample are still useful by examining the dispositional pattern of more recent felony arrests.

Over the years, the basic patterns have been surprisingly stable. In 1971, the number of felony arrests was 20 percent of the number of felony complaints; in 1978, felony arrests were 19 percent of complaints. Although the total number of felony arrests increased over those years, from 100,739 in 1971 to 107,135 in 1978, the distribution of arrests across the different types of crime has been relatively constant.*

---

* Although burglary, assault and grand larceny arrests now make up somewhat greater proportions of the total of felony arrests, the major changes in the arrest pattern occurred in the felony narcotics categories: there, arrests decreased dramatically, from 18 percent of all felony arrests in 1971 to 8 percent in 1978. Well before the 1973 Rockefeller Drug Law, there were major changes in this area brought about by shifts in New York City Police Department policy. In 1969, the Department had begun "street sweeps" of drug users, and arrests had risen from about 7,000 anually at the end of the 60s to over 26,000 in 1970; in 1970, Police Commissioner Murphy abandoned this policy and the number of narcotics felonies gradually decreased to the pre-1969 level. For a full account of this process, see Joint Committee of New York Drug Law Evaluation, *The Nation's Toughest Drug Law: Evaluating the New York City Experience* (New York: The Association on the Bar of the City of New York and Drug Abuse Council, 1977).

Most important, these arrests reach dispositions in a pattern that has shifted hardly at all from the pattern revealed by Vera's 1971 "wide sample." Figure 21 compares the dispositional pattern defined by the 1971 wide sample of arrests with the pattern of dispositions defined by official aggregate data* for the year 1977.

In most respects, the dispositional pattern of felony arrests in 1977 is virtually the same as that defined by 1971 wide sample data. In both years, only about 2% of felony cases reached disposition by trial in either Criminal Court or Supreme Court. The majority ended by guilty plea; roughly three-quarters of those pleas were to misdemeanors or lesser charges. Dismissals continued to account for approximately two-fifths of all felony arrests. In both years, approximately a quarter of the cases ended in prison or jail sentences. It remains the case that most felony arrests are not processed to disposition as felonies. It is hard to study Figure 21 and not

---

* Even when all available sources of official aggregate data are considered together, they permit only a rough approximation of the dispositional pattern of felony arrests. There is in New York's arrays of reports of aggregate data no offender-based tracking system that links felony arrests to dispositions. The preceding monograph is unique in that respect. Thus, although it is possible to approximate the dispositional pattern, by combining aggregate data reported by various agencies in a given year, it must be remembered that the arrests made in that year do not match the dispositions reported in that year—some of the dispositions will have occurred in cases commenced in earlier annual reporting periods and some of the arrests will not reach disposition until subsequent reporting periods. Some 1977 arrests, for example, were disposed in 1978, just as some 1977 dispositions are linked to arrests made and reported in 1976. We have used various annual reports of aggregate data (for felony arrests, dispositions of felony arrests in Criminal Court and dispositions of felony arrests in Supreme Court) to construct a picture of the dispositional pattern of 1977 felony arrest cases, but it is an artificial construction.

Another problem in attempting to approximate the pattern of dispositions in felony arrest cases arises because police data, Criminal Court data, and Supreme Court data actually count different things. The New York City Police Department's data report "arrests" by the number of individuals arrested in any incident, and each arrest is categorized by the most serious charge made against the defendant as a result of that incident. The Criminal Court counts "docket numbers"—there is usually, but not always, a one-to-one relationship between each docket number and each "arrest." The Division of Criminal Justice Services reports Supreme Court data by counting "defendant-indictments"—the number of defendants named on each indictment filed by the prosecutor. As more than one indictment may result from a single incident, the link between police "arrest" data and DCJS "defendant-indictments" data is not direct. When attempting to construct a picture of dispositional patterns from such diverse data, there is little choice but to assume that these differences are of marginal importance.

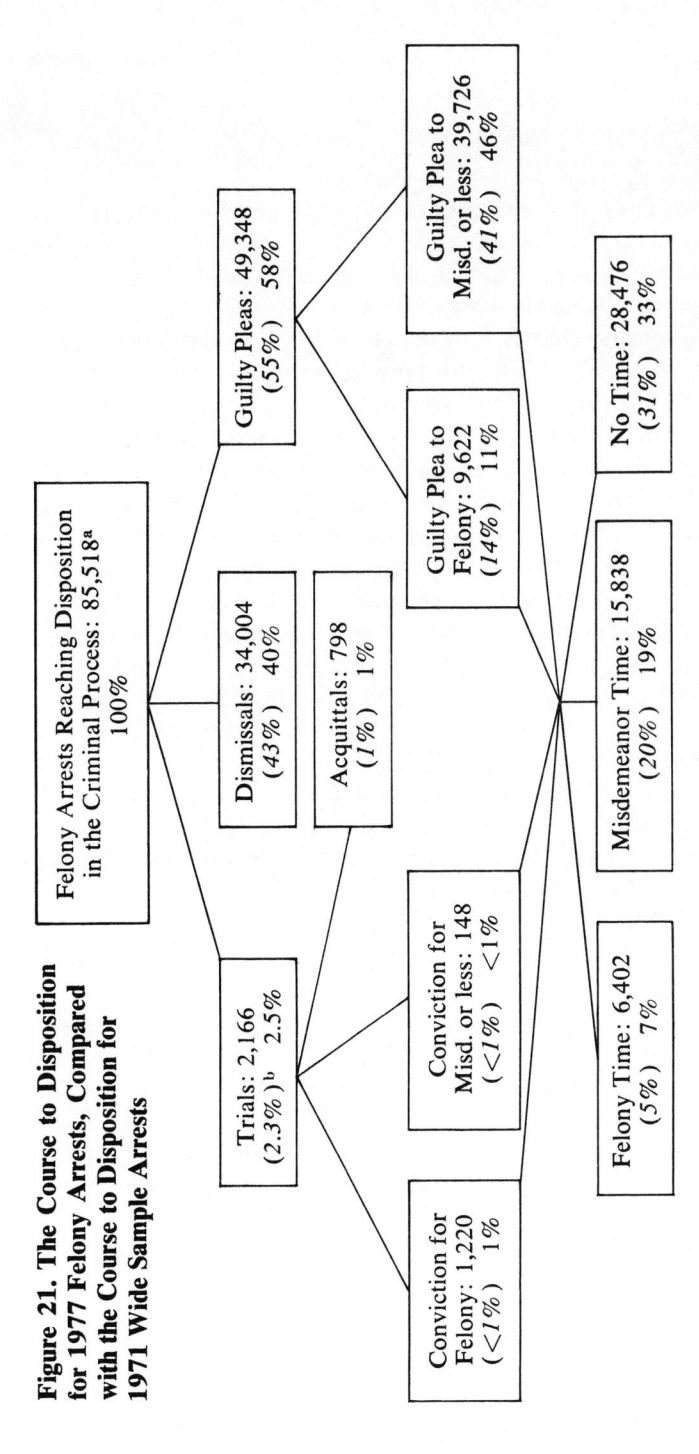

Figure 21. The Course to Disposition for 1977 Felony Arrests, Compared with the Course to Disposition for 1971 Wide Sample Arrests

Felony Arrests Reaching Disposition in the Criminal Process: 85,518[a] 100%

- Trials: 2,166 (*2.3%*)[b] 2.5%
  - Conviction for Felony: 1,220 (*<1%*) 1%
  - Conviction for Misd. or less: 148 (*<1%*) <1%
  - Acquittals: 798 (*1%*) 1%
- Dismissals: 34,004 (*43%*) 40%
- Guilty Pleas: 49,348 (*55%*) 58%
  - Guilty Plea to Felony: 9,622 (*14%*) 11%
  - Guilty Plea to Misd. or less: 39,726 (*41%*) 46%

- Felony Time: 6,402 (*5%*) 7%
- Misdemeanor Time: 15,838 (*20%*) 19%
- No Time: 28,476 (*31%*) 33%

Sources: Criminal Court of the City of New York, *Filings, Dispositions and Sentences by Charge: January–June 1977* and *July–December 1977*; New York State Division of Criminal Justice Services, *Crime and Justice: Annual Report 1977* and *New York State Felony Processing Quarterly Report: January–December 1977*.

---

a. This number does not include cases transferred to other jurisdictions or to Family Court, nor does it include dispositions listed as "other" in the reports of the New York State Division of Criminal Justice Services.

b. The italicized percentages express the patterns found in the 1971 wide sample data.

143

conclude that the patterns of behavior and circumstances characterizing felony arrests have changed very little.

However, it cannot be suggested that no change has taken place in the way the dispositional process is *managed*. There have been major changes there, since 1971, and the efficiency of the criminal justice system today is greatly increased. By the mid-70s, the District Attorney's Office in each borough had established procedures for more selective screening of felony arrests to identify, early on, cases that should be indicted.* Increased efficiency resulted in part from the establishment of the Early Case Assessment Bureaus in 1975, which placed experienced prosecutors in complaint rooms in the Bronx, Brooklyn and Manhattan. Assistant District Attorneys in these Bureaus were assigned to "track" felony arrest cases for dismissal, misdemeanor prosecution or felony prosecution, by identifying evidentiary and other problems early in the process. In addition, Early Case Assessment Bureaus helped focus Assistant District Attorneys on the early identification of particular subgroups of cases deserving priority prosecution.† As a result of these administrative innovations, the number of cases indicted has decreased (from a high of 27,185 in 1972 to a fairly constant 16,000 in 1976), and the conviction rate (and felony conviction rate) of cases indicted has increased.

Other important changes in the administration of the dispositional process flow from policy decisions by the court itself. Attempting to increase the speed of dispositions and to reduce backlog and delay problems, the courts' administrators selected for assignment to the arraignment parts of Criminal Court judges who had demonstrated an ability to bring to immediate disposition a substantial proportion of the incoming cases. To state it simply, the court acted on its perception that adjournment was unnecessary in many cases where facts known at the time of arraignment made it clear that dismissal, or conditional discharge, or a short jail term would be the ultimate disposition. A steady increase in disposition rates at arraignments resulted. Currently, 50% of all arrests (violations, misde-

---

* This process is fully outlined by Joyce Sichel, Janet Quint and John MacWillie in *Priority Prosecution in New York City* (draft title) (New York: Criminal Justice Coordinating Council, forthcoming).

† Other new programs in District Attorneys' offices continue the trend of selective screening of cases for indictment. Major Offense Bureaus, launched between 1973 and 1975 in all boroughs except Staten Island, focus prosecutorial efforts on the most serious felony cases. The Career Criminal Program, established in 1975 in Manhattan only, emphasizes the prosecution of repeat offenders, although the number of cases handled annually by the program is small.

meanors and some felonies) are disposed at arraignment, compared to 33% in 1973.

The Legislature also played a part in tightening up the dispositional process. A Second Felony Offender provision, added to the Penal Law in September 1973, required courts to impose a prison term on anyone convicted of a felony who had been convicted of a felony within the preceding ten years; the new provision also restricted sentencing discretion in ways intended to ensure that a second felony offender serving one of these mandatory prison terms would actually spend more time behind bars than if he had been imprisoned under ordinary Penal Law provisions. The Second Felony Offender provision, in conjunction with the Priority Prosecution Bureaus, is often cited as causing a trend toward increased sentence lengths for those sentenced to felony time.*

The impact of these efforts to tighten up the process for felony prosecutions seems to have been limited to the Supreme Court. Currently, cases indicted as felonies far more often result in felony conviction than they did 10 years ago, yet the proportion of all felony arrests that result in felony conviction is, in fact, slightly reduced (15% in 1971; 13% in 1977). Although the number of trials in Supreme Court has increased greatly over the decade, as a result of new policies in the District Attorneys' Offices (improved screening, priority prosecution), the proportion of all felony arrests that go to trial is unchanged. Sentences to felony time did increase from 33% of all felony convictions in 1971 to nearly 60% in 1977, and felony length sentences disposed of 7% of all felony arrests in 1977 compared to 5% in 1971. From these data, it is clear that the Supreme Court in New York City today deals more efficiently and more severely with cases indicted as felonies, and hands out more felony sen-

---

* This tendency is difficult to document using aggregate data, particularly for New York City alone. The Sichel report on priority prosecution bureaus, op. cit., does not show a significant increase in median maximum sentence length in Manhattan, the Bronx and Brooklyn after the institution of Major Offense Bureaus, yet the data are limited to relatively small samples in individual boroughs. Statewide aggregate data show little change in median maximum sentence length; but the data published by the Department of Correctional Services only go back to 1976, and the data supplied by the Department of Criminal Justice Services do not cover a full range of felonies. It is likely, however, that priority prosecution bureaus, the second felony offender provision and the Rockefeller Drug Law (mandating life sentences for class A narcotics felony convictions) all contributed to the tendency toward longer sentences acknowledged by the State Department of Correctional Services. See *Characteristics of New Commitments—1977* (State of New York, Department of Correctional Services, Albany, 1977).

tences for felony convictions. But these changes, however important and appropriate they are for the few felony arrests cases that reach the end of the process without charge reduction or dismissal, have not altered the overall dispositional pattern.

It is evident that changes in the overall dispositional pattern are hard to achieve. The data presented in the preceding monograph help explain why. Changes in legislation, in policy and in practice had little impact on the overall dispositional pattern for felony arrests because they affected the administration of justice, not the pattern of crime and not the pattern of police arrest activity. Figure 21 suggests that there has been no significant shift in felony arrest activity from prior relationship crime to predatory stranger crime. Perhaps the lesson is that we must look principally to the streets of New York—to the ways citizens behave and the ways police patrol and investigate crime—rather than to our court process, if we wish to change the basic pattern of dispositions.

Appendix: Note on Methodology

To provide both a description of the disposition process and an understanding of it, two samples were needed: a wide sample that would include enough cases to give a valid statistical picture of the disposition process and a deep sample small enough to allow extensive interviewing about each case. Because the samples were to serve different purposes, the methods of selection and the problems associated with selection and interpretation were different.

The wide sample was a probability sample from the 1971 Arrest Register, a current record of arrests maintained by the Police Department.* The register was used because it was the most accessible source for a complete list of all felonies. The year 1971 was chosen because most arrests in 1971 had been disposed by 1973, when data collection began.

In order to have a sample of approximately 500 felony arrests from each borough, one out of every 77 cases in Manhattan was selected, one out of every 24 in Queens, one out of every 65 in Brooklyn, and one out of every 50 in the Bronx. Of the cases screened, only felonies were kept, producing a sample of 1,888 cases. Approximately equal numbers of cases were selected from each borough to allow for comparisons among boroughs. (Such comparisons, however, are not presented in this monograph.) Since this monograph focuses on New York City as a whole, it was necessary to weight the cases so that together they produced an accurate city-wide picture. During 1971, there were 12,000 felony arrests in Queens and 30,000 in Brooklyn. We selected a sample of 502 cases of the 12,000 in Queens and 438 of the 30,000 in Brooklyn. Since the 502 Queens cases represent only 12% (approximately 12,000 of 100,000) of New York City felony arrests in 1971, while the 438 Brooklyn cases represent 31%, a case from Brooklyn was given more weight, and its disposition and other characteristics counted more heavily, in the city-wide profile.

Once the wide sample cases were selected, efforts were made to gather specific recorded data on each. The information sought on each defendant included: age, sex, ethnicity, type of counsel, criminal record, current charges, bail amount, bail made, time between arrest and disposition, type of disposition and sentence if convicted.

The first source of data for the wide sample was a form called the "JC 500," which is maintained by the Judicial Conference. However, since many of these

---

* Each arrest represents one defendant's case, which may consist of multiple complaints. For instance, if a defendant was initially charged with robbery, and drugs were later found on his person, the police would record the arrests as separate events. However, in this study all the complaints stemming from the same arrest are counted as one case.

forms were not complete and others were missing, it was necessary in many cases to go back to docket books, index books, and in some cases to the individual case folders. The criminal history of a defendant is not on the "JC 500" form, so these data were gathered from the State criminal justice computer system (NYSID).

From the original 1,888 cases, only 1,382 cases were followed through to disposition. Forty case folders could not be located. Another 466 cases are not discussed in this report because they were not adjudicated to disposition by September 1973, when data collection ended, or because they were transferred to another court.

Cases for the deep sample, selected to help explain the reasons behind dispositions, were chosen after the cases reached final dispositions. Thus, if a case ended by a conviction at trial or by guilty plea, selection into the sample occurred after the defendant was sentenced. Interviews were sought with the police officer, the assistant district attorney, the defense attorney and the judge about why the case had concluded as it had. The interviews were open-ended; structured questionnaires were not used.

The deep sample was not selected from the 1971 list of arrests, as was the wide sample, because it was thought that the participants would not remember well the decisions they made in cases disposed of a year or two previously. Selecting cases at disposition allowed a probability sample to be generated within ten months, while memory loss was minimized.

Ten cases were selected into the deep sample from each of the four major boroughs each month from January until October 1973. The target day in each borough was rotated to provide a representative sample. The court calendars were used to identify cases, originally arraigned as felonies,* that were disposed of on the target day in the Criminal and the Supreme Court. The day's quota for the sample was 10; therefore, if 46 cases that had been arraigned as felonies were disposed of on the target day, every fifth case was selected. Immediately after a case was selected, attempts began to locate and interview the participants. The interviews were supplemented by court records. A total of 369 cases (about 90 from each borough) were selected in this manner to form the deep sample.†

In this monograph, the deep sample data have not been weighted (as the

---

* All but three cases stemmed from felony arrests; in these cases an original misdemeanor arrest was elevated to a felony charge in the Complaint Room.

† An additional 34 cases were sampled from the Central Narcotics Court. Data from these cases have not been included in the monograph.

Appendix: Note on Methodology 149

wide sample data were); they are presented as illustrative of the reasons for the disposition patterns, and not as a statistically valid sub-sample. (However, weighting the deep sample data in the manner used to weight the wide sample data does not generate striking differences from the unweighted deep sample picture.)

Because the complexities of the criminal justice system are many, unanticipated problems arose in handling data. One problem was classifying the cases when there were multiple charges. Even the computer would find it unwieldy to trace changes in every charge from arrest to disposition. On the average, there were over two charges per arrest (and up to nine charges) and changes, up or down, could be made to each charge in the Complaint Room, Criminal Court Arraignment, Preliminary Hearing, Grand Jury, Supreme Court Arraignment and Supreme Court Pretrial Conference and Trial Parts. Therefore, only the "top" charge (at arraignment for the deep sample, at arrest for the wide sample) was used to classify a case. An A felony is a higher charge than a B felony, and so on. (See Table A, page 11, above.) But what is the top charge when a defendant is charged with two D felonies? If two charges were of the same class, then the case was classified for the sample as charged with the violent crime (homicide, rape, robbery, assault) where one of the charges fell into that group and other charges were for property or victimless crimes. If a defendant was charged with two violent crimes of the same class, the priorities were homicide first, then rape, then robbery, then assault. If two property crimes were charged, the priorities were burglary first, then grand larceny, then forgery, and then criminal possession of stolen property. If two victimless crimes were charged, the priorities were narcotics first, then possession of weapons, then gambling.

Major problems were encountered—particularly with respect to data collection for the wide sample—because criminal justice record-keeping is fragmented. For each case on which there was not a complete "JC 500" form, the researchers had to go to a number of different sources and ultimately, in some cases, to the individual court records for data. And even the court folders were often incomplete or unreadable. A special problem arose with criminal histories obtained from the state criminal justice computer system (NYSID), the only central source for criminal histories. To protect confidentiality of these data, NYSID required all identifiers and code numbers to be erased from our data tape after criminal history information had been added to it. As a result, errors or omissions discovered during subsequent analysis could not be investigated or corrected.

The deep sample presented its own set of problems. Participants were often difficult to locate for interviews, and poorly kept records sometimes made it difficult even to determine who had been present at disposition. (Resources were sufficient to interview attorneys and judges who were present at sentencing or dismissal of each case, but not to interview those who had made earlier decisions—for example, set bail or accepted a plea.) Naturally, the more cases a participant processes per day, the less time he has to allocate to each one; thus judges had the most difficulty remembering the specifics of individual cases, but police or private attorneys (for whom a felony case is more likely to be rare) generally found it easy to recall details. Sometimes interviews were not satisfactory because of the participant's lack of candor or inability to articulate the "real" reason for a decision. Occasionally a participant could not be located or refused to be interviewed.

In addition to the specific problems of collecting and organizing data for each sample, there were problems with applying to wide sample phenomena the reasons for decisions as they emerged from the deep sample interviewing. Some differences between the samples can be neatly accounted for: for example, because the wide sample was selected at arrest, it included cases dismissed or reduced to misdemeanors in the Complaint Room and, as such cases are not listed as felonies on the court calendars, the deep sample does not include cases dismissed or reduced in this way and thus is likely to evidence a higher rate of conviction. Also, cases siphoned off to Family Court and those cases in which the defendant jumped bail—for which there was therefore no criminal process disposition—were excluded from the deep sample, as were cases dismissed by the Grand Jury (because the Grand Jury files are sealed). Most of these differences can be eliminated by comparing deep sample data from only those wide sample cases that were disposed of in the criminal process.

Differences between dispositional patterns for cases adjudicated to disposition in the wide and in the deep samples are, however, more worrisome because we cannot disentangle differences which are by-products of methodological difficulties from those which represent "real" changes in dispositional patterns between the two sampling periods. The wide sample arrests occurred in 1971 and were disposed anytime between 1971 and 1973 (data from cases that did not reach disposition by 1973 were excluded from the study); the majority of deep sample arrests occurred in 1972 and 1973, and all were disposed in 1973. We know, for example, that substantial changes in processing narcotics cases resulted from creation of a city-wide Central Narcotics Court in 1972, between the sampling periods. (Because of other changes in the substantive law and penalty structure, enacted as the 1973 New York State Drug and Sentencing Laws, which went into effect August

Appendix: Note on Methodology 151

1, 1973, even the deep sample narcotics cases are no longer sufficiently representative of current disposition patterns in drug cases to warrant further analysis in this monograph.)

Other discrepancies, less obvious in origin, may be attributable simply to the time lag between the two samples. A new judicial administration was established in 1971 when Judge David Ross became the Administrative Judge for the Criminal Court of the City of New York. Priority was given to procedures aimed at clearing up the court backlog, and these efforts were reflected in the reduced time required for processing of arrests in the deep sample through to disposition.

A comparison of types of arrests making up the two samples reveals the following:

Types of Crimes	*Wide Sample*	*Deep Sample*
Against the person	27%	41%
Property	32%	28%
Victimless	41%	31%
	100%	100%

These data indicate that the deep sample included a higher proportion of crimes against the person and fewer victimless crimes than the wide sample. This difference arises partly from the methodological decision not to include narcotics arrests (victimless) in the deep sample but may also be attributable to more rapid increase over the years in the number of felony arrests for crimes against the person.

A comparison of the dispositions of wide and deep sample cases also indicates differences:

Type of Disposition:	*Wide Sample*	*Deep Sample*
Acquittal	2%	2%
Dismissed	43%	34%
Convicted	56%	64%
Convicted of a felony	*14%*	*15%*
Type of Sentence:		
Walk	52%	56%
Year or less	39%	33%
More than a year	9%	11%

The major difference is the higher conviction rate in the deep sample (64%) than in the wide sample (56%). This may be attributable to: (1) a "real" higher conviction rate of felony arrests in 1973, (2) a higher proportion of crimes against persons in the deep sample, or (3) sampling problems. The overall differences between the wide sample and the deep sample are reflected in the individual crime categories. The table on pages 148-149 summarizes the type of disposition and sentence for each of the major crimes.

While the differences are troubling because they suggest that we cannot confidently apply to the wide sample, on a statistical basis, the reasons for dispositions that we have discovered in the deep sample, these differences should not detract from the purposes of the two samples. The wide sample presents a statistical picture, and the deep sample illustrates reasons for the deterioration of felony arrests exhibited by the wide sample.

Comparison of Dispositions in Deep and Wide Samples for Five Crime Categories

	Assault		Robbery		Burglary		Grand Larceny		Weapons Possession	
	Deep Sample	Wide Sample	Deep Sample	Wide Sample	Deep Sample	Wide Sample	Deep Sample	Wide Sample	Deep Sample	Wide Sample
Type of Conviction:										
Felony Conviction	19%	23%	65%	53%	6%	16%	13%	16%	32%	27%
Misdemeanor Conviction	81%	77%	35%	47%	94%	84%	87%	84%	68%	73%
Type of Sentence:										
Walk	64%	69%	29%	34%	58%	31%	68%	41%	68%	75%
Misdemeanor time	33%	24%	41%	45%	42%	65%	25%	56%	25%	25%
Felony time	3%	7%	30%	21%	—	4%	7%	3%	7%	—

153